Android UI Fundamentals

DEVELOP AND DESIGN

Jason Ostrander

Android UI Fundamentals: Develop and Design

Jason Ostrander

Peachpit Press

1249 Eighth Street
Berkeley, CA 94710
510/524-2178
510/524-2221 (fax)

Find us on the Web at www.peachpit.com
To report errors, please send a note to errata@peachpit.com
Peachpit Press is a division of Pearson Education.

Editor: Clifford Colby
Development editor: Robyn Thomas
Production editor: Myrna Vladic
Copyeditor: Scout Festa
Technical editor: Jason LeBrun
Cover design: Aren Howell Straiger
Interior design: Mimi Heft
Compositor: Danielle Foster
Indexer: Valerie Haynes Perry

ISBN 13: 978-0-321-81458-6
ISBN 10: 0-321-81458-4

9 8 7 6 5 4 3 2 1

Printed and bound in the United States of America

To my lovely wife, Susan,
who tirelessly supports me in all of my adventures.

ACKNOWLEDGMENTS

I could write an entire book thanking people for their help along the way. Instead, I'll have to settle for this short paragraph:

Thanks to Chris H. for pushing me to consider writing a book and giving me endless encouragement and support. To Cliff C. for giving me the chance to write this book. To Robyn T. for keeping me on schedule despite my best efforts. To JBL for fixing my code and rocking a mean bass guitar. To Scout F. and Myrna V. for working tirelessly when I was late getting chapters to them. To Lucas D. and Rob S. for reading early chapters and giving me valuable feedback. To the entire team at doubleTwist for their dedication to making great Android software. To the Android team at Google for creating a great platform. To my family for their continuing support despite my dropping off the face of the earth. To Peachpit for giving me the opportunity to write this for you. And to you, the reader, for giving me the chance to teach you in whatever small way I can.

BIO

Jason Ostrander is a web and mobile software developer working at Silicon Valley startup doubleTwist, where he makes syncing media to Android phones simple. Prior to that, he solved networking problems at energy management startup Sentilla and defense company Northrop Grumman. Jason holds an MS in electrical engineering from UCLA. He lives with his wife in San Francisco's Mission District, where he spends his time searching for the perfect chile relleno.

CONTENTS

PART 2 THE VIEW FRAMEWORK

PART 3 ADVANCED UI DEVELOPMENT

INTRODUCTION

There is a revolution happening in the technology industry. Touchscreen interfaces, combined with low-cost and ubiquitous smartphones, have created a perfect storm for disruptive innovation. Android is at the forefront of this change, bringing a free and open-source platform on which developers can create the next generation of applications. With free development tools and an open market, anyone can develop applications that reach a worldwide market. But why choose to develop for Android?

Android now runs on the majority of smartphones in the United States. And it's quickly expanding into new markets and device types. The last year has seen the introduction of hundreds of Android-based tablets, including the hit Kindle Fire. Google has ported Android to TVs with its Google TV platform, and many manufacturers are beginning to ship TVs with Android built in. Boeing has selected Android as the entertainment platform for its new Dreamliner jet. Ford is integrating Android into its in-dash SYNC entertainment system. And Android is quickly gaining traction in the developing world, especially in Africa, where the need for low-cost handsets is greatest.

Yet for all of the platform's promise, the majority of Android applications still lack the visual polish of their iOS counterparts. This book aims to address that issue by providing developers with a solid foundation for building app UIs. It will cover the basics of UI development on Android, teach best practices for creating flexible layouts, and give you tips on how to optimize your UI for smooth, fluid performance. I created this book in the hope that it will help developers to create beautiful applications.

Who am I? I've been developing software professionally for almost ten years, and I've focused on embedded and mobile software for the last five. In my day job, I work for one of the top Android development companies and write code that millions of people use every day.

Android development can be difficult at times, and the challenges of supporting such a diversity of devices can be daunting. But with a good idea, a solid understanding of the framework, and a little persistence, anyone can create a great app that is used by millions of people.

I hope you'll enjoy reading this book as much as I enjoyed writing it for you.

WHO THIS BOOK IS FOR

This book is aimed at beginning Android developers who are interested in creating great user interfaces. You are expected to know basic Java programming and XML syntax. The focus of this book is on UI. While you don't need to have experience writing Android software, many basic Android concepts are only described in passing. It will help you to have a rudimentary knowledge of Android development.

WHO THIS BOOK IS NOT FOR

This book is not a general introduction to programming for Android. While it is intended for beginning Android developers, the focus is on user interface tools and programming. In particular, this book will not cover basic Android concepts such as intents, services, or content providers. Further, this book will not be an introduction to the Java programming language or to XML. You should know how to program and how to read XML.

HOW YOU WILL LEARN

Throughout this book, you'll learn by creating an actual app, a simple time tracker. Each chapter includes detailed examples of real Android code that you will compile and run. All code for the book can be found at the book's website: www.peachpit.com/androiduifundamentals.

WHAT YOU WILL LEARN

You'll learn how to create user interfaces for Android applications. From the most basic concepts, like activities and views, all the way to advanced graphics using RenderScript, this book covers everything you will use to build the user interface of your apps.

A NOTE ABOUT ANDROID VERSIONS

This book was written to Android version 4 APIs and best practices, but it is compatible back to Android version 2.2. When relevant, notes and tips are included to indicate when an API is deprecated or no longer appropriate. The Android compatibility library, a package of classes that back-port several newer features, will be used throughout the book.

WELCOME TO ANDROID

Throughout this book, you'll be writing your code using the Eclipse integrated development environment (IDE). You'll need to install the Android software development kit (SDK), along with the Android Developer Tools (ADT) plugin. This setup includes several other utilities to help you develop and test your application. Aside from the SDK, none of these tools are required, but they will make your application development easier.

THE TOOLS

The following tools are used throughout this book to build, test, and analyze your applications.

ANDROID SDK

The Android SDK is required to build and deploy Android applications. The SDK contains the tools you'll use to test and debug your application. It also contains tools for creating flexible layouts. You can download the Android SDK at http://developer.android.com/.

ECLIPSE

Eclipse is the recommended IDE for Android development and is the only IDE officially supported by Google. Google publishes a plugin called Android Developer Tools that integrates with Eclipse and provides features like a drag-and-drop interface builder. You are not required to use Eclipse, as the Android SDK fully supports command-line development. Throughout this book, however, it is assumed you are using Eclipse. You can download Eclipse at www.eclipse.org.

ANDROID SDK MANAGER

The Android SDK Manager is used to download and install the Android SDK. You will also use the SDK Manager to install add-on features like sample code, third-party emulators, and the compatibility library. The Android SDK Manager can also be used to create and launch emulated Android devices, called Android Virtual Devices. The Android SDK Manager can be found in the SDK `tools/` directory as `android`.

HIERARCHY VIEWER

This tool displays a graphical representation of your layout hierarchy and can help you debug layout performance issues by spotting overly complex layouts. It's also a good tool for understanding how Android layout works. You can find this tool in the SDK `tools/` directory as `hierarchyviewer`.

DDMS

The Dalvik Debug Monitor Server (DDMS) is used to debug application performance issues. It provides Java heap usage, running thread counts, and object allocation tracking. You also use it to take screen shots. The DDMS tool is built into Eclipse through the ADT or can be run standalone from the `tools/` directory of the SDK.

PART 1

BASIC
ANDROID UI

1

GETTING **STARTED**

Android is a powerful mobile operating system, built using a combination of the Java programming language and XML-based layout and configuration files. This chapter introduces the Android development environment, walks through the basic Hello World application, and covers the Android tools, with an emphasis on the user interface (UI) tools available in the Android Developer Tools (ADT) plugin. In this chapter you'll create a Hello World application; learn the Android project layout and purpose of each file and folder; learn basic Android UI concepts like the `Activity` class and XML layouts; and discover the tools available for creating user interfaces in Android.

HELLO WORLD

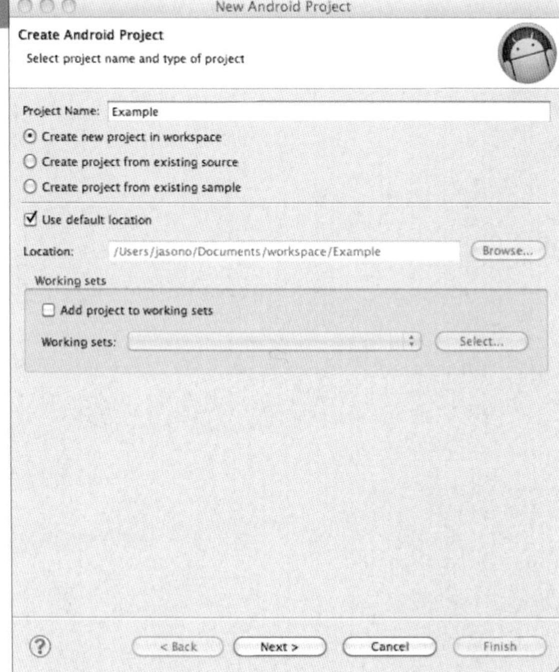

FIGURE 1.1 The Android project creation wizard

Before you create a basic Hello World app, you must download and install the Android developer tools available at developer.android.com. You will need to install the Android software development kit (SDK), Eclipse, and the ADT plugin. Follow the directions provided on the developer website to set up the Eclipse development environment. All examples in this book use Android SDK Release 13 and the Eclipse Helios release.

When ready, create the Hello World application using the following steps:

1. Start Eclipse.
2. Open the Java perspective by choosing Window > Open Perspective > Java.
3. Choose File > New > Android Project.
4. Leave all the defaults. Name the project **Example** and click Next (**Figure 1.1**).

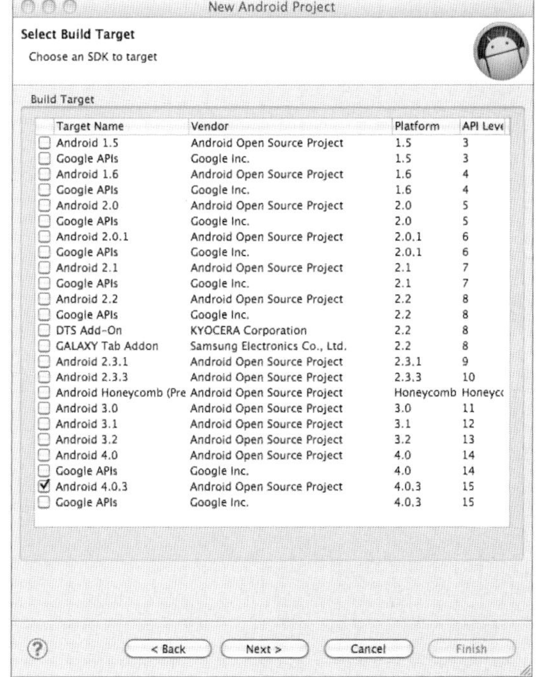

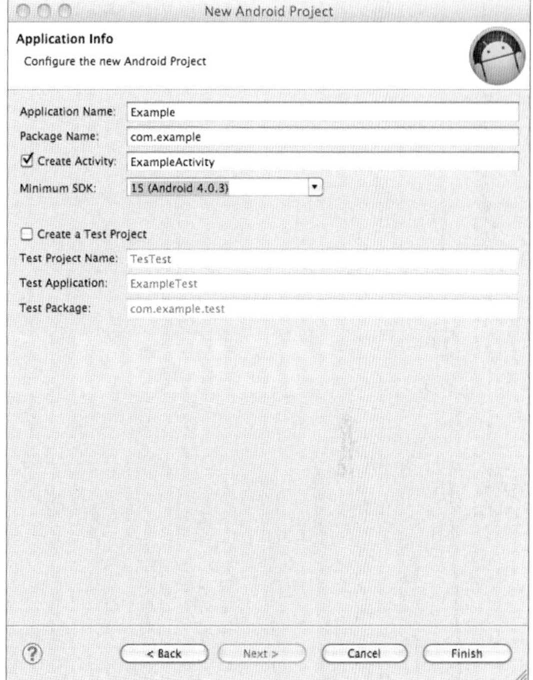

FIGURE 1.2 The Android project build target (left)

FIGURE 1.3 The Android project properties (right)

5. Set the Build Target option to Android 4.0 (**Figure 1.2**). You'll build to Android version 4.0 (API version 15) for all code in this book. Click Next.

6. Enter the package name `com.example` (**Figure 1.3**).

7. Click Finish, and the project will be created for you.

8. Run your app by right-clicking the Example project in the left-hand Package Explorer pane and selecting Run As > Android Application.

FIGURE 1.4 The AVD Manager

9. Select Yes when prompted to create a new Android Virtual Device (AVD). This will open the AVD Manager (**Figure 1.4**). Click the New button and configure it as shown in **Figure 1.5**. Click Create AVD when finished.

10. In the AVD Manager, select the AVD you just created and click Start. When prompted, click Launch. The emulator will start.

11. Once the emulator has loaded, close the AVD Manager, and the Android Device Chooser will open (**Figure 1.6**). Select the running emulator, and click OK.

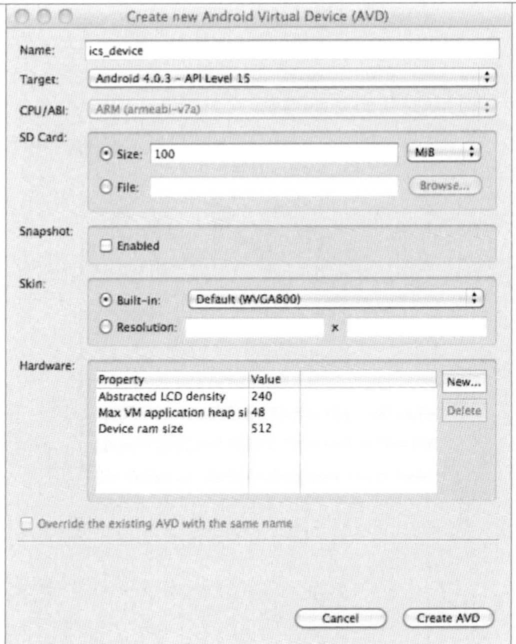

FIGURE 1.5 Android Virtual Device (AVD) creation dialog

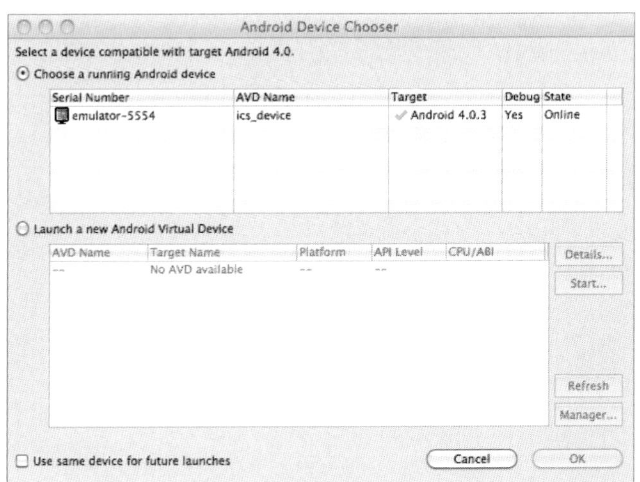

FIGURE 1.6 The Android Device Chooser

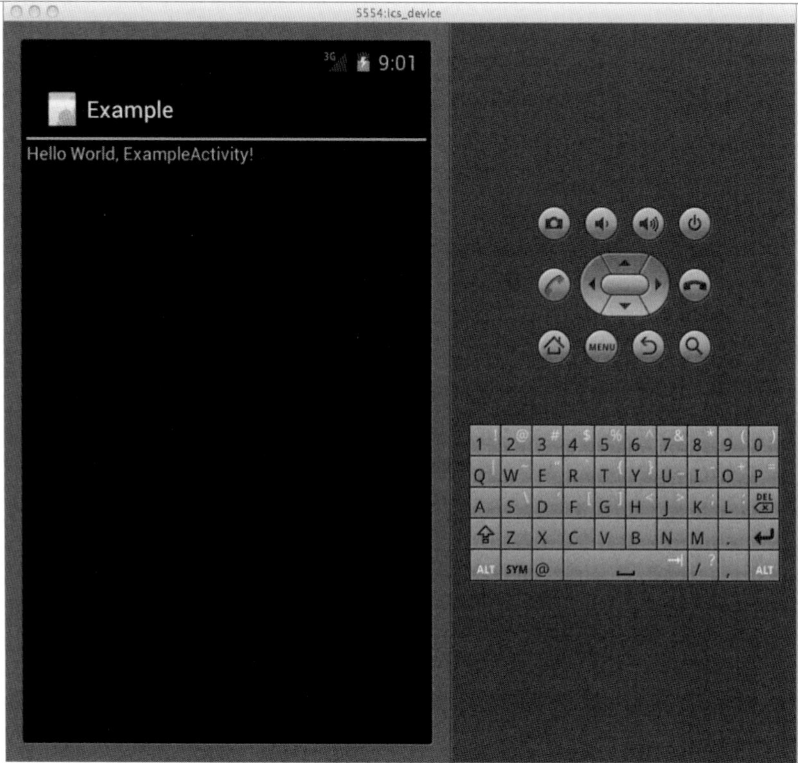

FIGURE 1.7 Hello World app running on Android emulator

Congratulations, you now have a running Android application (**Figure 1.7**).

RUNNING THE **EXAMPLE** APP ON A **PHONE**

If you want to run the Example app on your phone, follow these steps:

1. On your phone's home screen, press Menu > Settings > Applications. Select the "Unknown sources" checkbox to enable installation from your computer.
2. Open the Development menu and select the "USB debugging" checkbox.
3. Plug your phone into your computer.
4. Now close the emulator on your computer and run your application again. It should install on your phone. If the Android Device Chooser dialog appears, select your device from the list.

BASIC **STRUCTURE** OF AN **ANDROID APP**

The Eclipse IDE created an initial project structure for you when you started a new Android project. This project contains all the elements you need to build your application, and you should generally place all your work in this project. It's possible to create a library project for code-sharing between applications, but for most apps this is unnecessary. This section covers the basic structure of the project folder and where you should place your code, layouts, and resources.

FOLDER STRUCTURE

Expand the Example project folder in the Package Explorer and take a look at the project structure. Android uses a standard Java application layout. **Table 1.1** summarizes the project structure.

TABLE 1.1 Android Project Folder Structure

ITEM	EXPLANATION
`src/`	This folder contains your app's Java source code. It follows the standard Java package conventions. For example, a `com.example.Foo` class would be located in the folder `src/com/example/Foo.java`.
`res/`	This folder contains all the resources of your app and is where you declare the layout using XML. This folder contains all layout files, images, themes, and strings.
`gen/`	This folder is auto-generated when you compile the XML layouts in `res/`. It usually contains only a single file, `R.java`. This file contains the constants you need to reference the resources in the `res/` folder. Do not edit anything in this folder.
`assets/`	This folder contains miscellaneous files needed by your application. If your app needs a binary asset to function, place it here. To use these files, you need to open them using the Java File application programming interfaces (APIs).
`AndroidManifest.xml`	The manifest contains essential information about your app that the Android system needs. This includes the activites and services your app uses, the permissions it requires, any intents it responds to, and basic info like the app name.
`default.properties`	Lists the Android API build target.

ANDROID MANIFEST

The Android manifest contains all the information about your app's structure and functionality. It includes all the activities your app uses, the services it provides, any database content it makes available via a content provider, and any intents it processes.

```
<?xml version="1.0" encoding="utf-8"?>
<manifest xmlns:android="http://schemas.android.com/apk/res/android"
        package="com.example"
        android:versionCode="1"
        android:versionName="1.0">
    <uses-sdk android:minSdkVersion="14" />
    <uses-feature android:name="android:hardware.bluetooth"/>
    <supports-screens android:anyDensity="true"/>
    <application android:icon="@drawable/icon"
    → android:label="@string/app_name">
        <activity android:name=".ExampleActivity"
            android:label="@string/app_name">
        <intent-filter>
            <action android:name="android.intent.action.MAIN" />
            <category android:name="android.intent.category.
            → LAUNCHER" />
            </intent-filter>
        </activity>
    </application>
</manifest>
```

The manifest is where you declare the physical hardware features your app needs to run. For example, if your app requires a touchscreen device to operate properly, you would include the following line in the manifest:

```
<uses-feature android:name="android.hardware.touchscreen"
→ android:required="true" />
```

Declaring these hardware features as required by your application allows the Android Market to properly filter applications based on a user's hardware configuration. Users with non-touchscreen phones would not be able to download an app that requires a touchscreen to properly function.

You should strive to make your application as broadly compatible as possible. List features your app uses, but use code to dynamically determine their availability and gracefully degrade the user experience in your app.

The manifest is where you declare the permissions required by your app. Unlike hardware requirements, all the permissions necessary to run your application must be declared in the manifest. There are no optional permissions.

NOTE: Users are very unforgiving of applications that request overly broad permissions. This is especially true of location permissions. Carefully consider the needs of your application, and don't request permissions that you don't need.

The manifest is where you declare the icons and labels used by your application. You can assign these attributes to many of the XML elements in the manifest. The most important is the top-level `<application>` element. This is what will represent your application on the device home screen and app drawer. However, the icon/label combination doesn't just apply to the `<application>` element. You can use them on the permissions element, which displays when the user accepts your application to install. You can place them on the `<activity>` element, and the user will see them in the process monitor. These elements are inherited by any sub-components. Hence, if the `<application>` icon and label are set, but the `<activity>` and `<intent>` icons and labels are not set, then those elements will use the `<application>` icon and label by default. This setup allows you to use component-specific icons and labels for informing the user of your application's functions.

Lastly, the manifest is where you declare your supported Android API versions. It's important that you declare the API level properly, because attempting to reference unsupported APIs will result in your application crashing. This is also a good way to prevent your app from being installed on newer API releases that you may not have tested yet. See **Table 1.2** for more information on API levels.

TABLE 1.2 Android API Level Declaration

ITEM	EXPLANATION
`android:minSDKVersion`	Declares the minimum API level required by your application. Devices running Android versions lower than this will not be able to install your application.
`android:targetSDKVersion`	Declares the version of your application you are building against. This is what determines the features available to your app. If this differs from the `minSDKVersion`, you may need to use Java reflection to access APIs that are unavailable on the lower version.
`android:maxSDKVersion`	Declares the maximum SDK your application supports. Use this to prevent installation on newer devices that you may not be ready to support.

RESOURCES

Android apps store all resources in the `res/` folder. What are resources? Basically, resources are anything that isn't Java code. Images, layout files, app strings, localized strings, themes, and even animations go in the `res/` folder. Android uses the directory structure to separate resources for use in different device configurations. In the Hello World app, there are three drawable folders: `drawable-ldpi`, `drawable-mdpi`, and `drawable-hdpi`. These represent low-, medium-, and high-density resources. At runtime, the Android system will select the proper resource based on the device hardware. If no resource matches, it will select the most closely matching resource. This will be covered in depth in Chapter 3.

The `res/values/` folder is where you place constant values used in your layout. You should place all colors, dimensions, styles, and strings in this folder. In the example Hello World app, there is a single `strings.xml` file containing all the user-visible strings used in the app:

```
<?xml version="1.0" encoding="utf-8"?>
<resources>
    <string name="hello">Hello World, ExampleActivity!</string>
    <string name="app_name">Example</string>
</resources>
```

You should never use string literals in your Java code or XML layouts. Always declare any user-visible strings in the `strings.xml` file. This makes it easier to localize your resources later. When using these strings in your app, you reference them by the `name` attribute of the string element.

The `res/layout/` folder also contains the XML files that declare your application layout. Android UI can be created using either XML or Java code. It's recommended to use XML for layouts, because it provides a good separation between UI and application logic. Folder names are used to separate layouts for different device configurations.

ANDROID UI BASICS

FIGURE 1.8 The Android home screen, displaying widgets and the quick-launch bar

The user interface (UI) is the connection between your app and your users. In fact, to the user, the UI *is* the app. The Android UI framework is powerful enough to create complex UIs with graphics and animations, but it also has enough flexibility to scale from small-screen handheld devices to tablets to TVs. This section covers the basics of Android UI development so you can start to create great UIs for your apps.

HOME SCREEN AND NOTIFICATION BAR

To create Android apps, first you should understand the basic UI of the Android OS itself. The first screen an Android user encounters is the home screen (**Figure 1.8**). The home screen consists of sliding pages containing app launcher icons and widgets. You can press the launcher icons to start the corresponding applications. Widgets are like mini applications that present small chunks of data, such as weather or unread email counts. At the bottom of the screen are quick-launch icons for opening the phone dialer or email client. This also contains the launcher for the app drawer. The app drawer contains all the user's installed applications in a grid.

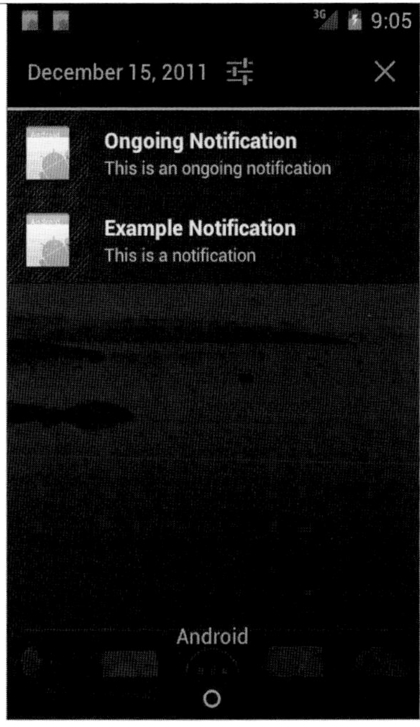

FIGURE 1.9 The Android notification tray

A key component of the Android UI is the notification tray (**Figure 1.9**). You access the tray by touching the status bar at the top of the screen and sliding your finger down. Android displays a list of all notifications in the notification tray: new mail notifications, currently playing music, system status info, and any long-running tasks such as downloads. Tapping a notification in the list typically opens the app that generated the notification.

NOTE: You should be aware that the user could replace the stock Android home screen with an alternative home screen. Generally, these alternatives follow the same UI conventions as the stock Android home screen. However, a few alternative home screens use radically different UI conventions, so it's a good idea not to rely on any particular home screen feature in your app.

XML LAYOUT

Android defines user interfaces using a combination of XML layout files and Java code. You can use Java to specify all layouts, but it's generally preferable to use XML to take advantage of Android's automatic resource selection. This allows you to declare layouts for different hardware configurations, and the Android system will select the most appropriate layout automatically.

Here is the code in the Hello World application's `main.xml` file.

```
<?xml version="1.0" encoding="utf-8"?>
<LinearLayout xmlns:android="http://schemas.android.com/apk/res/
→ android"
    android:orientation="vertical"
    android:layout_width="match_parent"
    android:layout_height="match_parent"
    >
<TextView
    android:layout_width="match_parent"
    android:layout_height="wrap_content"
    android:text="@string/hello"
    />
</LinearLayout>
```

The first line is basic XML boilerplate, listing the version and encoding. This is always the same and must be included at the beginning of every layout file. The next line defines one of Android's basic container types, the `LinearLayout`. This view arranges its child views linearly inside it. You will learn more about `LinearLayouts` in the next chapter.

NOTE: The `xmlns:android` attribute is necessary and must be declared in the top-level XML tag. This must always be present, or your resources will not build.

The LinearLayout is a simple container for displaying multiple sub-views in a linear fashion. For example, a series of items could be displayed inside a LinearLayout as a list. The android:orientation attribute declares the direction in which the sub-views are arranged. In this case, the layout uses the vertical orientation, and all sub-views will be arranged vertically. Finally, the width and height of the layout are declared to fill the entire parent view (more on this later).

Inside the LinearLayout is a single TextView. As the name implies, this view is used for displaying text to the user. The text attribute of the TextView declares the text displayed in that TextView. In this case, it's referencing a string defined in the strings.xml file. Android uses the @ symbol to reference other resources. You could have declared a string here, but it's better to declare all user-visible strings in the strings.xml file to aid localizing the app later. Also, you can change the text dynamically using Java code.

Each element in the layout is a view. A view is anything that can be drawn on the screen. Every text field, list item, web view, map, colorful spinning wheel, or button is represented by a view. The Android framework provides many views for you, such as the ListView and the TextView, but developers will need to create the more complex views that contain animations and special behavior.

TIP: Even when you plan to set the text of a TextView in code, it's a good idea to declare a default string. That way, you can see what your layouts will look like with full text.

THE ACTIVITY CLASS

Let's take a look at the source code for the Hello World application in the file src/com/example/ExampleActivity.java. In the manifest, you declared this activity and set it as the main activity to launch for the app. The Activity class is the main building block of Android applications. It represents a single screen of the application. Every screen your application contains will have an activity that represents it. In some cases, the content contained in an activity will be swapped without changing the activity (when using fragments, which you'll learn about later). For effective Android development, it's critical to understand the life cycle of the Activity class, because it has the most direct effect on the user experience.

```
package com.example;
import android.app.Activity;
import android.os.Bundle;
public class ExampleActivity extends Activity {
    /** Called when the activity is first created. */
    @Override
    public void onCreate(Bundle savedInstanceState) {
        super.onCreate(savedInstanceState);
        setContentView(R.layout.main);
    }
}
```

Android activities use a callback structure for creating UI events. The framework calls the appropriate overridden method during the creation or destruction of the activity. In the example activity, only a single method is implemented: `onCreate`. This method is called when an activity is first created. Typically this is where the setup of the activity takes place. This is where you create your views and set up any adapters you need to load your data. It's not strictly necessary to override any of the activity methods but `onCreate`.

The example just sets the view for the activity. It does this by calling `setContentView(R.layout.main)`. This references the `R.java` file that the Android developer tools built for you. In this case, it tells the system to load the `main.xml` file located in one of the layout directories. The Android runtime selects the most appropriate `main.xml` file (there is only one in this case) and loads it.

TIP: All Android callbacks occur on the main, or UI, thread. It's important to remember not to block this thread. Take care to perform long-running operations on a different thread, or the UI will become unresponsive.

FIGURE 1.10 Android tablet software buttons

The R.java file allows you to reference the generated ID of resources stored in the res/ folder. To reference layout files, use R.layout.file_name; to reference strings, use R.string.string_name; and so on.

Activities are short-lived objects. They are created and destroyed frequently. Each time the user rotates their phone, the activity that is currently displayed is destroyed and re-created. In addition, the Android system may destroy an activity if the device is running short of memory or resources. It's important to design your activities with the understanding that they can be killed at any time.

Take care to save any state the user might value. If your activity is destroyed, you don't want to frustrate your users by making them re-enter text. You will learn more about how to save activity states in the next chapter.

HARDWARE BUTTONS

Android devices prior to version 3.0 have four hardware buttons: Home, Back, Menu, and Search. Android version 3.0 and above have made the hardware buttons optional. In their place, Android presents onscreen software buttons that replicate the functionality of hardware buttons (**Figure 1.10**).

The Home button takes the user to the phone home screen. It's not generally available to applications, unless the app is a home-screen replacement.

The Back button is meant to navigate back in the Android activity stack. This allows the user to easily jump into an app and them immediately return to the previous screen.

TIP: To ensure that your app is a good Android citizen, always allow the user to return to a previous application if they have jumped straight into your app (for example, by pressing a notification or handling an intent created by another application). Don't force the user to back out of many screens of your app to return to their previous task.

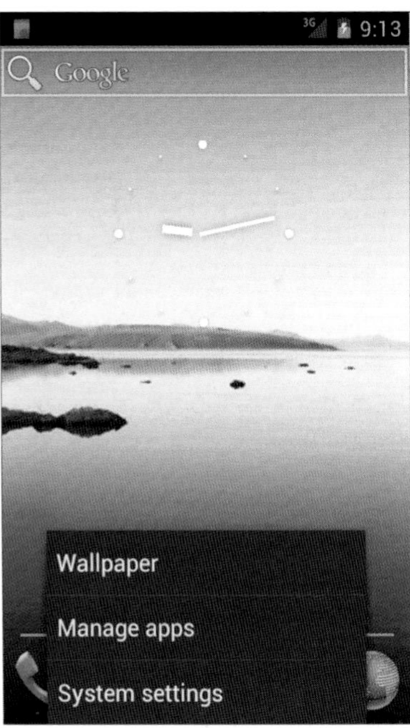

FIGURE 1.11 The options menu on the Android home screen

The Menu button displays a context-dependent list of options (**Figure 1.11**). Use the options menu for displaying infrequently used options for your application. On Android tablets and phones running version 3.0 or greater, this button is not available, and options are instead presented on the action bar. You'll learn about the differences between Android 4.0 devices and previous versions of Android in a later chapter.

TIP: It is often difficult for users to discover features hidden behind the Menu button. Carefully consider your application's needs, and provide space in your layout for all common operations that the user will need to take.

Finally, the Search button exists to provide a quick interface for launching a search on Android. Not all applications use this button, and in many applications, pressing this button does nothing.

In addition to these buttons, it is also possible to perform an alternative action on some hardware buttons. These actions are activated by long-pressing on the buttons. For example, long-pressing the Menu button will activate the software keyboard. Your application can take advantage of this feature to provide filtering in lists.

NOTE: Not all Android devices have all of these buttons. In particular, Android 4.0 devices omit the Search button, making it impossible for users to search in applications. Take care to evaluate the necessity of search to your application, and provide a button in your UI if search is an essential feature.

TOOLS

The Android SDK includes a suite of tools to assist in developing your apps. The suite consists of SDK tools and platform tools. The SDK tools, including ADT, are platform independent and are used regardless of which Android version you are developing against. The platform tools are specific to Android versions and are generally installed when updating the SDK to a new version. Let's focus on the SDK tools, specifically those used to develop the UI of an Android app.

ANDROID DEVELOPER TOOLS

The primary tool for developing Android apps is the Eclipse IDE using the ADT plugin. Eclipse is a powerful, multi-language development environment with features such as code completion, inline documentation, and automatic refactoring. You can use Eclipse to develop your application, debug it using the standard Eclipse Java debugger, and even sign a release package for publishing on the Android Market. There are many tools included in ADT, and you should familiarize yourself with all of them. Here, I'll focus on the tools that aid in creating the user interface of Android applications. Chief among these is the graphical layout editor.

THE GRAPHICAL LAYOUT EDITOR

The graphical layout editor allows you to drag and drop views to create your UI. In early versions of ADT, the graphical layout editor was sparse and not very helpful. Luckily, the latest version is quite powerful and can be used to create complex layouts containing compound components and animations.

Figure 1.12 shows the various components of the graphical layout editor.

1. The Configuration drop-down menu lets you change the way the layout is displayed. This is a quick way to view your UI for different hardware configurations, such as phones and tablets.

2. The Canvas displays the current layout as it will appear on your specified device configuration. The layout includes a set of context-specific buttons for quickly changing the parameters of selected views. You can drag views from the Palette and drop them here to build the UI. You can right-click components to get a context-specific list of available configurations. You can also use this list for refactoring the UI into reusable components.

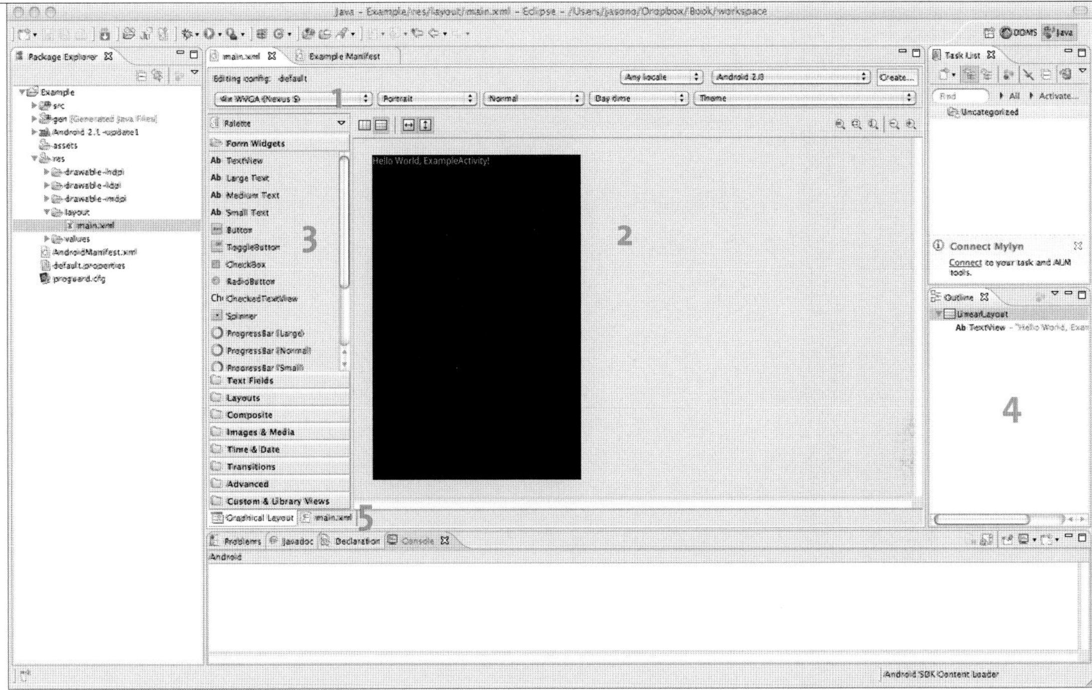

FIGURE 1.12 The graphical layout editor

3 The Palette contains the basic building blocks of Android user interfaces. This is where you can find the basic layout containers, the form controls (including buttons and text inputs), and even advanced features like transition animations. You can drag each of these components onto the Canvas to create your UI. When you drag components onto the Canvas, they will snap to the edges of the existing blocks, helping to align your layout.

4 The Outline displays an overview of your layout, with all components listed in a hierarchy. This makes it easy to see how the components are nested. It also makes finding hidden or invisible components easier. You can use this view to quickly reorder the components of your layout.

5 At the bottom of the graphical layout editor are tabs for switching to a standard XML view of your UI. While you can accomplish a lot using the graphical layout editor, it's recommended that you tweak your final layouts by hand-coding the XML.

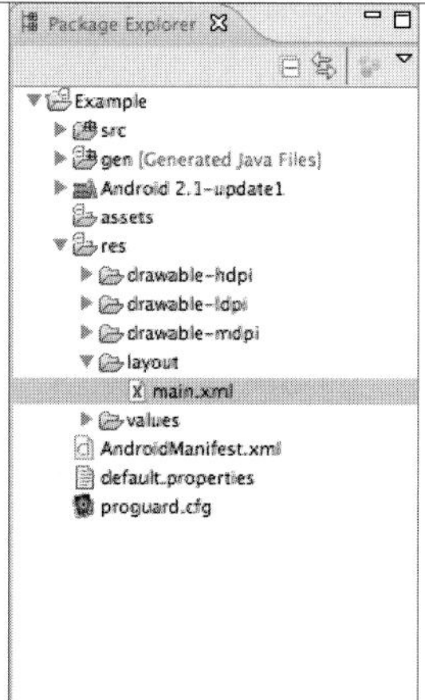

FIGURE 1.13 Package Explorer pane showing the `res/` folder (top)

FIGURE 1.14 The device configuration editor of the graphical layout editor (bottom)

The graphical layout editor is very powerful, and you should spend some time getting to know the options available within it. Let's experiment with the editor by adding a few buttons and text boxes to the layout.

1. In the Eclipse Package Explorer, expand the `res/layout` folder of the project.
2. Right-click the file named `main.xml` and select Open With > Android Layout Editor (**Figure 1.13**).

   This will display the graphical layout editor. You may need to set up a device configuration before you can start editing. At the top of the window are the controls for specifying the Android version, theme, locale, screen size, and orientation of the device.
3. Configure the options as seen in **Figure 1.14**. You may need to close `main.xml` and reopen it for the changes to take effect.

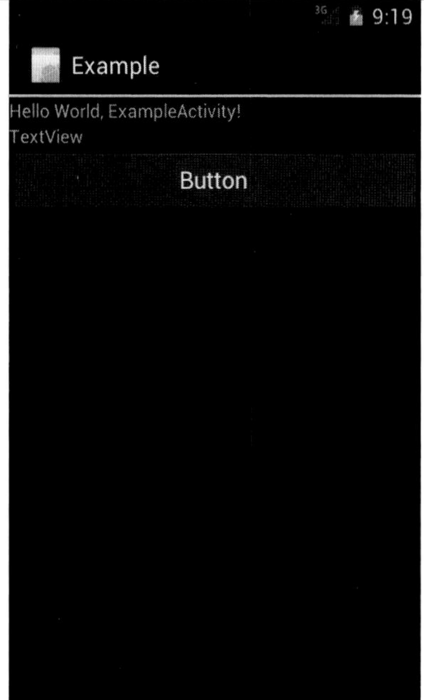

FIGURE 1.15 Hello World layout with an extra text view and button

4. Now try dragging a `TextView` onto the layout, just below the existing `TextView`.

   Notice that you can place the view only above or below the existing view. Remember the `LinearLayout` container from before? It was set up with a vertical orientation, so you can arrange views only vertically within it. Now try changing the size of the `TextView`.

5. Make it fill the width of the window.

6. Add a `Button` below your newly created `TextView`, and expand it to fill the width of the window.

   You should now have something that looks like **Figure 1.15**. As you can see, the graphical layout editor makes it possible to quickly create complex layouts with very little effort.

ANDROID VIRTUAL DEVICES

Android is designed to run on a wide range of hardware. It's important to test your code extensively before release to ensure that your app is compatible with most Android devices. This is where the Android Virtual Devices, or AVDs, come in. An AVD is an emulated Android device. It's not just a simulator; it actually runs the full Android framework, just as an actual device would. This is an important distinction, and it makes the emulator a far better representation of real-world devices than a simulator.

Because AVDs are emulated devices, they run the standard Android graphics stack. This can be very slow for high-resolution AVDs such as tablets. Google is working on improving this, but for now it's recommended to test your layouts in the graphical layout editor and only use the emulator for final verification. Of course, you can always use an actual Android device.

You already created an AVD when you ran the Hello World application. You did this using the AVD Manager. Using the AVD Manager, you can create a range of emulated devices with different hardware characteristics, including

- Screen size and default orientation
- Hardware support, such as accelerometers and gamepads
- The Android OS version
- SD card storage, emulated using your hard disk

In addition, many handset manufacturers make device-specific AVDs available to aid in testing on their hardware. You should create a range of virtual devices and test on all of them to ensure that your application has maximum device compatibility.

TIP: The emulator is useful for testing your app, but it cannot emulate all possible hardware features. For example, there is no support for emulating OpenGL graphics, Near Field Communication (NFC), or even Wi-Fi. To ensure maximum compatibility, you should always test your final application on a real hardware device.

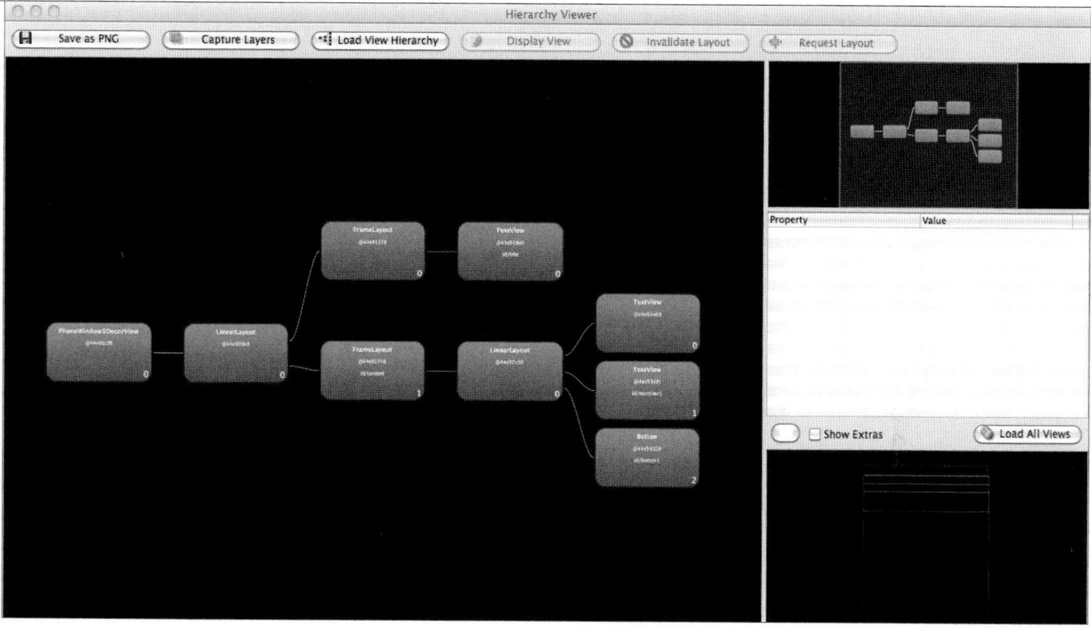

FIGURE 1.16 The Hierarchy Viewer displaying the modified Hello World app layout

HIERARCHY VIEWER

When developing any application, it is important that the app feel very responsive. Often, an unresponsive app is due to slowdowns in drawing the UI. To assist in debugging these situations, Android includes a tool called the Hierarchy Viewer. As the name suggests, this program will display the full layout hierarchy of your app, allowing you to optimize and debug potential issues.

NOTE: For security reasons, the Hierarchy Viewer will connect only to devices running developer versions of Android. In practice, you will be able to use Hierarchy Viewer only with the emulator or a phone that has been hacked to enable root access.

Use the Hierarchy Viewer by running the `tools/ hierarchyviewer` executable in the Android SDK directory.

1. Run `hierarchyviewer` now and select the Hello World app.
2. Click the Load View Hierarchy button, and you will see something like **Figure 1.16**.

There are four primary components in the Hierarchy Viewer:

- The left sidebar displays all connected devices, along with the running processes on each device. This is where you select your application.
- The Tree View displays a graphical representation of your UI layout. You can see exactly how many components make up your layout. Large layouts with many nested components will take much longer to draw than simple layouts. If you look closely, you will see colored circles on some components. These give you an at-a-glance indication of the time taken to draw the view and its children. Green is faster, red is slower. You can click a view to get more information about its draw time, along with a small preview of the view as it appears onscreen.
- The Tree Overview provides a quick zoomed-out view of the entire hierarchy, giving you a quick feel for the complexity of the layout. This pane also provides quick navigation around the Tree View pane.
- The Layout View shows an outline of the actual displayed application. This helps to orient the view components to the actual displayed UI. By clicking around in this pane, you can see which components make up each portion of the display.

If you look closely at the hierarchy displayed for the Hello World application, you may notice that it contains more components than are listed in the `main.xml` file. Here's a quick explanation:

- The topmost component is the `PhoneWindow`. This represents the display of the device. It is always present and is the base container for the entire display, excluding the notification bar.
- There is a `LinearLayout` directly below the `PhoneWindow`. This is not the `LinearLayout` in our `main.xml`. Rather, this layout is drawn by the system to display the title bar above the content. Notice the extra `FrameLayout` and `TextView`? That is the title bar of the app. If you run the app with no title bar, then this layout would be removed.
- The other `FrameLayout` is the application. This layout contains a child `LinearLayout`. The child `LinearLayout` is from the `main.xml` file in the example. It contains the two `TextView`s and the `Button` you created earlier in the Hello World app.

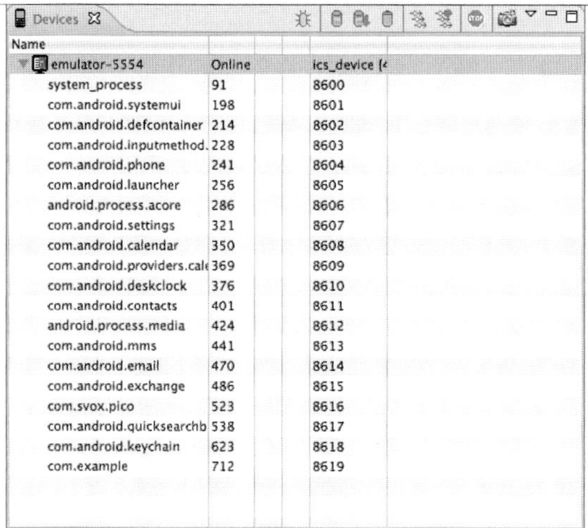

FIGURE 1.17 The DDMS Devices pane. To take a screenshot, click the camera icon.

The hierarchy view is especially useful for debugging nested `LinearLayouts`. If you start creating layouts with many layers of `LinearLayouts`, consider switching to a `RelativeLayout` to reduce complexity.

TAKING SCREENSHOTS WITH DDMS

The Dalvik Debug Monitor Server (DDMS) is a powerful tool for capturing the state of your application, including heap usage, running thread counts, object allocations, and logs. While these features are outside the scope of this book, DDMS also has a very important function that all app developers will need: It allows you to take screen shots of your application. To run DDMS, in Eclipse choose Window > Open Perspective > Other > DDMS. Select your device in the Devices pane, then click the camera icon (**Figure 1.17**). This will open the Device Screen Capture window. From here you can rotate the image, refresh it to recapture the screen, and save it.

> **NOTE:** Android version 4.0 and above has the ability to take screenshots without using DDMS. Simply hold the power and volume down buttons at the same time, and a screenshot will be saved to your device image gallery.

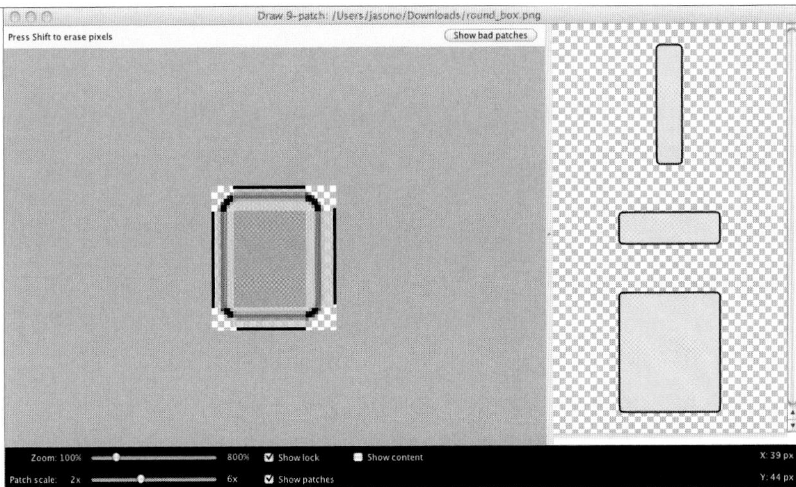

FIGURE 1.18 An example of the Draw 9-patch tool. The button can stretch, but the corners remain the same.

OTHER TOOLS

In addition to the common Android UI tools, there are some lesser-known tools that are useful for perfecting your app UI.

DRAW9PATCH

Images used in Android applications are often stretched to fit the available area on a device. This can distort the image, resulting in ugly graphics. Android uses an image called a 9-patch to handle scaling without distortion. For example, all buttons in Android are 9-patch graphics that stretch but maintain proper rounding on their corners (**Figure 1.18**). A 9-patch image is simply a standard image file with an additional 1-pixel border. By coloring the pixels in this border black, you can indicate which parts of the image should stretch as the image is scaled up. The Android SDK provides the `draw9patch` command-line tool for creating these images.

LAYOUTOPT

Optimizing layouts by hand can be a tedious job. The `layoutopt` tool can do some of the work for you by analyzing your layouts and displaying inefficiencies in the view hierarchy. This command-line tool takes a list of XML layout files, or a directory of files, and outputs the results of its analysis. While this isn't sufficient for debugging complex hierarchies, it can help in providing a first pass at fixing layout slowdowns.

ANDROID **ASSET STUDIO**

Creating image resources for different screen densities is necessary but tedious. Luckily, there is an excellent tool that will create these resources for you. Called the Android Asset Studio, this tool will take an uploaded image and create density-specific versions. It can also be used for creating launcher icons, menu bar icons, action bar icons and tab icons. For now, you can find the Android Asset Studio at this address:

http://android-ui-utils.googlecode.com/hg/asset-studio/dist/index.html

The Android Asset Studio is part of the Eclipse ADT plugin and can be accessed by selecting File>New>Android Icon Set.

MONKEY

When creating applications, it's important to thoroughly test every aspect of the user experience. It can be difficult to truly test a UI, because the developer of the app is familiar with the interface and won't try to do things that are unexpected or just plain weird—things like pressing multiple buttons at the same time while rotating the phone. This is where the Monkey tool comes in. The Monkey runs a specified number of iterations and randomly hits areas of the screen, changes the orientation of the device, presses volume and media keys, and generally just does crazy things. This is often a simple way of rooting out unexpected errors.

WRAPPING UP

This chapter introduced the Android framework by having you create the standard Hello World application and explore the tools available for building user interfaces on Android. Along the way, you learned that

- The `AndroidManifest.xml` file declares all the features used by your application. Use the manifest to prevent your app from running on unsupported hardware.
- Images and layouts are separated into folders that allow the Android system to select the best resources for the device's current configuration at runtime.
- The `Activity` class is the primary building block of Android applications. Understanding its life cycle is key to building great apps.
- The graphical layout editor provides a quick and easy way to create your applications.
- You should use the Hierarchy Viewer tool to debug performance issues in your views.
- You can use the DDMS tool to take screenshots of your application.

2

CREATING YOUR FIRST **APPLICATION**

Over the course of this book, you'll develop a simple time-tracking app. This app will eventually have all the features you would expect in a time-tracking application: a Start/Stop button, a running clock indicator, lists of previous times, editing capabilities, and a home-screen widget for fast time entry. But to begin, you'll create a basic app with a few buttons, a text view, and a list of times. In this chapter you'll learn the different layout containers and when to use them; explore XML options for getting the interface just right; learn the proper way to load data and display it as a list; and dive deep into the `Activity` class, a fundamental part of Android UI development.

CREATING AN APP

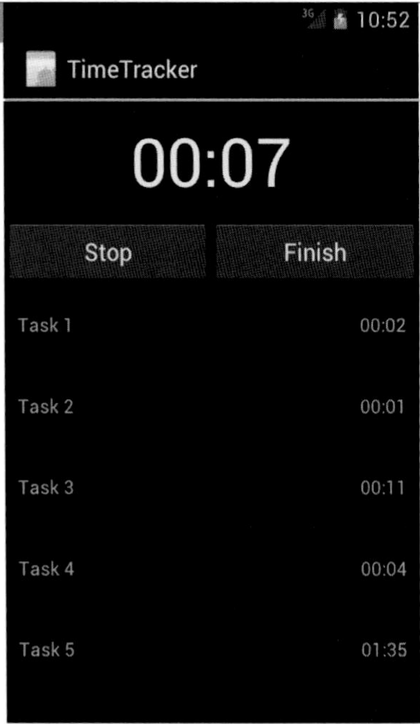

FIGURE 2.1 The time-tracking app you'll build by the end of this chapter

To get started, create a new project called **TimeTracker**. This will be your app project throughout the book. In this chapter, you'll work through some simple layouts and build a minimally functional application. **Figure 2.1** shows what you'll have built by the end of this chapter.

This book won't cover much of the back-end logic and will instead focus on the user interface code. However, all the code is available on the book's website, www.peachpit.com/androiduifundamentals, for you to download.

GETTING STARTED WITH ANDROID VIEWS

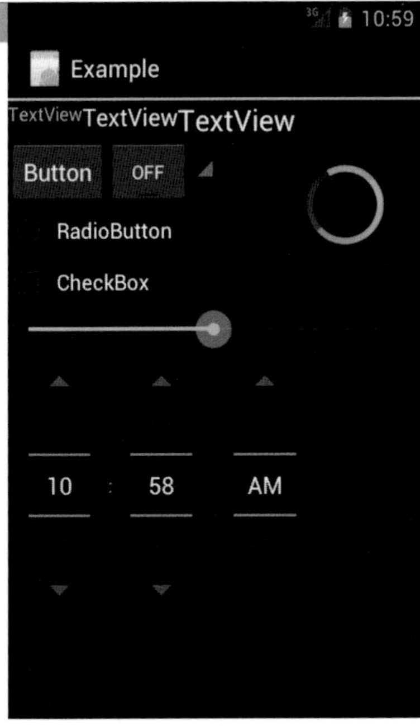

FIGURE 2.2 Some common form widgets available to your app

An Android application's UI is composed of a hierarchy of `View` objects. Each view represents an area on the screen. A `Button`, for example, represents a rectangular area that can be pressed by the user. Android apps arrange views in layout containers, also known as `ViewGroups`. Views have attributes that specify their look and arrangement within the container. The Android framework provides many views and containers. **Figure 2.2** shows a few of the common view elements available. However, there are many more, and you should spend some time using the graphical layout editor to discover all the available views. It's also possible to create custom views by subclassing a `View` class. You'll learn more about this later in the book.

COMMON VIEW ATTRIBUTES

To control how the views of your UI are arranged and displayed onscreen, Android provides a number of `View` attributes—you saw some of them in Chapter 1. `View` attributes exist as fields in `View` classes and are accessed using getter and setter methods. They are also specified as XML attributes in XML layout files. The attributes follow the form `android:attribute_name`, where *`attribute_name`* is the actual name of the attribute. All system attributes use the `android:` prefix. Here, we'll go over the most important attributes and behaviors, covering a few confusing aspects along the way.

NOTE: Android uses special dimension units called density-independent pixels, or dp. This is one way that Android handles varying screen sizes and densities. You'll learn more about this in Chapter 3. For now, know that you should almost always use dp units when specifying the size of your UI elements.

HEIGHT AND WIDTH

Every view in Android is required to have a height and width. These are specified using the `layout_height` and `layout_width` attributes. Values for width and height are specified by using exact dimensions or by using the special symbolic values `wrap_content` or `match_parent`. Android API version 8 renamed `fill_parent` to `match_parent`, but `fill_parent` is still allowed for backward compatibility. You should use `match_parent` in your layout files because `fill_parent` is now deprecated.

With `wrap_content`, the view will take only as much space as it needs to contain any content inside it. Using `match_parent` will make the view expand to fill the entire inside of its parent view. Alternatively, specifying an exact dimension will make a view take exactly that much space onscreen. So, for example, you can create a view with a width of 48px, and it will take exactly 48 pixels of space on the display. In general, you'll find that `match_parent` and `wrap_content` are the most useful for creating your layouts.

It can be tempting to use exact dimensions when creating your layouts. You should avoid this urge and instead use the more flexible `wrap_content` and `match_parent`. For example, you could have two views: one taking up a quarter of the screen and the other taking the remaining space. This will make your views flexible enough to fit any screen size.

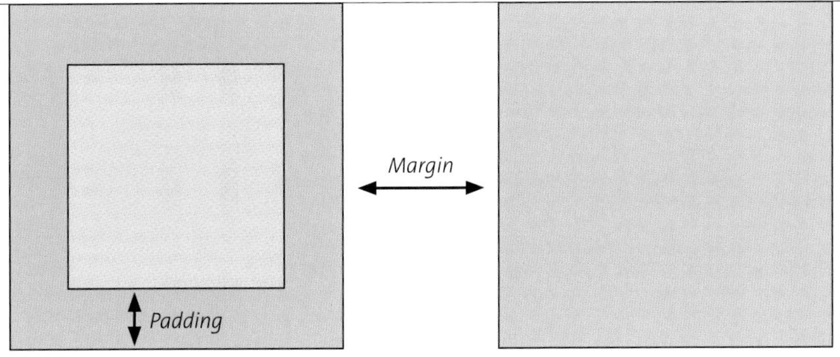

FIGURE 2.3 The difference between padding and margin

MARGINS AND PADDING

When creating your layouts, you'll want to add space around your views. This increases the usability of your app by increasing the target size of tappable areas. It can also add visual appeal to your app. Android uses two attributes for creating the space around views: `layout_margin` and `padding`. Margins create space on the outside of a view, which will separate the view from the surrounding views. Padding creates space inside a view. **Figure 2.3** shows the difference between them. You can use attributes to set the dimensions of padding and margin for all sides of a view or for just a single side.

GRAVITY

By default, Android will place views on the left side of the screen. To change this, you use the `gravity` attribute. The `gravity` attribute controls the default position of a view's children inside that view. For example, you can use the `gravity` attribute on a linear layout to position its child views on the right side of the screen. By default, layout containers have `gravity` set to `left`. Most other views have their default `gravity` set to `center`.

NOTE: When setting `gravity`, you must account for the size of the views. The `gravity` attribute only positions child views inside the parent view. If the parent view takes up half the screen, then `gravity` will position children only in that half of the screen. If you are trying to use `gravity` and not getting the results you expect, check the size of your views.

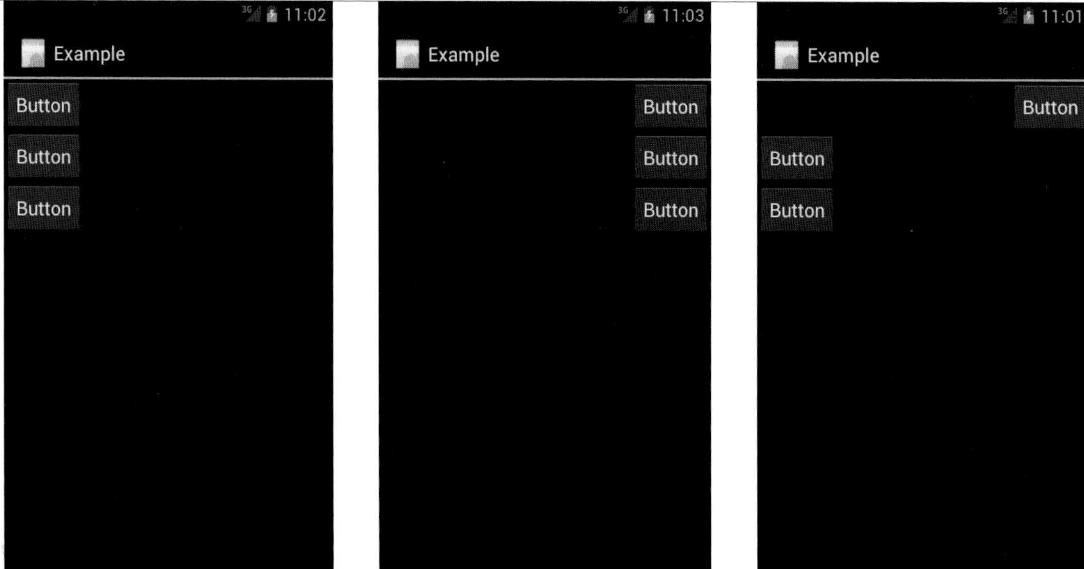

FIGURE 2.4 A linear layout with default `gravity`

FIGURE 2.5 A linear layout with `gravity` set to `right`

FIGURE 2.6 A linear layout with default settings; the first `button` has `layout_gravity` set to `right`.

Similar to the `gravity` attribute is the `layout_gravity` attribute. While `gravity` affects the position of the children of a view, `layout_gravity` specifies the position of a view to its parent. Taking the example of a linear layout again, if you keep the `gravity` at its default value, all views will be positioned on the left side of the screen. You can then set the `layout_gravity` attribute of one of the child views to `right`, and that single view will be positioned on the right side of the screen. **Figures 2.4, 2.5,** and **2.6** show three screens: default `gravity`, `gravity` set to `right`, and one button's `layout_gravity` set to `right`.

MORE OPTIONS

There are many more optional view attributes. Some of them are specific to particular views, like setting the source of an `ImageView` or the text of a `TextView`. Some are available on every view but have a default value, like the background used for images. Some can even be used to create animations for your views. You should explore these attributes and get familiar with the basics. You'll learn about more attributes throughout this book, but there are too many to cover them all.

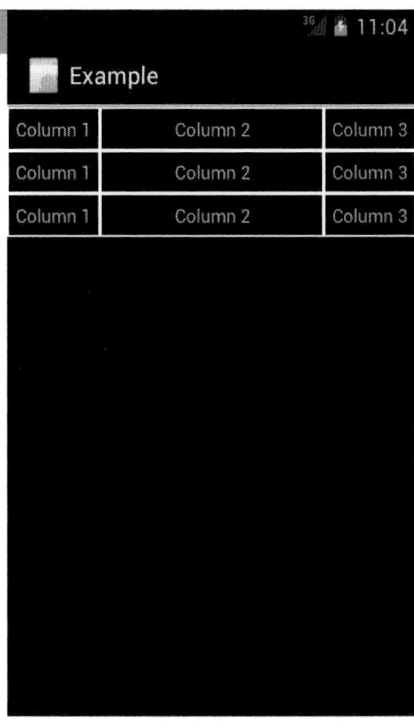

FIGURE 2.7 An example of a table layout. Cell borders are not normally displayed.

The Android view hierarchy starts with a layout container. These containers hold the child views and arrange them relative to each other. There are several container types with different characteristics, optimizing them for different situations.

FRAMELAYOUT

The simplest layout container is the `FrameLayout`. This container does not arrange child views at all. It simply presents each view, one on top of the other. The order of the views is based on their declaration in the XML file: Views declared later in the file are drawn on top. Use this layout whenever you want to create overlapping views.

`FrameLayout` is especially useful when creating customized tappable elements. You can use the `FrameLayout` to pair a button with an `ImageView`, setting the button background to be transparent. This gives you more control over the padding and scaling of button images than just setting a background does.

TABLELAYOUT

The `TableLayout` displays data in a tabular format (**Figure 2.7**). It arranges subviews into rows and columns, with each row contained in a `TableRow` container. A `TableLayout` will have as many columns as the `TableRow` with the most cells. Unlike the children of most views, the children of a `TableLayout` cannot specify a layout_width. This is handled by the TableLayout and will be set for you. Cells can be marked to span multiple columns and expand or shrink to fill available space.

You should use this layout only when displaying a table of data. In other cases, use a LinearLayout, a RelativeLayout, or the new GridLayout.

LINEARLAYOUT

You saw the LinearLayout in Chapter 1. You'll be using this container a lot in your apps. As the name implies, this container arranges child views in a single direction, vertically or horizontally. The orientation attribute sets the direction for a linear layout's child views. Child views specify how much space they will consume within the linear layout. They do this by setting a layout_weight. This parameter specifies the relative weight of one view versus the other views. By default, all views have a weight of 0. This means they will take up exactly as much space as they need to contain their content. Setting a weight higher than 0 will make a view expand to fill the remaining space in the layout. The relative value of the weight versus the weight of other views will determine how much space a particular view consumes.

The buttons in **Figure 2.8** are contained in a linear layout with orientation set to vertical. Each button takes up as much space as needed to contain its content. The top button has its weight set to 0 and is taking up only the space needed to display its content. The other two buttons have their weights set to 1 and 4, so in addition to their normal size, they expand to fill the remaining space. The bottom button has a higher weight and consumes more of the available space. It actually takes four-fifths of the remaining space, leaving one-fifth for the third button (1 + 4 = 5). Using layout weights allows you to create proportionally arranged views, greatly increasing the flexibility of your layouts.

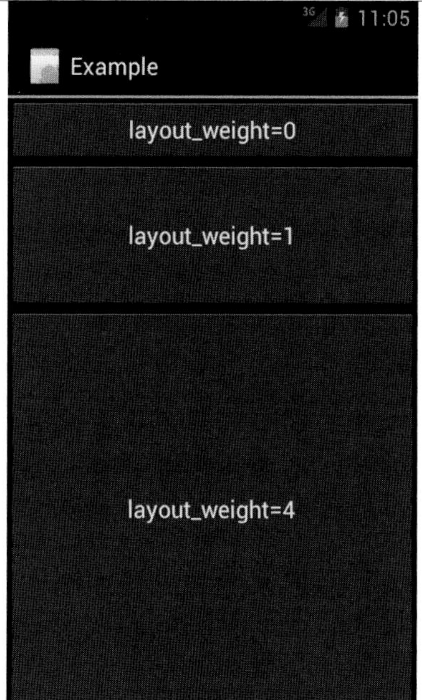

FIGURE 2.8 A linear layout with three buttons demonstrating `layout_weight`

NOTE: A somewhat confusing aspect of using `layout_weight` is its relationship to the `layout_height` and `layout_width` attributes. The weight will generally override the height and width, but not always. If you plan to use the `layout_weight` attribute, set the corresponding height or width to `0dp`. That way, the view size will be controlled by the weight and nothing else.

The linear layout is simple to use and perfect for the first version of the TimeTracker app. Remember Figure 2.1? Here is how you create that UI:

1. Open the TimeTracker project you created earlier.

2. Open the `res/main.xml` file that was created automatically. Replace its content with the following XML layout:

```
<?xml version="1.0" encoding="utf-8"?>

<LinearLayout xmlns:android="http://schemas.android.com/
→ apk/res/android"

    android:layout_width="match_parent"
    → android:layout_height="match_parent"

    android:orientation="vertical">

    <TextView android:id="@+id/counter" android:text="0"

        android:layout_height="wrap_content"
        → android:textAppearance="?android:
        → attr/textAppearanceLarge"

        android:gravity="center" android:padding="10dp"

        android:layout_width="match_parent"
        → android:textSize="50dp"></TextView>

    <LinearLayout android:layout_height="wrap_content"

        android:layout_width="match_parent"
        → android:orientation="horizontal">

        <Button android:text="@string/start"
        → android:id="@+id/start_stop"

            android:layout_height="wrap_content"
            → android:layout_width="0dp"

            android:layout_weight="1"></Button>

        <Button android:text="@string/reset"
        → android:id="@+id/reset"

            android:layout_height="wrap_content"
            → android:layout_width="0dp"
```

```
            android:layout_weight="1"></Button>
    </LinearLayout>
    <ListView android:layout_weight="1"
    → android:layout_width="fill_parent"
        android:layout_height="0dp"
        → android:id="@+id/time_list">
    </ListView>
</LinearLayout>
```

This XML code uses a linear layout to arrange three children: a text view to hold the current time, another linear layout that will hold the two buttons, and a list view that displays a list of all previous times. The buttons are arranged using a second linear layout with `orientation` set to `horizontal`. Note that you set the `layout_width` of both buttons to `0dp` and the `layout_weight` to `1`. This makes the buttons expand to fill the width of the layout and divide that space equally. The list view will display a list of times with a custom layout for each row. You'll learn more about using list views in the next section.

RELATIVELAYOUT

The other common layout container is the `RelativeLayout`. Relative layouts are more flexible than linear layouts, but they are also more complex. As its name implies, the relative layout arranges child views based on their position relative to the other views and to the relative layout itself. For example, to place a text view just to the left of a button, you would create the text view with the attribute `toLeftOf="@id/my_button"`. This flexibility allows you to create very complex UIs within this one container.

TIP: Views that reference other views in a relative layout must be declared after the referenced view.

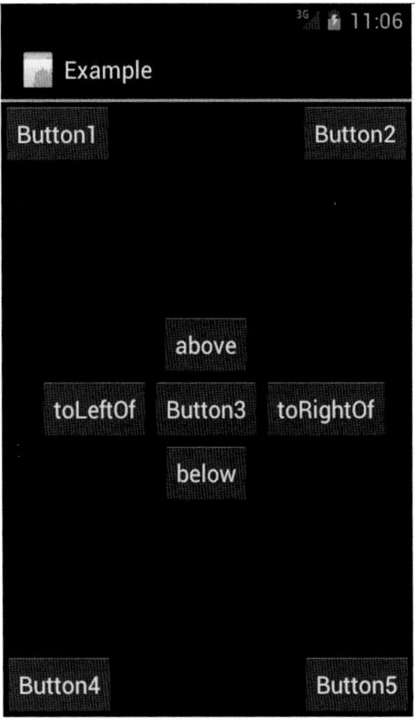

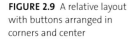

FIGURE 2.9 A relative layout with buttons arranged in corners and center

Figure 2.9 shows some buttons arranged in a relative layout. Buttons 1, 2, 3, 4, and 5 are positioned relative to the parent `RelativeLayout` container. The corner buttons have attributes aligning them with the top, bottom, left, and right of the relative layout. The center button is aligned with the center of the relative layout, and the remaining buttons are positioned relative to the center button. **Table 2.1** lists the attributes available for views inside a `RelativeLayout`, as well as how they are used.

NOTE: The child views of a relative layout are arranged in the order they are declared. So if a view is declared to be in the center of the layout, all subsequent views aligned to that view would be arranged based on the center of the view.

TABLE 2.1 XML Attributes for RelativeLayout

ATTRIBUTES	DESCRIPTION
layout_alignParentTop, layout_alignParentBottom, layout_alignParentRight, layout_alignParentLeft	These attributes will align the view with the parent. Use these to fix the view to the sides of the RelativeLayout container. The value can be true or false.
layout_centerHorizontal, layout_centerVertical, layout_centerInParent	Use these attributes to center a view horizontally or vertically or to directly center a view within the parent RelativeLayout. The value can be true or false.
layout_alignTop, layout_alignBottom, layout_alignRight, layout_alignLeft	These attributes are used to align the view with another view. Use these to line up views in the layout. The value must be the id of another view.
layout_alignBaseline	This attribute sets all the edges of a view to align with the specified view. This is useful when you have overlapping views and need them to exactly match. The value must be the id of another view.
layout_above, layout_below, layout_leftOf, layout_rightOf	Use these attributes to position a view relative to another view. This attribute sets rules on the view to ensure that it never crosses the boundary set by the edge of the target view. The value must be the id of another view.

It can be tricky to master using the relative layout, but it will pay off when you create more-complex UIs. Remember that if you find yourself creating multiple nested linear layouts, you should consider using a relative layout to optimize the drawing of your UI.

NOTE: You cannot have a circular dependency in a relative layout. So, for example, you cannot set the width of the RelativeLayout to wrap_content and use alignParentTop on one of the child views. This will generate an error, and your R.java file will not be generated.

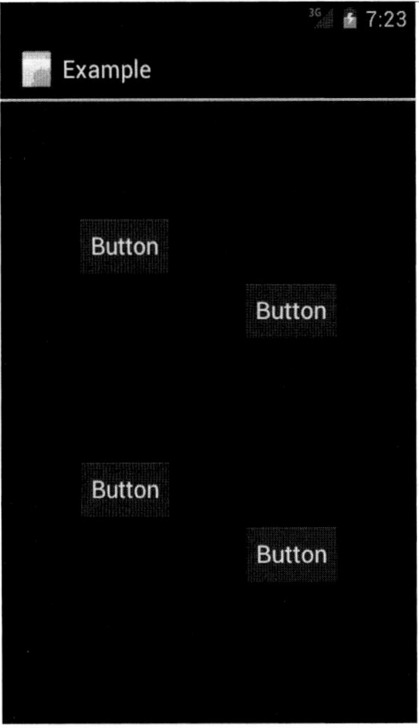

FIGURE 2.10 `GridLayout` produces complex layouts without nested containers.

GRIDLAYOUT

Android 4 brought a new layout container called `GridLayout`. As its name implies, it arranges views into a grid of columns and rows. This layout makes it easier to create the common "dashboard"-style UI seen in apps like Google+. You would normally create such a UI using a `TableLayout`, but `GridLayout` allows you to create the same layout with a flatter hierarchy. This improves performance by reducing the number of views that Android has to draw. `GridLayout` has also been designed to support drag-and-drop creation of UIs using the graphical layout editor. Developers will be able to create complex and efficient layouts just by using a `GridLayout` and the layout editor.

Figure 2.10 shows an example layout created using the `GridLayout` container. In this layout are four buttons arranged into rows and columns. The XML to create that layout is:

```
<?xml version="1.0" encoding="utf-8"?>
<GridLayout xmlns:android="http://schemas.android.com/
→ apk/res/android"
    android:layout_width="match_parent"
    android:layout_height="match_parent"
    android:columnCount="3" >
    <Button
        android:id="@+id/button1"
        android:layout_column="1"
        android:layout_row="1"
        android:text="Button" />
    <Button
        android:id="@+id/button2"
        android:layout_column="1"
        android:layout_gravity="bottom"
        android:layout_row="2"
        android:text="Button" />
    <Button
        android:id="@+id/button3"
        android:layout_column="2"
        android:layout_row="2"
        android:text="Button" />
    <Button
        android:id="@+id/button4"
        android:layout_column="2"
        android:layout_row="3"
        android:text="Button" />
```

Unlike a TableLayout, a GridLayout does not need explicit TableRow elements. The buttons themselves declare the rows and columns in which they should appear.

By default, this layout will not include any space between the buttons. To add space, you can use the traditional margin and padding parameters, or you can use a new view that was introduced in Android 4: Space. This view simply adds a gap between the elements of a layout. When using drag and drop to create a layout in the graphical layout editor, spaces are automatically inserted to achieve the desired appearance. Here are the Spaces created by the layout editor for the layout in Figure 2.10:

```
<Space
        android:layout_width="58dp"
        android:layout_height="1dp"
        android:layout_column="0"
        android:layout_gravity="fill_horizontal"
        android:layout_row="0" />
    <Space
        android:layout_width="128dp"
        android:layout_height="1dp"
        android:layout_column="1"
        android:layout_gravity="fill_horizontal"
        android:layout_row="0" />
    <Space
        android:layout_width="134dp"
        android:layout_height="1dp"
        android:layout_column="2"
        android:layout_gravity="fill_horizontal"
        android:layout_row="0" />
```

```
    <Space
        android:layout_width="1dp"
        android:layout_height="83dp"
        android:layout_column="0"
        android:layout_gravity="fill_horizontal"
        android:layout_row="0" />
    <Space
        android:layout_width="1dp"
        android:layout_height="180dp"
        android:layout_column="0"
        android:layout_gravity="fill_horizontal"
        android:layout_row="2" />
    <Space
        android:layout_width="1dp"
        android:layout_height="173dp"
        android:layout_column="0"
        android:layout_gravity="fill_horizontal"
        android:layout_row="3" />
</GridLayout>
```

DISPLAYING A LIST

One of the most common view types you'll use to develop an app is the ListView. This view presents a vertically scrolling list of items. Each row generally holds some text but will often include other views, such as ImageViews and Buttons (a good example of this is the Contacts app). Use a ListView whenever you have a list of data to present to the user. This view is so common that Android actually provides built-in activities that just display a list.

LISTACTIVITY

A ListActivity will bind to a default view containing a ListView. There is no need to call setContentView in the activity's onCreate method, because the ListActivity is already set to a ListView by default (though you can define a custom view if you choose). The ListActivity class also contains a few convenience methods for retrieving and setting the list data and for handling item selection. Although it's not necessary to use a ListActivity to display a list, you should consider using it whenever you want to display a list of data to the user.

ANDROID DEFAULT LAYOUTS

The ListActivity actually sets its content to a special layout built into the Android OS. This layout contains a single ListView as its content. There are other built-in layouts you can use when creating your app, a number of which are contained in the android.R.layout class. Here are two that you could use with a ListView:

- android.R.layout.simple_list_item_1 is used to display a single line of text in a row of a ListView.
- android.R.layout.two_line_list_item displays two lines of text per row of a list.

In addition to the layout files, Android also has built-in styles, menus, drawables, and other useful views. You should explore the Android package for useful defaults for your app.

XML LAYOUT

Displaying screens of lists is convenient, but sometimes you need to display more than just a list. In those cases, you can create a standard layout and use a list view to show the list. List views are defined the same way as other views in Android:

```
<ListView android:layout_width="match_parent"
    android:layout_height="match_parent" android:id="@+id/list">
</ListView>
```

List views have a few special attributes that you can use for more complex layouts. The first is the `android:entries` attribute. Use this attribute when you have a static, unchanging list of values to populate the list view. Using the `entries` attribute, you can simply reference a resource and not have to programmatically populate the list. Attributes for altering the appearance and behavior of the dividers between rows are also available. In general, you should stick with the defaults and not deviate from the platform look and feel.

ROW LAYOUT

Creating the layout for a list row is the same as for an activty: You create an XML file with a layout container and several views. Each row will contain that layout, allowing you to set values for text and images. The Android platform provides several default row layouts. These are generally sufficient for the list views that you will create. However, you can also create custom layouts for the rows of the list. To create a custom layout, you simply create a new layout file and use it when binding data to the list view.

The time-tracking app will require a custom layout for its list view. In the `res/` folder, create a new layout file called `time_row.xml`:

```
<?xml version="1.0" encoding="utf-8"?>
<LinearLayout xmlns:android="http://schemas.android.com/
→ apk/res/android"
    android:id="@+id/time_row" android:orientation="horizontal"
    android:layout_width="match_parent"
    → android:layout_height="wrap_content"
```

```
    android:gravity="center" android:paddingLeft="10dp"
    android:paddingRight="10dp" android:paddingBottom="20dp"
    android:paddingTop="20dp">
    <TextView android:id="@+id/lap_name"
    → android:layout_height="wrap_content"
        android:text="Lap 1" android:layout_weight="1"
        → android:layout_width="0dp" />
    <TextView android:id="@+id/lap_time"
    → android:layout_height="wrap_content"
        android:text="00:00:00" android:layout_weight="1"
        android:layout_width="0dp" android:gravity="right" />
</LinearLayout>
```

This file uses a simple linear layout to display two text views side by side: one for the name of the session and one for the time. The linear layout uses padding to create some space between the text views.

BINDING DATA TO THE LIST

The `entries` attribute of `ListView` works great if you already know what the list elements are going to be. But if you want to generate the list dynamically, you'll need to set up a list adapter. `ListAdapters` populate the elements of a `ListView` based on some internal data storage. There are `ListAdapters` for populating the list using a static map of values (similar to using the XML `entries` attribute), for loading rows from an array, and for loading data from a database. A `ListAdapter` is a list-specific instance of the `Adapter` class. Adapters are used to bind data to views in your UI (you'll learn more about them later in this book).

When you create a list adapter, you'll want to override the `getView` method. This method is called by the system for each row of the list view. It takes the list position, any existing layout for that row, and the parent view of the row, and it expects the row layout view to be returned. For the TimeTracker app, you'll use the row layout you created earlier. Create a new class called `TimeListAdapter` that extends `ArrayAdapter<Long>`. Then override the `getView` method to load the custom `time_row.xml` layout for every row of the list view:

```
public class TimeListAdapter extends ArrayAdapter<Long> {
    public TimeListAdapter(Context context, int textViewResourceId) {
        super(context, textViewResourceId);
    }
    @Override
    public View getView(int position, View convertView,
    → ViewGroup parent) {
        View view = convertView;
        if (view == null) {
            view = LayoutInflater.from(getContext()).inflate
            → (R.layout.time_row, null);
        }
        long time = getItem(position);
        TextView name = (TextView) view.findViewById(R.id.lap_name);
        String taskString = getContext().getResources().getString
        → (R.string.task_name);
        name.setText(String.format(taskString, position+1));
        TextView lapTime = (TextView) view.findViewById
        → (R.id.lap_time);
        lapTime.setText(DateUtils.formatElapsedTime(time));
        return view;
    }
}
```

This method inflates a custom layout for each row of the list view. Inflating a layout is the process of converting XML layouts into a set of `View` objects (you'll learn more about this in Chapter 3). As the user scrolls through the list, the system will call this method to create the rows of the list. Rows that are no longer visible will be garbage collected. You should take care to prevent needless allocation of memory in data adapters. Unnecessary garbage collection events are one of the primary causes of stutter in Android animations. You will learn some tricks for creating efficient data adapters later in this book.

TIP: Don't inflate new views unless you need to. In this code, the view is only inflated if it doesn't already exist. This is an optimization that prevents unnecessary object creation and garbage collection.

LOADERS

Loading data into a list adapter can be a tedious process: You need to handle things asynchronously to avoid performing too much work on the main thread; you need to keep the displayed data fresh by reloading the list adapter when the data changes; and you have to maintain the data across orientation changes, which destroy and re-create the activity. To simplify this process, Android 3 introduced a helper class called `Loader`. The `Loader` class takes a lot of the drudgery out of loading data asynchronously.

The `Loader` class is available to all versions of Android through the compatibility package. This package contains implementations of new Android APIs, like loaders and fragments, allowing you to use them in older versions of Android. You'll learn more about loaders and fragments in a later chapter, but for now just remember that you can simplify the binding of data to views by using the `Loader` class.

UNDERSTANDING **ACTIVITIES**

Android activities represent the interface to the user. All interaction with users takes place through activities. As a developer, it's important that you create a fast and responsive application that puts the user first. This can be as simple as using easy-to-read text views or as complex as saving the input to a data field as soon as the user types a query. Understanding activities is key to creating responsive and usable applications.

DECLARING ACTIVITIES

All activities must be declared in your application's manifest file. Failing to do so will result in your app throwing an exception when it first runs. Here is a sample activity manifest entry for the TimeTracker app:

```
<activity android:name=".TimeTrackerActivity"
    android:label="@string/app_name">
    <intent-filter>
        <action android:name="android.intent.action.MAIN" />
            <category android:name="android.intent.category.LAUNCHER" />
    </intent-filter>
</activity>
```

The manifest entry contains basic information about the activity, such as its class name and user label. Notice the "`.`" in the `name` attribute? That's a shortcut for using the full package name listed in the `<application>` element. This activity also declares an intent filter that is used to respond to intents sent by the system. In this case, it declares that this is the main activity for the app and that it should respond to the `android.intent.category.LAUNCHER` intent, which is sent when an app icon is tapped on the home screen. You should declare intents that launch activities in the manifest file.

UNDERSTANDING THE ACTIVITY LIFE CYCLE

Activities are short lived—they are continually being created and destroyed. It's up to the developer to properly handle these transitions as the user navigates an app. You create an activity by extending the `Activity` class and implementing a series of callbacks that the system calls when your activity transitions between states. Activities have three basic states, listed in **Table 2.2**.

TABLE 2.2 Activity States

STATE	EXPLANATION
Resumed or Running	In this state, the activity is focused and visible to the user. Users interact with your activity while it is in this state.
Paused	Your activity is still visible, but it is no longer focused. This occurs when something has popped up in front of your application, such as a dialog.
Stopped	Your activity is placed in this state when the user transitions to a new activity and your activity is no longer visible. The system will often destroy your activity to reclaim resources when it is in this state. If all activities of an app are stopped, the system will kill the entire app process to reclaim resources.

`onCreate` is called when an activity is first instantiated by the system. You should always implement this method. You'll perform basic setup of your activity in the `onCreate` method: binding data to the views, setting the layout for the activity, initiating any threads, and so on. You should also implement `onPause`. The `onPause` method is the first callback triggered when the activity is transitioning from the foreground; this is the method you should use to save any changes the user may have entered into your application.

TIP: The `onPause` method is where you should save any data the user would expect to keep. For example, if you created an email application, any text entered by the user should be saved to your database during the `onPause` callback.

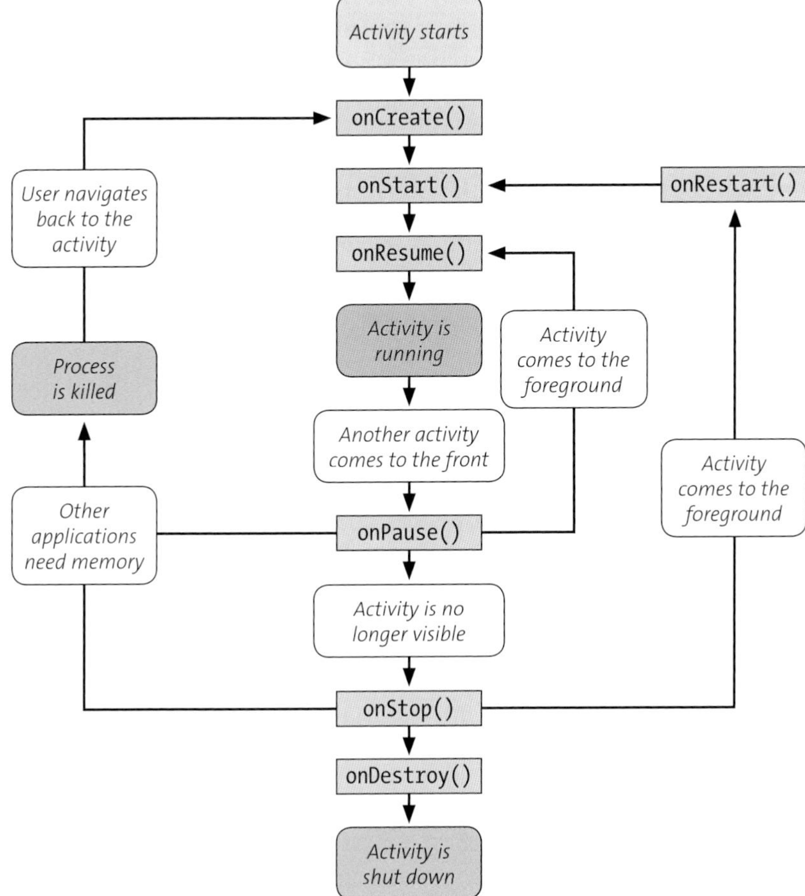

FIGURE 2.11 Activity callbacks showing the part of the life cycle from which they are called

You must always call the superclass implementation of activity callbacks that you implement. If you fail to do so, your activity will throw an exception.

As an activity transitions between the three states, the callbacks of the `Activity` class are triggered. **Figure 2.11** gives an overview of the callbacks and when they are triggered. There are two important things to remember about activities: The system will aggressively destroy your activity when it's not visible to the user; and the callbacks all run on the main thread, so you should not perform any long-running or computationally expensive operations in those callbacks.

The TimeTracker app will need to override the onCreate method for now. You'll also override onDestroy when you create the timer logic. Later, when you implement the database, you will want to override the onPause method to save any data the user has entered.

1. In the com.example package, create a file called **TimeTrackerActivity.java**:

```
public class TimeTrackerActivity extends Activity {
```

2. Override the onCreate method and set up the views using the following code:

```
@Override
    public void onCreate(Bundle savedInstanceState) {
        super.onCreate(savedInstanceState);
        setContentView(R.layout.main);
        // Initialize the timer
        TextView counter = (TextView) findViewById(R.id.counter);
        counter.setText(DateUtils.formatElapsedTime(0));
    if (mTimeListAdapter == null)
            mTimeListAdapter = new TimeListAdapter(this, 0);
        ListView list = (ListView) findViewById(R.id.time_list);
        list.setAdapter(mTimeListAdapter);
    }
}
```

This code sets the XML layout file for your activity by calling setContentView. The setContentView method inflates the XML layout and adds it to the activity view hierarchy. Next, the findViewById method retrieves a reference to the TextView that will hold the current time. It sets the default time value using a DateUtils format. Finally, the ListAdapter that you'll use to load data into the ListView is created and set on the ListView instance.

You should call setContentView in your activity's onCreate method. You may call it as many times as you want in onCreate, but only the last call will execute. Once the view hierarchy has been loaded, you cannot call setContentView again. However, you are still free to update the layout using Java APIs.

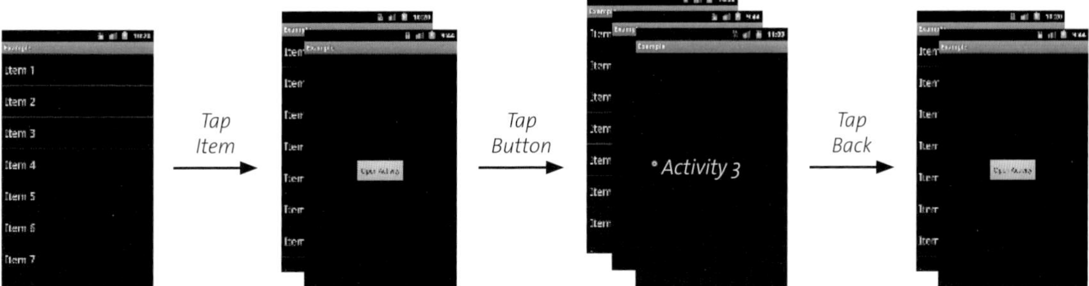

FIGURE 2.12 The back stack. Pressing the Back button will pop the most recent activity off the stack.

UNDERSTANDING TASKS AND THE BACK STACK

Android applications are typically constructed using a series of activities. The system groups these activities into tasks. Each task represents a set of activities as a stack, with activities being pushed onto the stack when the user navigates away from them and being popped off the stack when the user navigates back to them (**Figure 2.12**). This is called the *back stack*. New tasks are created when the user opens a new activity that is not associated with the current activity. Every task has its own back stack.

A **NOTE** ABOUT THE **MAIN THREAD**

The main, or UI, thread for an Android app is where all UI events are triggered. Every button you press generates an event that is dispatched via the main thread. For this reason, it is very important to use worker threads for handling long-running operations. However, updates to the UI are not thread safe. If you try to update the UI from one of your worker threads, an exception will result. Android provides a number of APIs for dealing with this:

- The `Activity.runOnUiThread` method
- The `View.post`, `View.postDelayed`, and `View.postInvalidate` methods
- The `AsyncTask` class
- Message handlers

If you need to update the UI of your application, make sure you either do it from the UI thread or use one of these APIs. You'll learn more about the `AsyncTask` class later in this chapter.

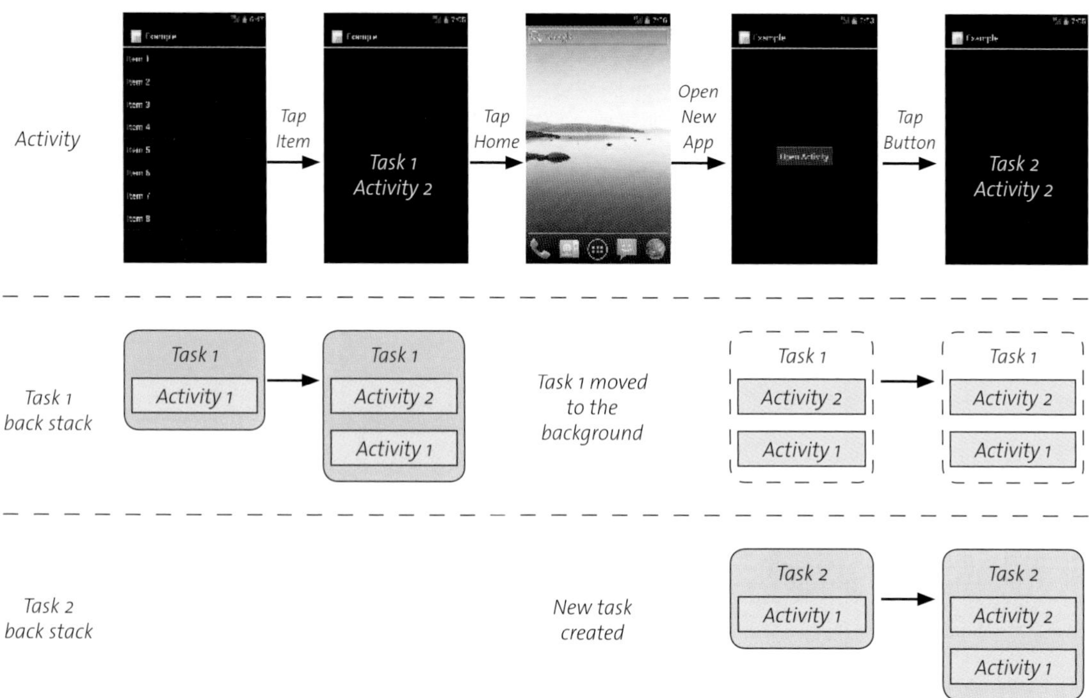

FIGURE 2.13 Two tasks and their back stacks

A simple example will demonstrate (**Figure 2.13**).

1. A user opens an application. This creates a new task. The example is a `ListView`.
2. The user navigates to a new activity by pressing a list item.
3. The user presses Home, then opens a new app. This creates a second task, containing the main activity of the new app.
4. The user navigates to a new activity in this task, again by pressing a list item.

There are now two tasks and two back stacks. The user can switch between the two tasks by pressing Home and tapping one of the application launchers. Alternatively, on Android 4.0 and later, users can press the task switcher button to switch tasks. The Back button will act on the active stack and pop the topmost activity from the task the user is viewing.

It is possible for the same activity to appear multiple times in the back stack. This occurs when the same activity can be started from multiple places. You should watch for these situations, because you could easily consume large amounts of memory storing multiple copies of the same activity. This will also be annoying to users, because they will have to press Back repeatedly to exit your app.

HANDLING CONFIGURATION CHANGES

A common situation that Android apps face is handling device configuration changes. What's a device configuration change? The most basic one is a change in orientation caused by rotating the device. This changes the screen from portrait to landscape. This configuration change results in your current activity being destroyed and re-created. Remember that activities are short lived and that even something as simple as rotating a device will result in a new activity being created.

How do you maintain the input data and state of your app when your activity is destroyed and re-created? You would normally save data in the `onPause` method of your activity. However, this is intended only for application data that the user might find important. In this case, you want to save data that is relevant only to the existing activity instance. To do this, you save the current state of your activity in the `onSaveInstanceState` callback. Unlike `onPause`, `onSaveInstanceState` is not always called by the system. It's only called if the activity is destroyed and will likely be re-created. You should use `onSaveInstanceState` to re-create the state of an activity before it was destroyed. A good use for it is to save the current scroll position in a list, so you can maintain that position across orientation changes. Here is an example that saves the current list position:

```
@Override
protected void onSaveInstanceState(Bundle outState) {
    ListView list = (ListView) findViewById(R.id.time_list);
    int pos = list.getFirstVisiblePosition();
    outState.putInt("first_position", pos);
    super.onSaveInstanceState(outState);
}
```

When `onCreate` is called, retrieve the list position from the input `Bundle` and re-scroll the list. Handling details like this makes your app user friendly.

PREVENTING ANRS

An Android application runs in its own process, which is sandboxed from all other applications. The application is run by a single thread: the main, or UI, thread. To keep the app responsive, Android limits the time that any function call may take. If the function exceeds this time limit, an Application Not Responding (ANR) dialog will be shown to the user, asking them to either wait or force the app to close. You want to avoid causing an ANR at all costs. ANRs happen when you perform long-running operations on the main thread; examples include network I/O, disk I/O, database queries, and CPU-intensive calculations.

TIP: Anytime you receive a callback from the Android system, it is done by the main thread. This includes activity and service callbacks, event handlers, button listeners, and so on. Remember not to perform any blocking operations in these callbacks. If you do need to perform such an operation, start a background thread or an `AsyncTask` to handle it.

STRICTMODE

Android 2.3 introduced a new developer tool called `StrictMode`. This tool will detect disk or network operations occurring on the main thread and take action to warn the developer. It provides a number of methods for warning the developer, from simple logging statements to full-blown application crashes.

`StrictMode` is not guaranteed to find all disk and network I/O occurring on the main thread. In particular, any accesses occurring through a Java Native Interface (JNI) will not be detected. Be aware that although `StrictMode` is helpful, it is not sufficient for creating responsive applications.

DECLARING STRICTMODE

Here is a simple `StrictMode` declaration that detects all types of network and disk I/O:

```
StrictMode.setThreadPolicy(new StrictMode.ThreadPolicy.Builder()
    .detectAll()
    .penaltyLog()
    .penaltyDialog()
    .build());
```

This will detect any network and disk I/O on the executing thread and take two actions: printing a warning to the log and displaying a warning dialog to the user. This example sets the warning only on the current thread. To detect violations on any thread, use the `setVmPolicy` call:

```
StrictMode.setVmPolicy(new StrictMode.VmPolicy.Builder()
    .detectAll()
    .penaltyLog()
    .penaltyDeath()
    .build());
```

It's recommended that you enable `StrictMode` in all projects you create. It's better to catch these cases earlier in development, when significant architecture changes will not be required.

DISABLING STRICTMODE

While `StrictMode` is very helpful for creating responsive applications, you should disable it when you release your app in the market. Otherwise, users may encounter the policy violation dialogs or even experience app crashes. A simple method of handling this is to enable `StrictMode` only if the app is built in debug mode (signed with a debug key). To detect if an app is running in debug mode, check the `ApplicationInfo` flags. The following code snippet checks if your app was built using the debug signing key:

```
public static boolean isDebugMode(Context context) {
    PackageManager pm = context.getPackageManager();
    try {
        ApplicationInfo info = pm.getApplicationInfo
        ➥ (context.getPackageName(), 0);
        return (info.flags & ApplicationInfo.FLAG_DEBUGGABLE) != 0;
    } catch (NameNotFoundException e) {
    }
    return true;
}
```

BACKGROUND TASKS

A common situation that you'll encounter is the need to perform some long-running operation that can't be done on the UI thread—things like downloading RSS feeds, writing a file, or running a timer. These tasks could potentially take many seconds to run and would block the UI thread from updating. There are several strategies you can take to handle these situations. Typically, you will create a new thread that can perform the task, updating the UI or application state when finished. Here are some strategies for implementing this behavior.

HANDLERS AND MESSAGE QUEUES

Running a thread in the background is a good way to prevent blocking of the UI thread. However, when the task is complete, you will often want to update the UI. Updates to the UI can be performed only by the UI thread, or an exception will be generated. To do this, you use the `Handler` class. A handler allows you to send messages to be processed by the handler at some later time. These messages can be processed immediately or scheduled for processing at some time in the future. Handlers process messages in a `handleMessage` method.

By default, a `Handler` instance is bound to the thread that creates it (typically the main thread). Binding the handler to the UI thread provides a convenient method for updating the UI asynchronously. However, you also have the option of running the handler on a separate thread by supplying an optional `Looper` instance. A looper is used to run a message loop for a thread. Using a looper, you can send messages and have them executed by any thread instance.

NOTE: The `Looper` class creates and manages a `MessageQueue` object that holds all messages for a thread. The UI thread already has a message queue and looper set up for you.

The ability to post messages to be processed at later times makes handlers ideal for implementing timing-based behavior. Here is a simple handler that the TimeTracker application will use to track time intervals:

```
private Handler mHandler = new Handler() {
    public void handleMessage(Message msg) {
        long current = System.currentTimeMillis();
        mTime += current - mStart;
        mStart = current;
        TextView counter = (TextView) TimeTrackerActivity.this.
        → findViewById(R.id.counter);
        counter.setText(DateUtils.formatElapsedTime(mTime/1000));
        mHandler.sendEmptyMessageDelayed(0, 250);
    };
};
```

This code updates two fields of the enclosing `Activity` class that keep the current time. Then it updates the UI (remember that the `Handler` callback will run on the UI thread by default unless you explicitly give it another thread to run on). Finally, it schedules another message for 100 milliseconds in the future. The `sendEmptyMessage` method also takes an integer parameter that distinguishes it. Here, there is only a single message, so set it to 0. Using the handler messaging API, you can create convenience methods for using the timer:

1. Create a `startTimer` method in the `TimeTrackerActivity` class. This method will record the current system time and send a message to the handler, starting the timer. To prevent the possibility of having started the timer twice, remove any existing messages before sending the next one.

   ```
   private void startTimer() {
           mStart = System.currentTimeMillis();
           mHandler.removeMessages(0);
           mHandler.sendEmptyMessage(0);
       }
   ```

2. The stopTimer method just removes any messages from the handler message queue.

```
private void stopTimer() {
    mHandler.removeMessages(0);
}
```

3. The resetTimer method will call stopTimer and then add the current time to the list adapter, which will display it in the list.

```
private void resetTimer() {
    stopTimer();
    if (mTimeListAdapter != null)
        mTimeListAdapter.add(mTime/1000);
    mTime = 0;
}
```

   Finally, you will need to know if the timer is stopped.

4. Create a method that checks for messages in the message queue.

```
private boolean isTimerRunning() {
    return mHandler.hasMessages(0);
}
```

You now have all the logic for the timer completed.

Activity.runOnUIThread

It's very common to use a handler just to update the UI from a background thread. Android provides a shortcut for these situations with the Activity.runOnUiThread method. This method takes a runnable and posts it to the UI thread message handler. When available, the main thread will then run the code contained in that runnable.

ASYNCTASK

It's very common to start a background thread to perform some task and then update the UI when finished. You could just use a thread to perform these tasks and then use the `runOnUiThread` method to display that data to the user. But what happens if you need to display progress? Posting runnables to the UI message handler is too heavyweight for these situations. Luckily, Android includes a class called `AsyncTask` designed specifically for that scenario.

You can extend the `AsyncTask` class to create a simple thread to perform background tasks and publish the results on the UI thread. It includes methods for updating the UI before and after a task has completed, along with progress updates along the way. Here is the basic form of an `AsyncTask`:

```
private class DownloadFilesTask extends AsyncTask<URL, Integer, Long> {
    protected Long doInBackground(URL... urls) {
    while (true) {
        // Do some work
        publishProgress((int) ((i / (float) count) * 100));
    }
    return result;
    }
    protected void onProgressUpdate(Integer... progress) {
        setProgressPercent(progress[0]);
    }
    protected void onPostExecute(Long result) {
        showDialog("Result is " + result);
    }
}
```

The three type arguments given to the task are used to specify the type of the parameters given at execution time, the type of the parameters given to set progress, and the result type returned when the background task has completed. You can use `onPreExecute` to update the UI before your task runs, `onProgressUpdate` to update a UI progress indicator, and `onPostExecute` to update the UI when the task finishes. These methods all run on the main UI thread, so there is no danger in updating your views. All code runs in the `doInBackground` method, which you can think of as just being the run method of a thread.

`AsyncTask` is most useful for quick one-off tasks that need to update a UI component (such as downloading new posts from Twitter and then loading those posts into a timeline).

FINISHING THE TIMETRACKER

You almost have everything completed for the first version of the TimeTracker app. It just needs some logic to handle the button presses.

1. Back in the onCreate method of your TimeTrackerActivity, add the following code:

```
Button startButton = (Button) findViewById(R.id.start_stop);
startButton.setOnClickListener(this);
Button stopButton = (Button) findViewById(R.id.reset);
stopButton.setOnClickListener(this);
```

   This sets the TimeTrackerActivity class to be the listener for Button events. You'll learn more about event handling in the next chapter, but for now, update the TimeTrackerActivity to implement the OnClickListener interface.

2. Override the onClick method. This method will be called each time one of the buttons is pressed.

```
@Override
    public void onClick(View v) {
        TextView ssButton = (TextView) findViewById
        → (R.id.start_stop);
```

3. Check which button was pressed. If the user pressed the Start/Stop button, check the state of the timer. If it's stopped, you need to start it and change the button text to "Stop"; otherwise, stop the timer and change the button text to "Start":

```
        if (v.getId() == R.id.start_stop) {
            if (isTimerStopped()) {
                startTimer();
                ssButton.setText(R.string.stop);
            } else {
                stopTimer();
                ssButton.setText(R.string.start);
            }
```

FIGURE 2.14 Your first app

4. If the user pressed the Reset button, reset the timer and counter TextView and then set the Start/Stop button text to "Start":

```
        } else if (v.getId() == R.id.reset) {
            resetTimer();
            TextView counter = (TextView) findViewById
            → (R.id.counter);
            counter.setText(DateUtils.formatElapsedTime(0));
            ssButton.setText(R.string.start);
        }
    }
```

You can now run the app! It should look like **Figure 2.14**.

You should be able to start and pause the timer and record the previous values in the list. In the next chapter, you'll go further—you'll extend the app to work on multiple screen sizes, add some notifications, and make the timer work in the background.

WRAPPING UP

This chapter introduced the common Android views and layout containers, along with the attributes used to display them. You also started building a basic time-tracking app. Along the way, you learned that

- Android provides many basic form widgets for building your UI.
- There are several layout container types, and they each have specific situations in which you should use them.
- Any updates to your app UI must take place on the UI thread.
- You can use a `ListView` to display lists of data to your users, and you can bind data to that `ListView` by using a `ListAdapter`.
- Understanding the activity life cycle is fundamental to building a responsive app.
- You can use `StrictMode` to prevent Application Not Responding (ANR) errors.

3

GOING **FURTHER**

Now that you have a basic app, it's time to add some more features. To start, you'll need to handle some more events from the user, create an ongoing notification, and list extra options in a menu. Along the way, you'll learn the specifics of supporting multiple device configurations; explore event callbacks and multiple event filtering; create notifications, toasts, and dialogs to alert the user; and learn when and how to create menus.

SUPPORTING **MULTIPLE** SCREEN **SIZES**

Android is designed to operate on a wide range of hardware devices, but writing a separate interface for every device would be a nightmare. Luckily, the Android OS provides a number of abstractions that support this diverse set of hardware.

RESOURCE QUALIFIERS

Android has many features that are inspired by the web (not surprising given that it was created by Google). Nowhere is this more apparent than in the design philosophy of Android views. In contrast to iOS devices, Android apps don't know the screen resolution, size, or aspect ratio of the devices they run on, but you can use the `View` classes to stretch and shrink layouts to fill the available space, just as you can on the web.

You've already seen how to create Android layouts, and you've learned how to create a layout that stretches to fill the available space. This creates a flexible layout, but it's usually not enough to make your app work on every device configuration. Often, you need to do more than just adjust the size of elements—you actually need to create a different layout to provide a useful interface. To make this easier, Android uses a series of layout qualifiers that define different device configurations. The layout qualifiers are appended to the resource folder names. Using these folders, you can create a layout for a specific set of device configurations; Android will automatically select the appropriate layout file for the user's device.

For example, when a phone is held in portrait, the basic XML layout file for that device will be loaded and displayed. When a phone is rotated to landscape, a landscape-specific layout can be loaded, but only if it is available; if no landscape version is available, the standard portrait version will be loaded. Layout qualifiers exist for screen density, orientation, screen size, mobile country codes, region, platform version, primary navigation mode, and much more. **Table 3.1** summarizes the important qualifiers.

TIP: The number of layout options may seem overwhelming at first. Don't worry. In general, you will only need to handle the orientation, screen size, and screen density qualifiers.

In the Hello World app you created in Chapter 1, the call to `setContentView` will load the XML layout file and display it to the user. To add a new landscape version of the layout, follow these steps:

1. In the `res/` directory, create a new folder named **`layout-land/`** and put a copy of the `main.xml` file into it.
2. Open the new file and change the string to `"Hello Landscape"`.

Now when you start the app, you will see the standard layout in portrait but the new layout in landscape.

TABLE 3.1 Common Layout Resource Qualifiers

CONFIGURATION OPTION	EXAMPLE	DESCRIPTION
Screen orientation	`port` `land`	The orientation of the device. This changes often while your application is running.

Screen pixel density	`ldpi`
	`mdpi`
	`hdpi`
	`xhdpi`
	`nodpi`
		The number of pixels per square inch of the display. An image will appear as different physical sizes depending on the pixel density of the screen. Use these qualifiers to create images of different sizes for each screen density (use `nodpi` to provide image resources that you do not want to scale based on the screen density). Most Android devices on the market now are `mdpi` and `hdpi` devices. `xhdpi` was introduced in API level 13 and is intended for tablet devices.

Screen size	`small`
	`normal`
	`large`
	`xlarge`
		A rough approximation of the physical screen size. Most Android devices are normal to large. The `xlarge` qualifier represents tablet devices. Consider using smallestWidth, available width, and available height for Android 3.2 and above.

smallestWidth, available width, available height	`sw320dp`
	`sw720dp`
	`w720dp`
	`h720dp`
		The available screen pixels for width and height. These qualifiers were added by Android 3.2 and make it easier to create layouts for specific screen sizes.

API version	`v6` `v14`	The minimum API version supported by the device. For example, the qualifier `v7` means these resources should be used for all devices running Android API version 7 and later.

Note that this is not an exhaustive list of qualifiers. Consult the Android documentation for all the available options.

RESOURCE QUALIFIER PRECEDENCE

Android selects the appropriate resources at runtime, based on the device configuration. Since multiple resource folders could match, Android establishes precedence for qualifiers to resolve conflicts. This precedence determines which resources are selected. Consult the Android documentation for the full list of qualifiers and their precedence.

When selecting resources, these are the general steps that Android takes to determine the proper folder:

1. Eliminate all folders that contradict the device configuration.
2. Select the next qualifier in precedence.
3. If any folders match this qualifier, eliminate all folders that do not match. If no folders match this qualifier, return to step 2.
4. Continue until only one resource folder remains.

The exception to these rules is screen pixel density. Android will scale any resources to fit the screen; therefore, all pixel densities are valid. Android will select the closest density that is available, preferring to scale down larger densities.

TIP: When creating resource folders, you must list qualifiers in their precedence order. Your app will not compile otherwise.

An example will better illustrate how Android selects resources. Consider a device with the following configuration:

- Screen orientation: landscape
- Screen pixel density: `hdpi`
- Screen size: large
- Touchscreen type: `finger`

You have the following resource folders in your app:

```
/res/layout/
/res/layout-notouch/
/res/layout-land/
```

/res/layout-land-ldpi/

/res/layout-land-finger/

/res/layout-hdpi/

Android will run through its steps to select the best resource:

1. Eliminate the /res/layout-notouch/ folder because it conflicts with the touchscreen qualifier.
2. There are no folders with screen-size qualifiers, so skip to the next qualifier.
3. Orientation is the next highest precedence, so eliminate all folders that do not have the land qualifer. This leaves three folders: /res/layout-land/, /res/layout-land-ldpi/, and /res/layout-land-finger/.
4. The next qualifier is pixel density. There is no exact match, so continue to the next qualifier. If no other qualifiers match, select the nearest pixel density.
5. The last qualifier is touchscreen type. In this case, finger means that the device has a capacitive touchscreen, so eliminate all folders that do not contain the finger qualifier.
6. The only remaining folder is /res/layout-land-finger/. Select the layouts in this folder.

Android performs this procedure for every resource your layouts require. Often, resources will be mixed from multiple locations. For example, the layout may be taken from the /res/layout-ldpi/ folder, but the drawable resources could be taken from the /res/layout-hdpi/ folder. Remember that Android selects each resource independently and will pick the best match. If you start getting strange problems with your layouts, check the precedence on your resource folders. Android may be loading different resources than you expect!

NOTE: Android will select only screen size resource qualifiers that are smaller than or equal to the device configuration (excluding the pixel density qualifier). If you have only xlarge resources and the device has a small screen, then your app will crash when it runs.

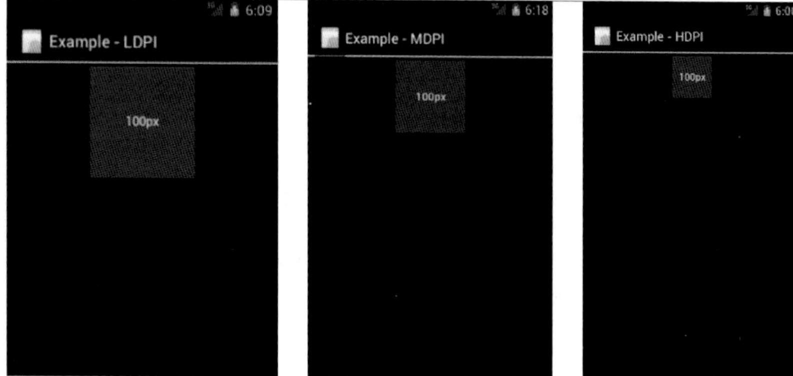

FIGURE 3.1 A button with a fixed pixel size. At different screen resolutions, it appears as a physically different size.

DENSITY-INDEPENDENT PIXELS

Using resource qualifiers and Android's layout containers will let you create layouts that stretch and compress to fill available space. But sometimes you need to specify the exact dimensions of a view. If you've done GUI programming, you're probably used to specifying exact sizes in pixels. Android supports this, but you should avoid using absolute pixel or dimension values when you create your app. The pixel density of devices varies greatly, and the same resource will appear as a different physical size on each device. **Figure 3.1** shows an example of a button that has its height and width values specified in pixels. At each screen density, the relative size of the view is different.

To handle this, Android has several ways of declaring dimensions in a density-independent manner, summarized in **Table 3.2**.

Figure 3.2 shows the previous example, but with the height and width of the button specified in dp. The buttons appear much closer to the same size on the screen.

In general, you should use dp for all units of measure (or sp for text sizes). Using these units will make your layouts appear consistent across device sizes and densities. This will ensure you get maximum device compatibility and will help you avoid layout headaches later.

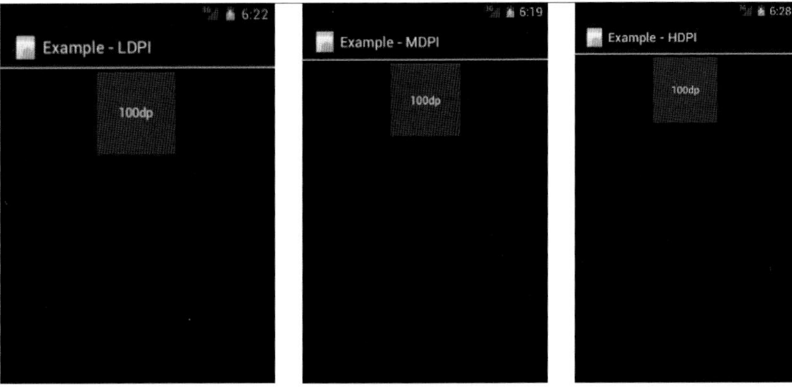

FIGURE 3.2 A button with density-independent pixels will appear as the same physical size, regardless of screen density.

TABLE 3.2 Android Dimension Units

UNIT	DESCRIPTION
px	The physical pixels on the device. This will make a view take up an exact number of pixels on the screen. However, since every device has a different number of pixels, and the pixels might be different physical sizes, this unit should be avoided.
in	Inches on the screen. This will make a view take up an exact number of inches on the screen. Again, since every device has a different screen size, this unit should be avoided.
mm	Millimeters on the screen. This will make a view take up an exact number of millimeters on the screen. Like inches, this unit should be avoided.
pt	Points, which are 1/72 of the physical screen size. Much like in and mm, points are based on the physical size of the device and generally are not used.
dip, dp	Density-independent pixel. This is an abstract unit representing a single pixel on a device with a resolution of 160 dpi. The view will be scaled based on the dpi of the running device. This is the unit you should use for all layouts. Note that dip is interchangeable with dp.
sp	Scaled pixel. This is the same as dp, but it is scaled based on the user's font size preference. You should use this unit when specifying font or text sizes that need to be adjusted based on the user's preferences.

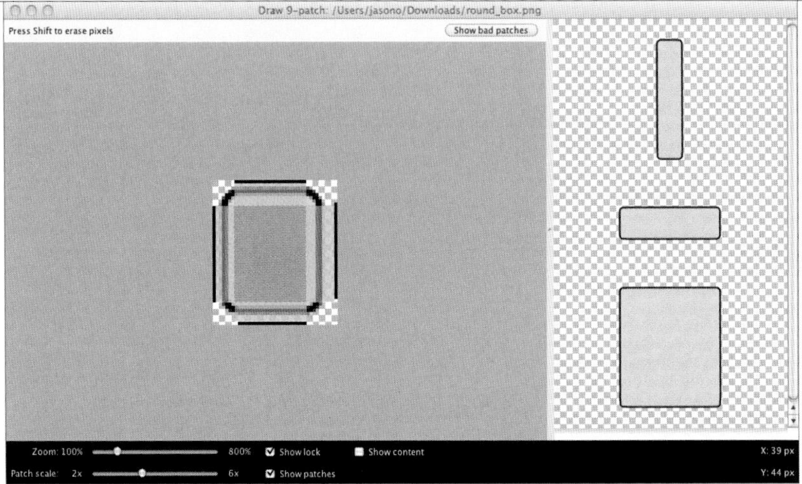

FIGURE 3.3 The Draw 9-Patch tool

9-PATCH GRAPHICS

Using the resource folders and density-independent pixels will get you most of the way to a flexible layout, and Android will scale your images appropriately in most situations. But often you will need to create image resources with rounded corners. These images won't stretch properly and will appear distorted. To handle that case, Android supports a feature known as a 9-patch graphic. This is simply a PNG file with a 1-pixel border around it. The Draw 9-Patch tool (see Chapter 1) provides an easy way to create 9-patch graphics (**Figure 3.3**). These images can be stretched in the areas indicated by the shaded region (marked with black pixels in the border of the image). By using the Draw 9-Patch tool, you ensure that your image will stretch but will maintain the proper rounding on corners. All of the stock Android button resources use 9-patch graphics.

BEST **PRACTICE**

Creating flexible layouts may seem arduous at first, but it will soon become second nature. Remember these points, and you should be able to build an app that is compatible with the majority of Android devices:

- Always use density-independent pixel values in your layout.
- Use `wrap_content` and `match_parent` whenever possible. This will make your layout much more flexible than layouts using hard-coded dimension values.
- Provide alternate image resources for each density to ensure that your images look appropriate on all screen densities.
- Use 9-patch graphics for any resources that can't stretch without distortion.

TIP: Remember that if you haven't yet adapted your app to a particular screen configuration, you can specifically declare which configurations your app supports in the Android manifest. This will prevent your app from being installed on unsupported hardware.

HANDLING **NOTIFICATIONS**

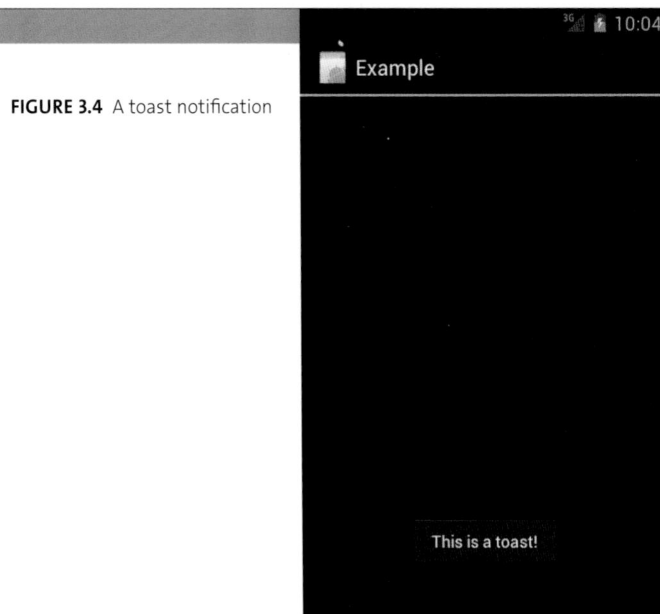

FIGURE 3.4 A toast notification

Android is designed to run on portable devices that are carried everywhere and used in sporadic bursts. To ensure that users get the full benefit of these devices, Android supplies a robust set of notification techniques to ensure that users are immediately aware of any events. This section covers the notification options in order of increasing interruption to the user.

TOASTS

A toast is the most basic and least intrusive notification. This is a simple message that is flashed on the screen for a short time (typically 5 to 10 seconds). It's intended to give the user immediate feedback on some event that is relevant to their current situation. For example, if a social networking app is attempting to update a user's status, it could use a toast to inform the user when the status is successfully updated. **Figure 3.4** shows an example toast.

To create a toast, use the static makeText method on the Toast class to create a Toast object. Give it a context, the text you want to display, and a duration. The duration can be either Toast.LENGTH_SHORT or Toast.LENGTH_LONG. Calling show() on the Toast object will display it to the user. The following code snippet creates a simple toast:

```
Context context = getApplicationContext();
CharSequence text = "Hello toast!";
int duration = Toast.LENGTH_SHORT;
Toast toast = Toast.makeText(context, text, duration);
toast.show();
```

Toasts include options for setting their position on the screen. Use the setGravity method to change the default display location. And as with most views in Android, you can override the default layout of a toast and create a custom toast.

Use toasts when you want to give quick feedback to the user but don't expect them to take any action.

TIP: It's possible for toasts to be shown when your application is not in the foreground. For example, a toast generated by a background service could be displayed during any application. Carefully think through the situations that might generate a toast in your application, and choose appropriate text.

STATUS BAR NOTIFICATIONS

The primary notification method in Android is the notification tray. This tray can be pulled down from the top of the screen and contains all ongoing and immediately important notifications. A notification in the tray consists of an icon, title text, and message text. Tapping the notification will take the user to the app that generated the notification (more on this in a bit).

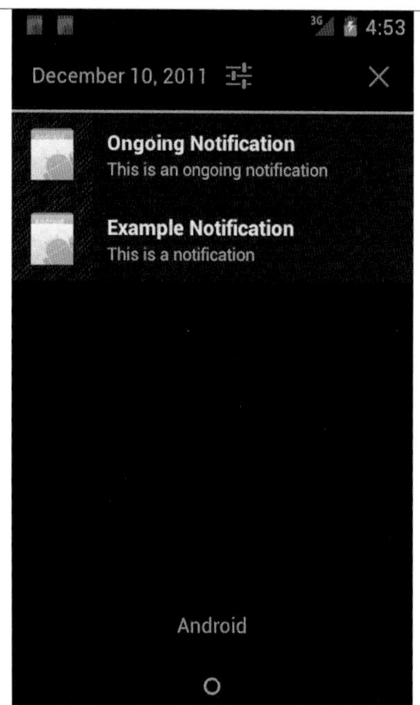

FIGURE 3.5 One-time and ongoing notifications in the Android notification tray

If you need to create a notification, it should generally go in the notification tray. It's the easiest way to notify the user, it is unobtrusive, and users will expect it. **Figure 3.5** shows some example notifications.

Notifications have a few basic parameters you can set:

- An icon to display in the status bar.
- Optional ticker text that will be displayed in the status bar when the notification is first shown.
- The title and message to display in the notification tray. This is also optional.
- A required `PendingIntent` to trigger when the user taps the notification.

TIP: Take care not to generate an excessive number of notifications. This will clutter the user's notification tray, and they will likely uninstall your app. Instead, collapse all notifications into a single summary notification (such as total number of messages received).

A PendingIntent is simply a holder for an intent and target action. It allows you to pass an Intent object to another application and invoke that Intent as if it were invoked by your application. In this way, the PendingIntent can be used to trigger actions in your app. The PendingIntent is used by the notification tray application to trigger an event in your app when the user taps your notification.

Here is an example notification:

```
int icon = R.drawable.icon;

CharSequence ticker = "Hello World!";

long now = System.currentTimeMillis();

Notification notification = new Notification(icon, ticker, now);
```

A notification is created with an icon, ticker text, and timestamp. This example creates a notification with the resource located at /res/drawable/icon, the ticker text set to the string "Hello World!", and the time set to the current time.

Once you have created a notification, use the NotificationManager to display that notification to the user:

```
NotificationManager nm = (NotificationManager)
→ getSystemService(NOTIFICATION_SERVICE);

Context context = getApplicationContext();

CharSequence message = "Hello World!";

Intent intent = new Intent(this, Example.class);

String title = "Hello World!";

String message = "This is a message.";

PendingIntent pendingIntent = PendingIntent.getActivity(this, 0,
→ intent, 0);

notification.setLatestEventInfo(context, title, message,
→ pendingIntent);

nm.notify(ID, notification);
```

MORE **NOTIFICATION OPTIONS**

You can do more than just update the status bar with notifications—you have the option of playing a sound, flashing an LED, or vibrating the device when the notification is triggered. You do this by using the `notification.defaults` option. For example, to play the default notification sound, set the defaults option to:

```
notification.defaults |= Notification.DEFAULT_SOUND;
```

This will play the user-configured notification sound when your notification is displayed. You can also use a custom sound for the sound option:

```
notification.sound = Uri.parse("file:///sdcard/mysound.mp3");
```

There are custom options for LED flashing and vibrations as well. Check out the `Notification` class in the Android documentation for all options available. Keep in mind that not all devices will have LED indicators or vibration capability.

Use the `setLatestEventInfo` method to update the contents of the notification. Here, the `PendingIntent` is set to display the example activity when the notification is tapped. Call `notify` to display the notification in the tray. The device status bar will also display the notification briefly before returning to its usual state. You can update a notification that is already displayed by calling `setLatestEventInfo` and then `notify` again.

TIP: Android 3.0 (Honeycomb) introduced the `Notification.Builder` class for creating notifications. This builder replaces the existing constructor for the `Notification` class and makes creating notifications easier. The notification ID for each notification should be globally unique in your app. You should list all these IDs in a common file to ensure their uniqueness, or strange behavior may result.

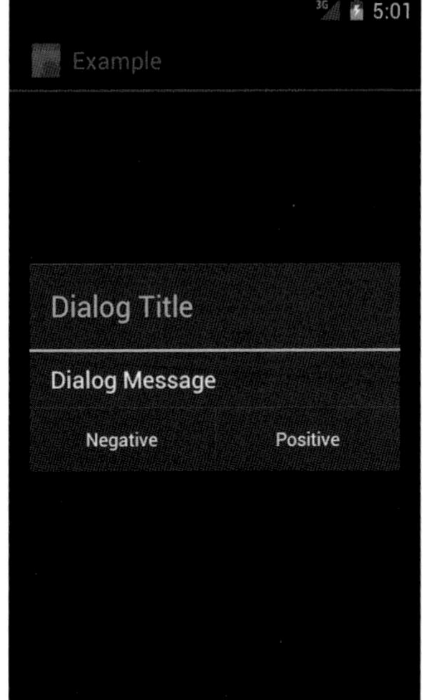

FIGURE 3.6 An alert dialog

DIALOGS

Notifications are great for most events, because they don't interrupt the user. However, sometimes you need to inform the user of something immediately—perhaps you need to alert the user to some failure in your app or confirm that they want to perform an action. To do this, you use a dialog.

Dialogs are small windows displayed over your application (**Figure 3.6**). They block all user input into your app and must be dismissed before the user can continue using your app. This makes them the most intrusive of all notification types. Android provides several types of dialogs, with different use cases: an `AlertDialog` with simple Accept and Cancel buttons, a `ProgressDialog` for displaying long-running progress, and date- and time-picker dialogs for accepting user input.

To create a dialog, extend the `DialogFragment` class and implement either the `onCreateView` or `onCreateDialog` method. Use `onCreateView` to set the view hierarchy (what is displayed inside it) for the dialog; use `onCreateDialog` to create a completely custom dialog. A typical scenario is to override `onCreateDialog` and return an `AlertDialog`. An `AlertDialog` is a dialog with some text and one, two, or three buttons.

PRE-3.0 **DIALOGS**

Dialogs have traditionally been managed as part of the activity life cycle. However, Android 3.0 introduced a new method of creating dialogs: the `DialogFragment` class. This class uses the new `Fragments` framework to create and manage the life cycle of dialogs. This is the primary method of creating a dialog for future versions of Android. The `DialogFragment` class is available to previous versions of Android through the compatibility library, a collection of classes that allows you to use the new fragments APIs on older versions of Android. You should use `DialogFragments` for all of your applications.

Add a confirm dialog to the TimeTracker app you created in Chapter 2 by following these steps:

1. Create a new class, `ConfirmClearDialogFragment`, that extends `DialogFragment`:

```
public class ConfirmClearDialogFragment extends DialogFragment {
}
```

2. Override the `onCreateDialog` method and return a new `AlertDialog`:

```
@Override
public Dialog onCreateDialog(Bundle savedInstanceState) {
    return new AlertDialog.Builder(getActivity())
    .setTitle(R.string.confirm_clear_all_title)
    .setMessage(R.string.confirm_clear_all_message)
    .setPositiveButton(R.string.ok, null)
    .setNegativeButton(R.string.cancel, null)
    .create();
}
```

Here, an `AlertDialog.Builder` class is used to create the `AlertDialog` that will be returned by the `onCreateDialog` method. Note that it uses the string resources defined in `strings.xml` to set the title, message, and button text of the dialog. In this example, the buttons are set to do nothing when clicked by setting the `onClickListener` to `null`. You will learn more about handling events using click listeners in the next section.

3. Add the following code to the onCreate method to create the dialog and display it to the user:

```
FragmentManager fm = getSupportFragmentManager();
if (fm.findFragmentByTag("dialog") == null) {
    ConfirmClearDialogFragment frag =
    → ConfirmClearDialogFragment.newInstance(mTimeListAdapter);
    frag.show(fm, "dialog");
}
```

If you run the app now, the dialog should appear immediately. Dismiss it by pressing any button. Fragments let you decompose your application into reusable components, such as this dialog. You'll learn more about fragments in Chapter 5.

NOTE: Fragments, including the DialogFragment, require a public no-argument constructor. Failing to provide one will result in odd behavior in your app.

HANDLING **EVENTS**

Like most GUI frameworks, Android uses an event-based model to handle user interaction. When the user taps the screen, a touch event is fired and the corresponding `onTouch` method of the tapped view is called. By extending the views in your UI, you can receive these events and use them to build gestures into your app; similar methods exist for handling focus and key change events.

These event callbacks form the basis of Android event handling. However, extending every view in your UI is not practical. Further, the low-level nature of the events requires work to implement simple interactions. For this reason, Android has a number of convenience methods for registering listeners on the existing `View` class. These listeners provide callback interfaces that will be called when common interactions, like tapping the screen, are triggered. To handle these common events, you register an event listener on a view. The listener will be called when the event occurs on that view. You generally want to register the listener on the specific view the user will interact with. For example, if you have a `LinearLayout` container with three buttons inside, you would register the listeners on the buttons rather than the container object. You have already seen an example of this with the `onClick` method in the TimeTracker app.

NOTE: Android event callbacks are made by the main thread (also called the UI thread). It's important that you not block this thread, or you will trigger an Application Not Responding (ANR) error. Make sure to perform any potentially long-running operations on a separate thread.

SCREEN TAPS

The simplest type of event is a simple tap on the screen. To listen for this event, you register an onClickListener that has a single method: onClick. This method will be called every time a user taps that view on the screen. An onClickListener can be registered on any view. In fact, a button is just a view with a background that appears tappable and that responds to focus and press events by changing state.

In the previous section, you saw an example of an AlertDialog with buttons. In that example, the button event listeners had been set to null, disabling them. You can add custom button-click actions to the dialog by creating implementations of the OnClickInterface:

```
AlertDialog.Builder(getActivity())
    .setTitle(R.string.confirm_clear_all_title)
    .setMessage(R.string.confirm_clear_all_message)
    .setPositiveButton(R.string.ok,
    → new DialogInterface.OnClickListener() {
        @Override
        public void onClick(DialogInterface dialog, int which) {
            dialog.dismiss();
            mAdapter.clear();
        }
    })
    .setNegativeButton(R.string.cancel, null)
    .create();
```

This code creates a confirmation dialog. The positive button uses a click listener that will dismiss the dialog and clear the list adapter. The negative button again just clears the dialog.

TIP: To avoid creating anonymous classes for click handling, you can implement the click interfaces in your activity and simply pass in this when registering a click listener.

LONG PRESSES

A long press is triggered when the user taps and holds on the screen. It is used to create an alternate action for a view. This can be used to create a context-specific menu, trigger an alternate action, or drag an icon on the screen. You can think of the long press as analogous to the right-click on a traditional desktop application.

Long presses are handled by registering an onLongPressListener. Other than the name, the setup of a long-press listener is exactly the same as a standard click listener. Here is a simple example of a long press listener that displays a toast message:

```
View view = findViewById(R.id.my_view);
view.setOnLongClickListener(new View.OnLongClickListener() {
    @Override
    public boolean onLongClick(View v) {
        Toast.makeText(TimeTrackerActivity.this, "Long pressed!",
        → Toast.LENGTH_LONG).show();
        return false;
    }
});
```

The most common usage of long pressing in a UI is for creating a context menu. For those cases, you don't create a long press listener but instead create a context-menu listener. You'll learn more about context menus in the next section.

NOTE: Android will propagate events up the view hierarchy. Returning true from an event handler will stop the propagation, as the event has been reported as handled. Make sure you want to stop handling events when you return true.

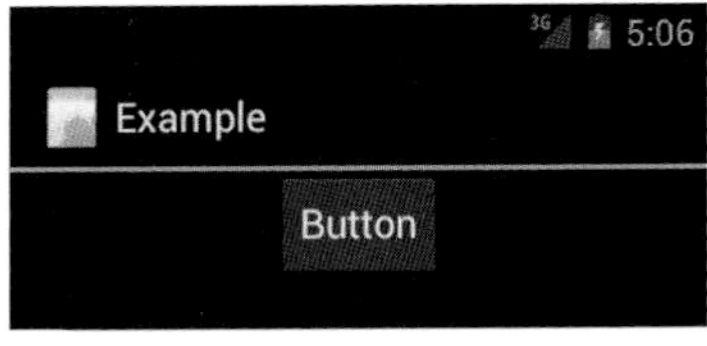

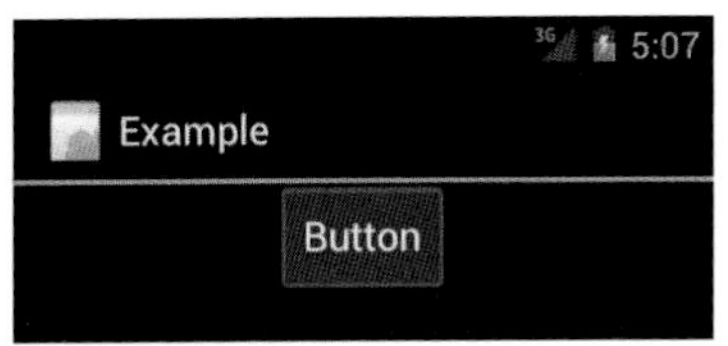

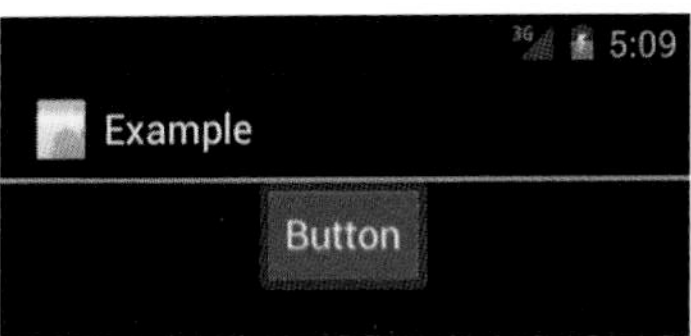

FIGURE 3.7 Different states of a button: default (left), focused (middle), pressed (right)

FOCUS EVENTS AND KEY EVENTS

The majority of Android devices have a touchscreen interface. However, Android is also designed to work on devices that use a keyboard-style input. In this case, the touch/click events don't apply. To handle those cases, Android uses focus events and key events. **Figure 3.7** shows an example of the different states of a button.

The focus event is triggered when a view on the screen gains focus. This happens when a user navigates to it using a trackball or the arrow keys on a keyboard. It is called again when the view loses focus; this is typically used on devices that have a trackball. When the user actually presses an action button on your view, the key event will be called. You can intercept this event using an `OnKeyListener`, which will trigger the `onKey` event when the user presses a button. You can also directly override the `onKeyUp`, `onKeyDown`, or `onKeyPress` methods of the `View` class, providing a lower level of event handling.

While these events may seem unnecessary in an age of touchscreen devices, there are important uses for focus and key events. If you're designing apps for the Google TV platform, you will want to use these events to handle navigation in your app, because the user will likely be using a remote control. Also, properly handling focus and key events is key to adding accessibility features to your application. Users with disabilities that require screen readers or other alternate input methods will appreciate an app that is designed to work without a touch interface.

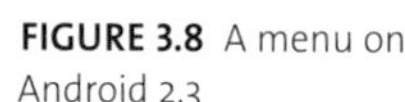

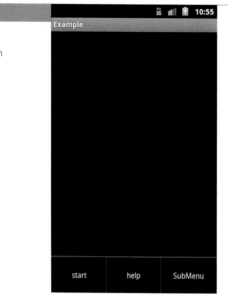

FIGURE 3.8 A menu on Android 2.3

All Android devices before version 3.0 include a menu button. This menu button creates an activity-specific menu that you can use to provide extra functionality in your app (**Figure 3.8**). This frees you to design your UI with only the most important actions and to hide optional functionality. On Android versions 3.0 and later, the menu button is generally part of the application UI; it appears as a button in the action bar. You will learn more about the action bar in Chapter 6.

TIP: You should take care not to provide too much functionality via the options menu. Common user actions should be available with a single touch in your UI. Users may not even know that an action is available if it is buried in a menu.

MENU LAYOUT

Like all other Android layouts, menus can be defined using XML or Java code. It's generally a better idea to use XML, because you can quickly create the menu options and their order without any boilerplate code.

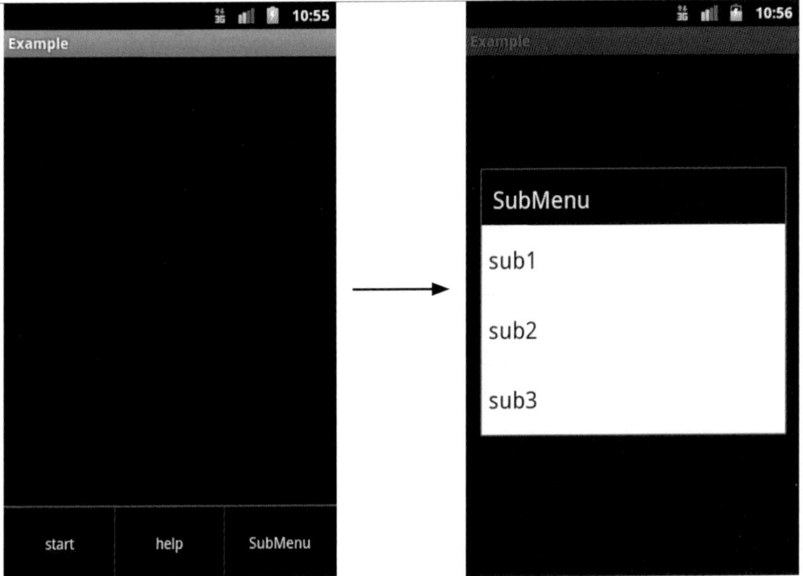

FIGURE 3.9 A submenu is opened when the user taps the Submenu menu option.

Add a menu to the TimeTracker app to clear the current list of times:

```
<?xml version="1.0" encoding="utf-8"?>
<menu xmlns:android="http://schemas.android.com/apk/res/android" >
    <item
        android:id="@+id/clear_all"
        android:title="@string/clear_all"/>
</menu>
```

The basic structure of the menu layout is quite simple: A top-level menu element contains the item elements; each item element defines a single menu option. The `android:id` attribute is required for each item and is how you will reference the options in your code. The `android:title` attribute provides the string resource name that will appear in your app. Although a title is not required, you should always provide one; otherwise, your menu option will appear as a blank space.

You can optionally assign to your menu items an icon that will be displayed alongside the text. Icons can help the user quickly understand the available options in your menu. Menus can be nested inside items, creating submenus. **Figure 3.9** shows an example of a menu leading to a submenu.

There are many more options available for menu items. You should explore the range of options available and take advantage of menus in your application.

MENU CALLBACKS

To provide an options menu in your activity, you need to override the callback methods `onCreateOptionsMenu` and `onOptionsItemSelected`. The `onCreateOptionsMenu` callback is called when the user presses the menu button; this is where you create the menu by using the layout resource file. To do this, inflate the layout file by using the `MenuInflater` class. The following code snippet provides an example:

```
@Override
    public boolean onCreateOptionsMenu(Menu menu) {
        MenuInflater inflater = getMenuInflater();
        inflater.inflate(R.menu.menu, menu);
        return true;
    }
```

Once the menu has been created, you override `onOptionsItemSelected` to handle the menu selection. This method is called with the menu item that the user selected. You then select the appropriate action based on the selected menu item.

LAYOUT **INFLATION**

The process of converting a layout XML file into a hierarchy of views is called inflating. This is typically done using the `LayoutInflater` class, although the `MenuInflater` is used for inflating menu layouts. Inflating a view is optimized by the Android resource compiler and requires a compiled XML file. You can't inflate a generic XML file, only those contained in the `R.java` file.

You can inflate a view by using `View.inflate` method or by calling inflate on the `LayoutInflator` system service. You can retrieve a reference to the `LayoutInflator` by calling `getSystemService` and passing it the `Context.LAYOUT_INFLATER_SERVICE` string.

You only need to inflate views that are added to your layout at runtime. Calling `setContentView` will inflate the views in your layout for you. When using `findViewById` to retrieve a view, the result is already inflated.

Add an option to clear all tasks to the TimeTracker application:

1. Override the onOptionsItemSelected method:

```
@Override
public boolean onOptionsItemSelected(MenuItem item) {
    switch(item.getItemId()) {
    case R.id.clear_all:
        return true;
    default:
        return super.onOptionsItemSelected(item);
    }
}
```

2. Move the dialog creation code from the onCreate method. The result is a dialog confirming that the user wants to clear all the tasks:

```
@Override
public boolean onOptionsItemSelected(MenuItem item) {
    switch(item.getItemId()) {
    case R.id.clear_all:
        FragmentManager fm = getSupportFragmentManager();
        if (fm.findFragmentByTag("dialog") == null) {
            ConfirmClearDialogFragment frag =
            → ConfirmClearDialogFragment.
            → newInstance(mTimeListAdapter);
            frag.show(fm, "dialog");
        }
        return true;
    default:
        return super.onOptionsItemSelected(item);
    }
}
```

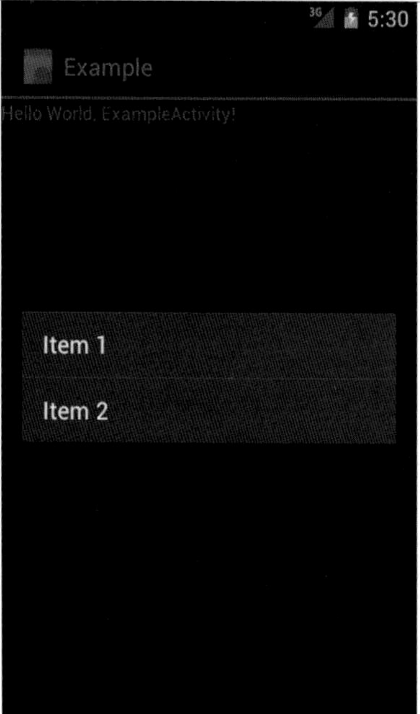

FIGURE 3.10 Context menus are opened when the user long-presses a view.

The method returns `true` when it has finished creating the dialog to indicate that the event has been handled and should not be propagated to any other handlers.

CONTEXT MENUS

A context menu is like a right-click menu in a standard desktop computing environment. Context menus work the same way as options menus but are triggered when the user long-presses a view. To create a context menu, you set the context menu listener for a view and implement the `onCreateContextMenu` method. In this method, you inflate the context menu to display to the user. Finally, you implement the `onContextItemSelected` method to handle user selections. You register the context menu listener using either `View.setOnCreateContextMenuListener` or `Activity.registerForContextMenu`. **Figure 3.10** shows an example context menu. Here is the code to create that menu:

```
TextView tv = (TextView) findViewById(R.id.text);
tv.setOnCreateContextMenuListener(this);
// Alternatively, use Activity.registerForContextMenu(tv);
@Override
public void onCreateContextMenu(ContextMenu menu, View v,
        ContextMenuInfo menuInfo) {
    super.onCreateContextMenu(menu, v, menuInfo);
    MenuInflater inflater = getMenuInflater();
    inflater.inflate(R.menu.context_menu, menu);
}
@Override
public boolean onOptionsItemSelected(MenuItem item) {
    switch(item.getItemId()) {
    case R.id.item1:
        return true;
    case R.id.item2:
        return true;
    default:
        return super.onOptionsItemSelected(item);
    }
}
```

IMPLEMENTING THE TIME TRACKER

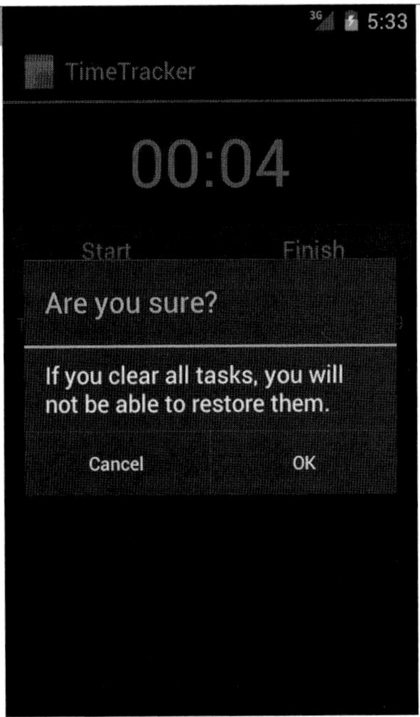

FIGURE 3.11 TimeTracker app with notification and confirm dialog

Now that you've added a notification, a menu, and a dialog to the TimeTracker app, you should have something that looks like **Figure 3.11**. It still runs only while the app is in the foreground, though. To fix this, you'll need to create a service to handle running the timer and updating the notification. A service is how you perform background tasks on Android. Its life cycle is similar to that of the activity, but it does not have a UI component. Anytime you need to execute code when the user is not actively using your app, you should create a service.

NOTE: The service life cycle callbacks are run by the Android main thread. Just as with activities, you should avoid performing long-running operations in those methods. Instead, start a thread or use message handlers with background workers to perform the actual background work.

1. Create a new `TimerService` class that extends `Service`. Move all the `Handler` code from the `TimeTrackerActivity` to the `TimerService`, and add some convenience methods for stopping and resetting the timer:

```
public class TimerService extends Service {
    private static final String TAG = "TimerService";
    public static int TIMER_NOTIFICATION = 0;
    private NotificationManager mNM = null;
    private Notification mNotification = null;
    private long mStart = 0;
    private long mTime = 0;
    public class LocalBinder extends Binder {
        TimerService getService() {
            return TimerService.this;
        }
    }
    private final IBinder mBinder = new LocalBinder();
    private Handler mHandler = new Handler() {
        public void handleMessage(Message msg) {
            long current = System.currentTimeMillis();
            mTime += current - mStart;
            mStart = current;
            updateTime(mTime);
            mHandler.sendEmptyMessageDelayed(0, 250);
        };
    };
    @Override
    public void onCreate() {
        Log.i(TAG, "onCreate");
        mNM = (NotificationManager)getSystemService
        ➥ (NOTIFICATION_SERVICE);
    }
```

```
@Override
public int onStartCommand(Intent intent, int flags,
→ int startId) {
    // Show notification when we start the timer
    showNotification();
    mStart = System.currentTimeMillis();
    // Only a single message type, 0
    mHandler.removeMessages(0);
    mHandler.sendEmptyMessage(0);
    // Keep restarting until we stop the service
    return START_STICKY;
}
@Override
public void onDestroy() {
    // Cancel the ongoing notification.
    mNM.cancel(TIMER_NOTIFICATION);
    mHandler.removeMessages(0);
}
@Override
public IBinder onBind(Intent intent) {
    return mBinder;
}
public void stop() {
    mHandler.removeMessages(0);
    stopSelf();
    mNM.cancel(TIMER_NOTIFICATION);
}
public boolean isStopped() {
```

```
        return !mHandler.hasMessages(0);
    }
    public void reset() {
        stop();
        timerStopped(mTime);
        mTime = 0;
    }
}
```

You still need to update the activity, though, so the service will need to notify the activity of the current time via the `updateTime` method.

2. Create the `updateTime` method, and inside it create a broadcast intent to send the current time:

```
private void updateTime(long time) {
    Intent intent = new Intent(TimeTrackerActivity.
    → ACTION_TIME_UPDATE);
    intent.putExtra("time", time);
    sendBroadcast(intent);
}
```

3. Create a `timerStopped` method to notify the activity that the timer has finished:

```
private void timerStopped(long time) {
    // Broadcast timer stopped
    Intent intent = new Intent(TimeTrackerActivity.
    → ACTION_TIMER_FINISHED);
    intent.putExtra("time", time);
    sendBroadcast(intent);
}
```

4. In the TimeTrackerActivity onCreate method, create an IntentFilter to be called when the intent is broadcast:

```
IntentFilter filter = new IntentFilter();
filter.addAction(ACTION_TIME_UPDATE);
filter.addAction(ACTION_TIMER_FINISHED);
registerReceiver(mTimeReceiver, filter);
```

   Now when the service updates the time, the activity will be notified and can update its counter. This will also come in handy later when you create a widget.

5. Add the notification code to the service, and call it when the timer is updated:

```
private Notification mNotification;
private void updateNotification(long time) {
    String title = getResources().getString
    → (R.string.running_timer_notification_title);
    String message = DateUtils.formatElapsedTime(time/1000);
    Context context = getApplicationContext();
    Intent intent = new Intent(context,
    → TimeTrackerActivity.class);
    PendingIntent pendingIntent =
    → PendingIntent.getActivity(context, 0, intent, 0);
    mNotification.setLatestEventInfo(context, title, message,
    → pendingIntent);
mNM.notify(TIMER_NOTIFICATION, mNotification);
}
```

You should now be able to run the timer in the background (**Figure 3.12**).

FIGURE 3.12 The ongoing timer notification is even present on the home screen.

WRAPPING UP

This chapter introduced basic Android UI concepts for supporting multiple device configurations, notifications, and options menus. Along the way, you learned that

- Android uses a combination of folder naming conventions, image scaling, and density-independent dimensions to create flexible layouts for different device configurations.
- Touch, focus, and key events are available, but you'll probably want to use an event listener to handle common user actions such as tapping on the screen.
- Notifications are the primary method of notifying your users, but dialogs and toasts can be used when you need more or less urgency.
- Menus allow you to add functionality to your app without cluttering the layout, but you should take care not to hide essential actions from the user.

PART 2

THE **VIEW FRAMEWORK**

4

BASIC **VIEWS**

The most basic element of Android user interfaces is the `View` class. A view represents an area of the screen. Buttons, lists, webpages, and even empty spaces are represented by views. Android contains a rich array of pre-built `View` classes that provide much of the functionality you will need. When the built-in views aren't enough, it's possible to create special views that are just right for your application. In this chapter, you will learn about the basic view types you can use to build your layout, discover how to load and display images, and explore the more advanced views available in Android: `MapView` and `WebView`.

CREATING A BASIC FORM

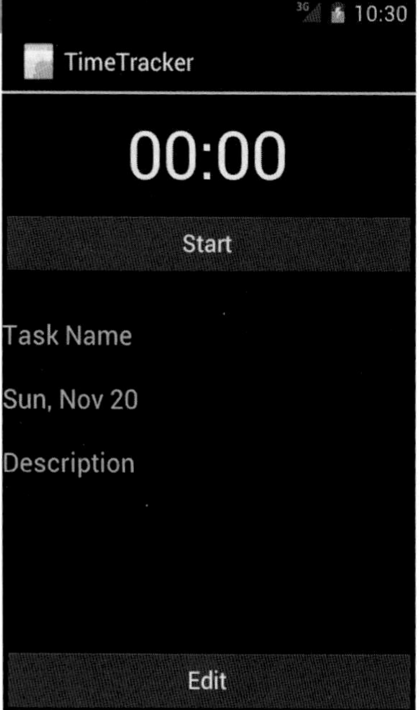

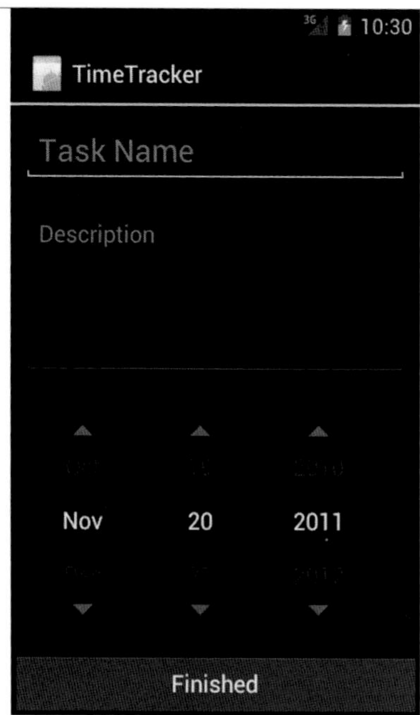

FIGURE 4.1 The TimeTracker app will have task detail and task edit screens.

The TimeTracker app looks pretty good so far, but it's time to add more than just a list of times. In this chapter, you'll add some text entry forms and split the app into multiple activities. When you're finished, you'll have something that looks like **Figure 4.1**. This section will cover the basic widgets you see in the image, as well as how to arrange them.

TEXTVIEW AND EDITTEXT

The most basic view available on Android is the `TextView`, which allocates an area of the screen to display text. You will use this view a lot in your layouts. An `EditText` is a `TextView` that is configured to allow the user to edit the text inside it (**Figure 4.2**). Tapping an `EditText` will display a cursor and the device software keyboard, allowing the user to enter new text or edit the existing text. The `TextView` has optional attributes such as size, font, and color that allow you to change the appearance of the text.

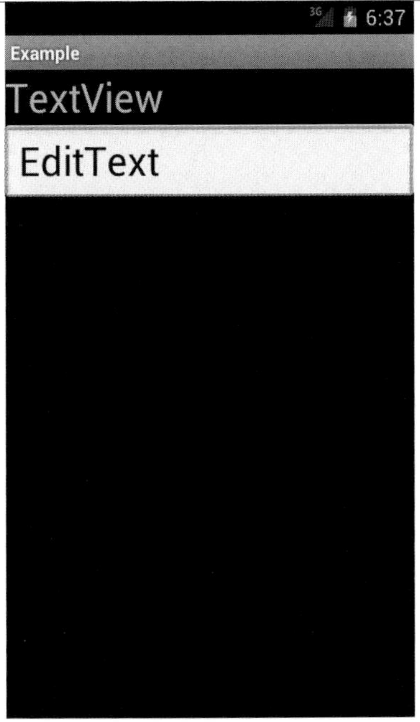

FIGURE 4.2 A TextView and an EditText

CREATING THE TEXTVIEW

To create the new UI for the TimeTracker app, you'll need to create two new layouts: `task_detail.xml` and `edit_task.xml`. They will look very similar, but `edit_task.xml` will use `EditText` instead of `TextView`. Here is the XML for `task_detail.xml`:

```
<LinearLayout
    android:layout_width="match_parent"
    android:layout_height="match_parent"
    android:orientation="vertical" >
    <TextView
        android:id="@+id/counter"
        android:layout_width="fill_parent"
        android:layout_height="wrap_content"
```

```
        android:gravity="center"
        android:padding="10dp"
        android:text="@string/sample_time"
        android:textAppearance="?android:attr/textAppearanceLarge"
        android:textSize="50sp" >
    </TextView>
    <Button
        android:id="@+id/start_stop"
        android:layout_width="match_parent"
        android:layout_height="wrap_content"
        android:layout_marginBottom="30dp"
        android:text="@string/start" />
    <TextView
        android:id="@+id/task_name"
        android:layout_width="match_parent"
        android:layout_height="wrap_content"
        android:layout_marginBottom="20dp"
        android:text="@string/task_name"
        android:textSize="20dp" >
    </TextView>
    <TextView
        android:id="@+id/task_date"
        android:layout_width="match_parent"
        android:layout_height="wrap_content"
        android:layout_marginBottom="20dp"
        android:text="@string/date_select"
        android:textSize="20dp" />
```

```
    <TextView
        android:id="@+id/task_desc"
        android:layout_width="match_parent"
        android:layout_height="0dp"
        android:layout_marginBottom="20dp"
        android:layout_weight="1"
        android:text="@string/description"
        android:textSize="20dp" />
</LinearLayout>
```

This XML layout keeps the counter and the Start/Stop button from Chapter 2, but the task list is replaced with the new task detail fields. Note the use of `layout_weight` on the description to fill the entire display.

SIMPLIFYING TEXT ENTRY

In addition to general text entry, you will probably want your users to enter textual data in a particular format. Data such as email addresses, phone numbers, and passwords are particularly common on a mobile device. With a hardware keyboard, the user just enters data normally, but because Android devices have a software keyboard, the keys can be changed to make entry of certain data types easier. For example, if you have a field that accepts only numerical data, the keyboard will display just the number pad.

NOTE: In addition to changing the input, Android supports changing the entire software input editor, or IME. The typical IME is a software keyboard, but Android also supports IMEs like voice input, handwriting recognition, or even Palm OS-inspired graffiti. While this is not something you control with your app, you can give hints about the actions that should be taken when inputting data into forms; those hints will then be used to select the appropriate IME.

FIGURE 4.3 The keyboard displayed when the `inputType` of an `EditText` is set to `phone`

The `inputType` attribute of your `EditText` class is a simple bit mask that defines the type of data you expect the user to enter. The system can then display an appropriate keyboard type. You can combine `EditText` flags (attributes) so that the system creates a targeted input keyboard. For example, the following `EditText` attributes will make the keyboard a number pad for easy entry of phone numbers (**Figure 4.3**):

```
<EditText
    android:layout_width="match_parent"
    android:layout_height="wrap_content"
    android:inputType="phone" />
```

Along with changing the keyboard, you can use `inputType` to change the behavior of the `EditText`; for example, use flags like `textCapSentences` and `textAutoCorrect` to add capitalization and autocorrection to what the user types. In addition to configuring the input options, you can use an IME option to set the text for the Enter button, which appears in the lower-right corner of the stock Android keyboard: Use the `imeOptions` attribute to select `actionGo`, `actionSearch`, `actionSend`, `actionNext`, or actionDone to give the user a visual indication of what action will be taken when they are finished entering text.

Now you can create the content of the edit_task.xml layout. Create the file, and add the following XML:

```
<LinearLayout
    android:layout_width="match_parent"
    android:layout_height="match_parent"
    android:orientation="vertical" >
    <EditText
        android:id="@+id/task_name"
        android:layout_width="match_parent"
        android:layout_height="wrap_content"
        android:hint="@string/task_name"
        android:layout_margin="10dp"
        android:textSize="24dp" >
    </EditText>
    <EditText
        android:id="@+id/description"
        android:layout_width="match_parent"
        android:layout_height="0dp"
        android:layout_weight="1"
        android:layout_margin="10dp"
        android:hint="@string/description"
        android:gravity="top|left" />
    <DatePicker
        android:id="@+id/datePicker1"
        android:layout_width="wrap_content"
        android:layout_height="wrap_content"
```

```
        android:layout_gravity="center_horizontal"
        android:calendarViewShown="false"
        android:layout_margin="10dp" />
</LinearLayout>
```

Here you're using the `android:hint` attribute rather than `android:text`. This displays the desired preset text but removes it as soon as the user starts typing a value into the field. This `edit_task.xml` layout also uses the `DatePicker` view to make date entry easier.

BUTTONS

You've already used buttons to build the current TimeTracker UI. Buttons are simply `TextViews` that have a special background image—this background is actually an XML file that lists the images that should be used for the different button states (normal, hovered, focused, and pressed). This type of XML resource is called a *state list* resource, and you'll learn more about creating it later in this chapter.

1. Add a Finished button to the `edit_task.xml` layout:

```
<Button
    android:id="@+id/finished"
    android:layout_width="match_parent"
    android:layout_height="wrap_content"
    android:text="@string/finished" >
</Button>
```

2. Add an Edit button to the `task_list.xml` layout:

```
<Button
    android:id="@+id/edit"
    android:layout_width="match_parent"
    android:layout_height="wrap_content"
    android:text="@string/edit" >
</Button>
```

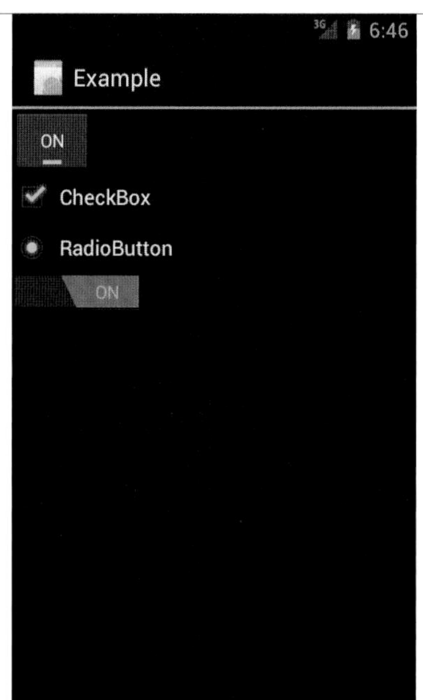

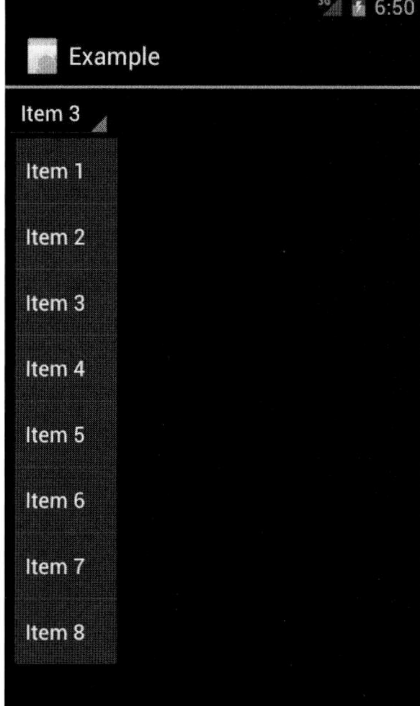

FIGURE 4.4 Boolean buttons on Android 4.0

FIGURE 4.5 A spinner on Android 4.0

BOOLEAN BUTTONS

Buttons are convenient for indicating on/off states. Android has a number of views, including toggle buttons, checkboxes, and radio buttons, that subclass the `Button` class and present a toggle between a `true` value and a `false` value. In addition, Android 4.0 introduced an option called the switch. **Figure 4.4** shows all these options for the 4.0 release of Android.

SPINNERS

A spinner looks like a button and displays a list of choices when pressed. **Figure 4.5** shows an example of a spinner choice list. The options presented by a spinner can be specified using the XML `android:entries` attribute, or you can use a data adapter to load entries programmatically (you'll learn more about loading entries into views via data adapters in Chapter 6).

MANAGING SETTINGS

Often, you will want to give users the ability to change the general options of your app through settings screens. It's not necessary to create a form, because Android includes a set of classes designed to create settings screens. The basic class is the `Preference`, and there are several different preference forms, mimicking the standard UI form widgets. The user's preferences will be saved to a key-value store that is local to your app.

Prior to Android 3.0 (Honeycomb), you would use a `PreferenceActivity` class for displaying application preferences. Honeycomb and later releases use the new `PreferenceFragment` class to handle settings preferences. However, this class is not available in the compatibility library, so you will need to continue using the `PreferenceActivity` class for applications that are designed to run on Android 2.3 and earlier.

SCROLLVIEW

Adding entry fields to a form is simple, but what happens if you cannot fit all the views on one screen? In these cases, it's often useful to allow scrolling in order to fit more elements in a single activity. To achieve this effect, you need to wrap your views in a `ScrollView` container. A `ScrollView` allows you to create a view that is larger than the physical screen on a device and scroll it to reveal the full contents. `ScrollView` is actually a subclass of `FrameLayout`, but it adds the ability to scroll its content. You typically place another layout container inside the `ScrollView` to arrange the child views.

TIP: You should never use a `ListView` inside a `ScrollView`. The behavior will be erratic and unpleasant to the user. If you find yourself wanting to use both, consider redesigning your app to use one or the other.

Since you want the user to enter an arbitrary amount of description text in the time tracker, you'll want to use a ScrollView so they can see it all. Wrap the existing LinearLayout contents in a ScrollView:

```
<ScrollView xmlns:android="http://schemas.android.com/apk/res/android"
    android:layout_width="match_parent"
    android:layout_height="match_parent"
    android:fillViewport="true" >
    <LinearLayout>
    <!-- Rest of code here -->
    </LinearLayout>
</ScrollView>
```

This code should be self-explanatory by now. The ScrollView simply wraps the LinearLayout, which contains the text and buttons you have already created. Notice the android:fillViewPort attribute? This prevents some odd behavior, which you'll learn about next.

THE FILLVIEWPORT ATTRIBUTE

A common issue you may experience with ScrollView is its interaction with child views that are smaller than the display. When the child view is larger than the display, the ScrollView behaves as expected, allowing you to scroll to see the full view. However, when the child view is smaller than the display, the ScrollView will automatically shrink itself to match the size of its content. The proper way to handle this is to use the fillViewPort attribute, which will cause the child views of a ScrollView to expand to the size of the display, if necessary; if they are already larger than the display, nothing happens. A simple example will demonstrate.

FIGURE 4.6 The desired `ScrollView` result, with a long block of text scrolling to reveal a button

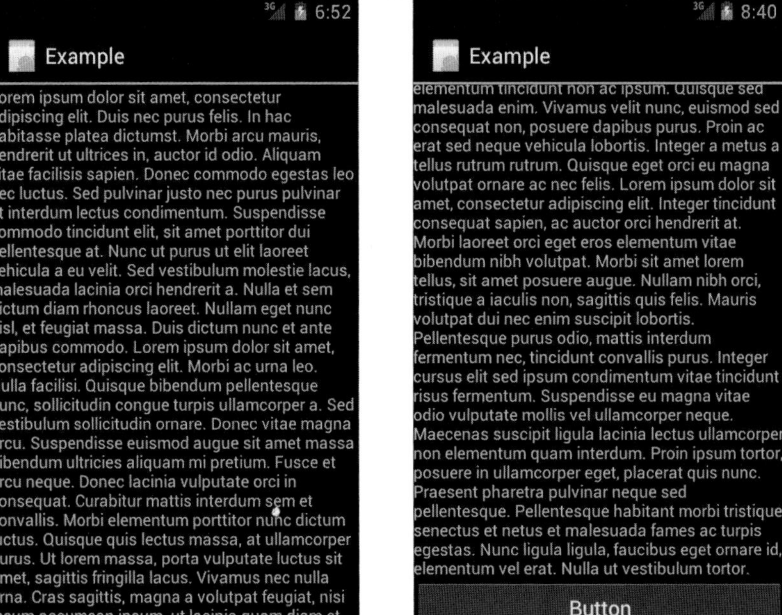

A frequent task is displaying a block of text with a button at the bottom (such as in a license agreement to which a user must agree). **Figure 4.6** shows the desired result: a long block of text that scrolls to reveal a button. When the text is smaller than a single screen, the naive implementation of `ScrollView` results in **Figure 4.7**—the button should still be pinned to the bottom of the screen but is instead directly below the text. The `ScrollView` only takes up as much space as its content. To fix this, set the `fillViewPort` attribute to `true`. Here is the code to correctly implement scrolling for any size of text, resulting in **Figure 4.8**.

```
<?xml version="1.0" encoding="utf-8"?>
<ScrollView xmlns:android="http://schemas.android.com/apk/res/android"
    android:layout_width="fill_parent"
    android:layout_height="fill_parent"
    android:fillViewport="true" >
    <LinearLayout
        android:layout_width="fill_parent"
        android:layout_height="wrap_content"
```

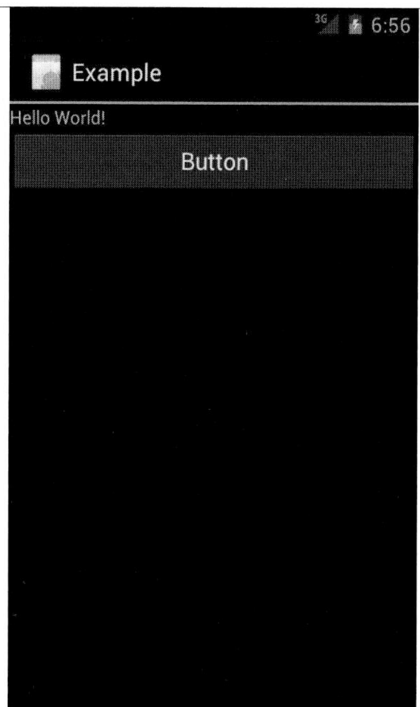

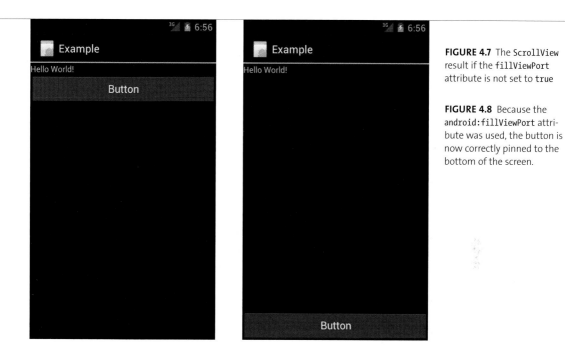

FIGURE 4.7 The ScrollView result if the fillViewPort attribute is not set to true

FIGURE 4.8 Because the android:fillViewPort attribute was used, the button is now correctly pinned to the bottom of the screen.

```
        android:orientation="vertical" >
        <TextView
            android:layout_width="fill_parent"
            android:layout_height="0dp"
            android:layout_weight="1.0"
            android:text="@string/hello" />
        <Button
            android:layout_width="match_parent"
            android:layout_height="wrap_content"
            android:text="Button" />
    </LinearLayout>
</ScrollView>
```

Try using ScrollView with and without the fillViewPort attribute to see how its behavior changes.

DISPLAYING IMAGES

Android phones feature large, high-resolution displays that are perfect for displaying images in your application. Images are an important way of conveying information to your users without explicitly stating it. Typically, images are displayed using the built-in image view. This view takes care of the loading and optimizing of the image, freeing you to focus on app-specific details like the layout and content. Unless you need special optimizations for your application, you should take advantage of the built-in image view whenever possible.

IMAGEVIEW AND RESOURCES

The simplest way to display an image is to declare an `ImageView` in your layout file and set its source to a resource in your project. Image resources are placed in the `/res/drawable` folders. This example will display an image named "icon":

```
<ImageView
    android:id="@+id/image"
    android:layout_width="match_parent"
    android:layout_height="match_parent"
    android:scaleType="center"
    android:src="@drawable/icon" />
```

The `ImageView` handles all the loading and scaling of the image for you. Note the `scaleType` attribute? This defines how the images will be scaled to fit in your layout. In the example, using scale type `center`, the image will be displayed at its native resolution and centered in the view, regardless of how much space the view consumes. Other scaling options fit the image to the dimensions of the image view or scale the image based on the width and height of the device. **Table 4.1** lists the scale type options and how they alter the image.

TABLE 4.1 ImageView Scale Types

SCALE TYPE	DESCRIPTION
`center`	Displays the image centered in the view with no scaling.
`centerCrop`	Scales the image such that both the *x* and *y* dimensions are greater than or equal to the view, while maintaining the image aspect ratio; crops any part of the image that exceeds the size of the view; centers the image in the view.
`centerInside`	Scales the image to fit inside the view, while maintaining the image aspect ratio. If the image is already smaller than the view, then this is the same as `center`.
`fitCenter`	Scales the image to fit inside the view, while maintaining the image aspect ratio. At least one axis will exactly match the view, and the result is centered inside the view.
`fitStart`	Same as `fitCenter` but aligned to the top left of the view.
`fitEnd`	Same as `fitCenter` but aligned to the bottom right of the view.
`fitXY`	Scales the *x* and *y* dimensions to exactly match the view size; does not maintain the image aspect ratio.
`matrix`	Scales the image using a supplied `Matrix` class. The matrix can be supplied using the `setImageMatrix` method. A `Matrix` class can be used to apply transformations such as rotations to an image.

TIP: The `fitXY` scale type allows you to set the exact size of the image in your layout. However, be mindful of potential distortions of the image due to scaling. If you're creating a photo-viewing application, you will probably want to use the `center` or `fitCenter` scale types.

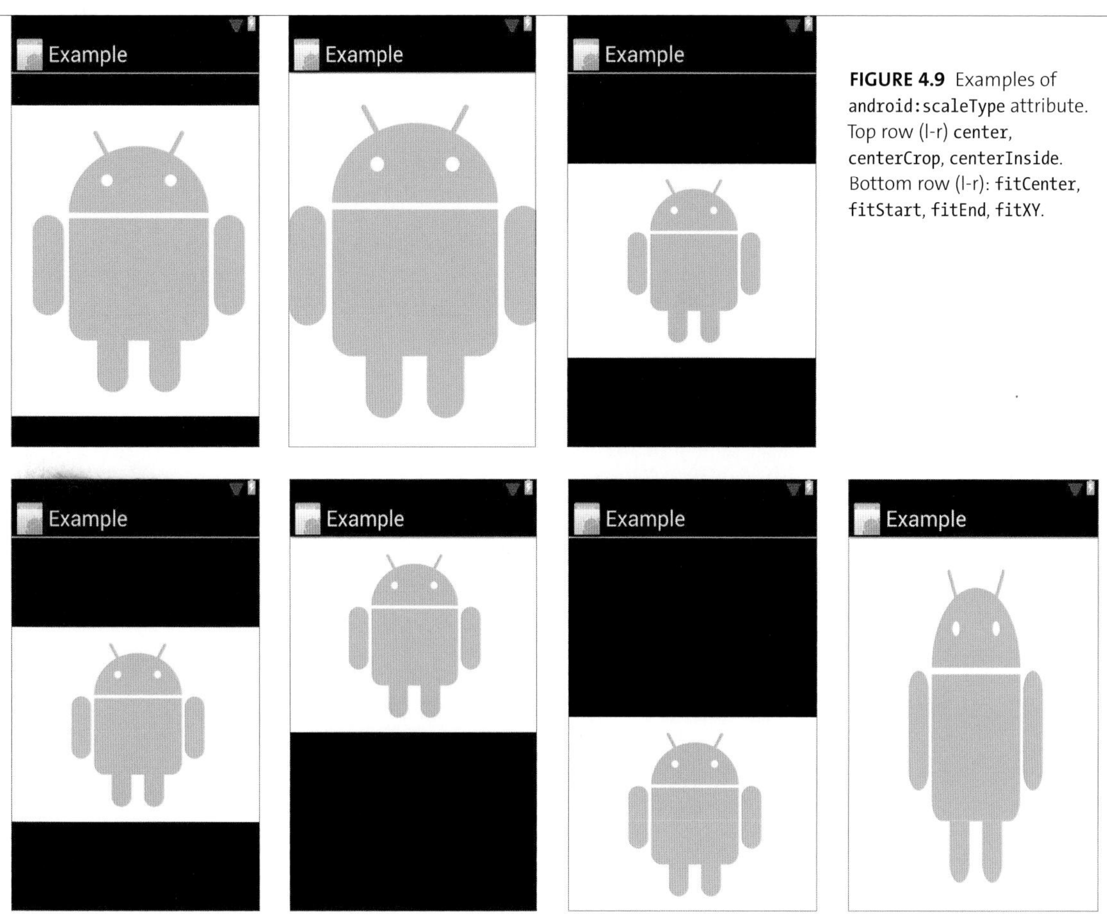

FIGURE 4.9 Examples of `android:scaleType` attribute. Top row (l-r) `center`, `centerCrop`, `centerInside`. Bottom row (l-r): `fitCenter`, `fitStart`, `fitEnd`, `fitXY`.

Figure 4.9 shows examples of the scale types. Using the correct scale type is important if you want to properly display images.

BITMAPS

Images used in your application are stored in the `/res/drawable` folders. These folders follow the device-configuration naming scheme to provide different images for different devices. Typically, you will create four different versions of each image and place them in the following folders: `drawable-ldpi`, `drawable-mdpi`, `drawable-hdpi`, and `drawable-xhdpi`. These represent the increasing resolutions of each device, and appropriately sized images should be placed in each. Use the same filename for each of the different versions, and then when you specify the drawable name, the Android resources manager will choose the image from the appropriate folder.

It's not always necessary to create an image for a particular resolution; Android will display whatever image is the best match. In general, Android will prefer scaling an image down in size so that images are always crisp and not blurred. By default, you should create hdpi-resolution images. However, you should strive to create resources for all resolutions to prevent unnecessary hardware scaling, which slows down the drawing of your UI. Once your image resources are placed in the `res/drawable` folders, you can reference them the same way you reference your layout files: via the `R.java` file.

> **NOTE:** Image resources in your project should be in one of three formats: PNG (preferred), JPEG (acceptable), and GIF (discouraged). Of course, 9-patch images are also accepted.

Including images in the `res/drawable` folders is a simple way of adding images to your app. However, it's also possible to create images at runtime and add them to your layout. For example, you may want to download an image from the Internet and display it to the user. To do this, you create a `Bitmap` object to encapsulate the image, and then load it into your UI. The `Bitmap` class is simply an object that references a bitmap image. You can use a `BitmapFactory` to create a bitmap image from any source: a resource in your app, a file, or even an arbitrary `InputStream`. A bitmap can then be loaded into an image view by calling `setImageBitmap`. Here is an example:

```
Bitmap bitmap = Bitmap.createBitmap(100, 100, Bitmap.Config.ARGB_8888);
ImageView iv = (ImageView) findViewById(R.id.image);
iv.setImageBitmap(bitmap);
```

DRAWABLES

Not all graphics need to be images—Android also lets you create graphics by using XML or writing custom drawing code. You'll learn more about creating custom graphics using Canvas and other classes in Chapter 11. To create graphics using XML, you use the Drawable class. A drawable represents something that can be drawn on the screen. This can be an image, an XML resource, or a custom class. The Drawable class is the general abstraction for representing all of these in your UI.

The Android framework makes extensive use of drawables for all the built-in UI views. One of the most common is the Button class, which uses an XML file to define the possible states a button can have. Here is an example XML file for Button:

```
<?xml version="1.0" encoding="utf-8"?>
<selector xmlns:android="http://schemas.android.com/apk/res/android">
    <item android:state_pressed="true"
        android:drawable="@drawable/button_pressed" />
    <item android:state_focused="true"
        android:drawable="@drawable/button_focused" />
    <item android:state_hovered="true"
        android:drawable="@drawable/button_hovered" />
    <item android:drawable="@drawable/button_normal" />
</selector>
```

This is called a StateListDrawable. It defines a set of drawables associated with different states. In this example, there are four possible states the button can be in: normal, hovered, focused, and pressed. Each item in the StateListDrawable defines a drawable that will be displayed when the button is in the specified state. In this case, the android:drawable attribute references an actual image drawable. The StateListDrawable does not select the best matching item, but rather selects the first item that meets the criteria for the current state. It performs this search from top to bottom, so the order in which you place each item is important. Using different drawables for button states provides feedback to the user when they are interacting with the UI.

There are more options than just defining states for a drawable. There are formats that create simple transformations of an existing bitmap or add padding and dithering to an image. You can combine several bitmaps to create a composite image. Or you can use XML to actually draw a shape using the `ShapeDrawable` class. You can add gradients, shadows, and rounded corners. The full range of XML drawable options is outside the scope of this book, but you should familiarize yourself with the available options. If you find yourself contemplating creating custom graphics to achieve the effects you want, consider using a drawable resource that may already be available.

In addition to displaying images using drawables and bitmaps, you have the option to create custom graphics using classes like `Canvas`, `SurfaceView`, and `TextureView`. You'll learn more about this in Chapter 11.

NOTE: Drawing images into a view uses the system's standard drawing process. In Android versions earlier than 3.0, this process is not fully hardware accelerated. Be aware that graphics-intensive applications using this process will not perform well on older versions of Android.

CREATING MAPS AND DISPLAYING WEBSITES

The typical Android device ships with a built-in GPS receiver and an always-on network connection. This provides tremendous opportunities for developers to leverage these features and create compelling location-aware applications. Android devices include access to Google's mapping technology, which you can use to add full-fledged navigation to your app. And the built-in Webkit browser gives you the power to create your own web-browsing applications. The next sections cover the basics of using these advanced views.

MAPVIEW

Unlike other views and classes in Android, maps are not part of the core library. They are provided by Google and are available to any application running on an Android-compatible device. Notably, this does not include devices that do not conform to the Android Compatibility Definition, such as the Kindle Fire. You will be unable to use Google Maps on those devices. However, most devices meet the Android specifications and support Google Maps integration.

TIP: Make sure you properly declare your permissions in the application manifest file. If you want to use location features in your application, you will need to request the location permissions in your app.

You can set up your project to use maps as follows:

1. Visit the Google APIs site (http://code.google.com/android/add-ons/google-apis/), and register for a map key. Map views are provided as part of the `com.google.android.maps` package, and you will need to register for a Google Maps API key in order to use this package.
2. Using the Android SDK Manager, download the Google APIs version of the Android SDK that you intend to support. You can use this SDK to create a new AVD image that supports `MapView`. Make sure you select a Google APIs target for your image.

3. Declare that your application requires the external Google Maps library to run by adding this to your manifest under the <application> element:

```
<uses-library android:name="com.google.android.maps" />
```

4. Google Maps requires a network connection, so you need to add the android.permission.INTERNET permission to your manifest:

```
<uses-permission android:name="android.permission.INTERNET" />
```

With those tweaks, you can use maps in your application. You add a map view to your layout like you would add any other view:

```
<com.google.android.maps.MapView
    android:id="@+id/mapview"
    android:layout_width="fill_parent"
    android:layout_height="fill_parent"
    android:apiKey="Your Maps API Key"
    android:clickable="true" />
```

Note that the element name highlighted in the code is the full package name—anytime you use a custom view that is not part of the core Android library, you need to specify the full package name. You will need to declare the ID of the MapView as mapview. Also, there are two new attributes here. The first is the apiKey attribute, which is where you will place the Google Maps API key you get from Google. This enables you to use Google's mapping service. The second new attribute is the clickable setting. Setting this to true allows the user to tap and scroll on the MapView in your UI; setting it to false will prevent all interaction with the map.

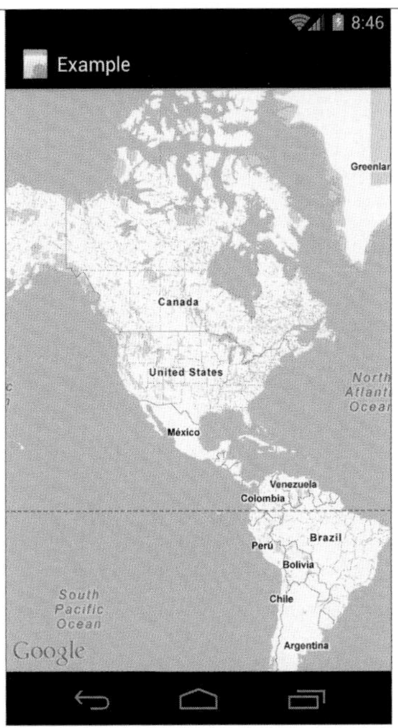

FIGURE 4.10 A MapView example.

To actually use a map view in your layout, your activity will need to extend `MapActivity`, which handles all the setup of the map view, and override the `isRouteDisplayed` method, which is required by the Google Maps license agreement and should return a Boolean that indicates whether there is active routing information displayed on the map (**Figure 4.10**).

NOTE: Because your activity must extend `MapActivity`, you cannot use fragments from the compatibility library and use a map view at the same time. For Android 3.0 and above, the fragment framework is built in to the `Activity` class, so this is not an issue.

WEBVIEW

Android includes a Webkit-based HTML rendering engine backed by the V8 JavaScript interpreter. You can use these technologies in your own application by using the `WebView` class. A web view renders HTML from web URLs, files stored on the device, or arbitrary strings you create in your app. Android's `WebView` includes standard browser features like history, plugins, zooming controls, and JavaScript support. You can also enable advanced gestures like pinch to zoom, providing easy navigation on touchscreen devices.

Like the map view, the web view can be added to your application with a simple XML element:

```
<WebView
    android:id="@+id/webview"
    android:layout_width="match_parent"
    android:layout_height="match_parent" />
```

You will need to enable the `INTERNET` permission in your manifest for your web view to access online webpages. The web view does all downloading and rendering of webpages, and you won't need to extend any special activities or use a special ID. With a web view in your UI, loading a webpage is as simple as adding the following code:

```
WebView webView = (WebView) findViewById(R.id.webview);
webView.loadUrl("http://www.google.com");
```

With that, you can display any webpage to the user in your custom UI layout. Note that the supplied content highlighted in the example is an actual webpage URL. It's also possible to load an arbitrary string containing HTML for display.

The web view defaults don't include JavaScript or Flash support. To enable that, you'll need to use a `WebSettings` object:

```
WebSettings webSettings = webView.getSettings();
webSettings.setJavaScriptEnabled(true);
webSettings.setPluginState(WebSettings.PluginState.ON);
```

This enables JavaScript and plugins—including Flash, if it's installed—in the web view. Adding zoom controls and pinch-to-zoom functionality is also simple:

```
webSettings.setSupportZoom(true);
webSettings.setBuiltInZoomControls(true);
```

The first line indicates that the web view will support zooming its contents. The second line uses the web view's built-in zoom controls for performing the zoom (this includes the tap-to-zoom and pinch-to-zoom functionality).

Finally, you will likely want to override the loading of new URLs in your web view. If you don't do so, when the user taps on a new URL in the web view, the default browser will open to load the new link. To force the load to occur in your web view, add the following code:

```
webView.setWebViewClient(new WebViewClient() {
    @Override
    public boolean shouldOverrideUrlLoading(WebView view, String url) {
        view.loadUrl(url);
        return true;
    }
});
```

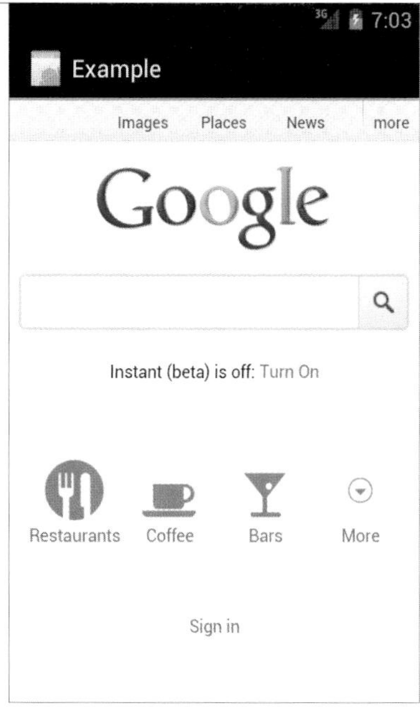

FIGURE 4.11 The web view displaying Google's homepage

Here the URL loading behavior is overridden, and the new URL is loaded in the existing web view. Returning `true` will discontinue the propagation of the event up the view hierarchy and prevent the browser from opening. **Figure 4.11** shows the screen of this activity.

The web view allows you to present any HTML content to the user and provides an easy way to load pages from the Internet. You should take advantage of it whenever your application needs to display HTML content.

WRAPPING UP

This chapter introduced the basic building blocks used to build a form on Android. You used these to refactor the TimeTracker app into a series of activities for displaying and entering tasks. You still need to save the data and display it, which we'll cover later in the book. In this chapter, you learned that

- Android provides a set of simple input widgets that you can use to build forms.
- Use the proper `android:scaleType` attribute when displaying an image using `ImageView`.
- With the `Drawable` class, you can create complex image types using only XML.
- Adding a map to your application is as simple as extending `MapActivity` and adding the map view to your layout.
- Android's Webkit-based `WebView` class allows you to display any HTML content.

5

REUSABLE **UI**

In the last chapter, you got an introduction to some of the common views available on Android and used those views to create a new interface for the TimeTracker app. Now you will expand that knowledge to create reusable components that you can use throughout the application. In this chapter, you'll learn that views can be abstracted and reused in other layouts by using the `<include>` tag; that using the `ViewStub` class can reduce the performance impact of the `<include>` tag; that themes can be applied to your entire application with a simple XML file; and that the new fragments APIs can be used to further abstract your UI into logical blocks that are suitable for phones, tablets, and televisions.

ABSTRACTING YOUR LAYOUTS

Reusing components is one of the hallmarks of good object-oriented design, and Android supports abstracting your views to provide a similar level of componentization. By separating your UI into discrete components, you can reuse them throughout your app. This provides your app with a consistent look and makes design changes much easier to implement.

THE <INCLUDE> TAG

Android provides a simple method for including one layout inside another: the `<include>` tag. Using this tag, a different layout can be included in your view hierarchy just as if it had been written in the original XML. This makes adding reusable components to your UI a snap. Here is an example of the `<include>` tag:

```
<?xml version="1.0" encoding="utf-8"?>
<LinearLayout xmlns:android="http://schemas.android.com/
→ apk/res/android"
    android:layout_width="match_parent"
    android:layout_height="match_parent"
    android:orientation="vertical" >
    <include layout="@layout/sub_layout" />
</LinearLayout>
```

The only required attribute of the `<include>` tag is the `layout` attribute (note that it does not include the `android:` prefix). This attribute specifies the layout file that will be included. In this example, a new layout called `sub_layout` will be included in the existing layout. You can override `layout_*` attributes of the included layout's root view by adding them to the `<include>` tag. Only the `android:layout_*` attributes and the `android:id` attribute can be overridden; all other attributes are ignored. The new attributes will be applied only to the root node of the included layout. This example shows another `include` tag, but this time with the `android:id` and layout attributes overridden:

```
<include
    android:id="@+id/sub_id"
    android:layout_width="match_parent"
    android:layout_height="wrap_content"
    layout="@layout/sub_layout" />
```

After inflation, the ID of the sub_layout root element will be set to sub_id. Similarly, its android:layout_width and android:layout_height attributes will be changed to match_parent. Using the <include> tag allows you to abstract common components in your UI and use them throughout your application.

NOTE: If you wish to override one of the android:layout_* attributes, then you must override the android:layout_width and android:layout_height attributes. Otherwise, the system will fail to apply your new layout attributes. This is also required to properly align included views inside a layout container (a LinearLayout, for example).

The TimeTracker app could use a better-looking detail page:

1. Create a new layout named detail_item.xml. This layout will contain two TextViews: one for the name of the field and one for the actual text. Here is the code for the new detail_item.xml layout file:

```
<?xml version="1.0" encoding="utf-8"?>
<LinearLayout xmlns:android="http://schemas.android.com/
→ apk/res/android"
    android:id="@+id/name"
    android:layout_width="match_parent"
    android:layout_height="wrap_content"
    android:orientation="horizontal"
    android:gravity="center_horizontal"
    android:paddingLeft="3dp"
    android:paddingRight="3dp" >
```

```
    <TextView
        android:id="@+id/name"
        android:layout_width="0dp"
        android:layout_height="wrap_content"
        android:layout_weight="1"
        android:text="@string/detail_name" />
    <TextView
        android:id="@+id/text"
        android:layout_width="0dp"
        android:layout_height="wrap_content"
        android:layout_weight="3"
        android:text="Text" />
</LinearLayout>
```

2. Open task_detail.xml, and remove the TextViews for task_name, task_date, and task_desc. Then add three new detail_item.xml layouts as includes:

```
<include
    android:id="@+id/task_name"
    android:layout_width="match_parent"
    android:layout_height="wrap_content"
    android:layout_marginBottom="20dp"
    layout="@layout/detail_item" />
<include
    android:id="@+id/task_date"
    android:layout_width="match_parent"
    android:layout_height="wrap_content"
    android:layout_marginBottom="20dp"
    layout="@layout/detail_item" />
```

```
<include
    android:id="@+id/task_desc"
    android:layout_width="match_parent"
    android:layout_height="wrap_content"
    android:layout_marginBottom="20dp"
    layout="@layout/detail_item" />
```

By using the `<include>` tag, you now have six text fields instead of three, but you have not changed the amount of XML in the `task_detail.xml` layout.

3. The final piece is adding a convenience method to set the fields, which is a little more work:

```
private void setNameAndText(View v, int nameId, String value) {
    TextView name = (TextView) v.findViewById(R.id.name);
    TextView text = (TextView) v.findViewById(R.id.text);
    String s = getResources().getString(nameId);
    name.setText(s);
    text.setText(value);
}
```

The `setNameAndText` method takes three parameters: the included view, the ID of the name string resource, and the actual string value of the task field. The method first retrieves the name and value `TextViews`. It then gets the string resource of the name `TextView` and sets it. Finally, it sets the value `TextView`.

You now have a much nicer display of task data, all using the same abstracted layout.

NOTE: `View.findViewById` rather than `Activity.findViewById` is used here. They work the same way, but `View.findViewById` only searches through the child views of that view.

THE <MERGE> TAG

If you use the <include> tag often, your layouts may become overly nested and slow down the drawing of the UI. The <merge> tag was created to address this problem. The <merge> tag instructs the system to remove the topmost container of your sub-layout. When you include a sub-layout, the contained views are merged into the primary layout, but without the additional container view. For example, given this layout:

```
<?xml version="1.0" encoding="utf-8"?>
<LinearLayout xmlns:android="http://schemas.android.com/
→ apk/res/android"
    android:layout_width="match_parent"
    android:layout_height="match_parent"
    android:orientation="vertical" >
    <include layout="@layout/merge_text">
    <include layout="@layout/merge_text">
</LinearLayout>
```

...and a sub-layout containing this:

```
<?xml version="1.0" encoding="utf-8"?>
<merge xmlns:android="http://schemas.android.com/apk/res/android" >
    <ImageView
        android:id="@+id/icon"
        android:layout_width="wrap_content"
        android:layout_height="wrap_content"
        android:src="@drawable/icon"
    <TextView
        android:id="@+id/textView"
        android:layout_width="wrap_content"
        android:layout_height="wrap_content"
        android:text="Hello merge" />
</merge>
```

...the resulting layout hierarchy after the system merges the included sub-layout looks like this:

```
<?xml version="1.0" encoding="utf-8"?>
<LinearLayout xmlns:android="http://schemas.android.com/
→ apk/res/android"
    android:layout_width="match_parent"
    android:layout_height="match_parent"
    android:orientation="vertical" >
    <ImageView
        android:id="@+id/icon"
        android:layout_width="wrap_content"
        android:layout_height="wrap_content"
        android:src="@drawable/icon"
    <TextView
        android:id="@+id/textView"
        android:layout_width="wrap_content"
        android:layout_height="wrap_content"
        android:text="Hello merge" />
    <ImageView
        android:id="@+id/icon"
        android:layout_width="wrap_content"
        android:layout_height="wrap_content"
        android:src="@drawable/icon"
    <TextView
        android:id="@+id/textView"
        android:layout_width="wrap_content"
        android:layout_height="wrap_content"
        android:text="Hello merge" />
</LinearLayout>
```

The containing <merge> tag has been removed. Although this is a trivial example, <merge> tags offer a convenient method for building complex layouts out of similar components.

NOTE: Using the <merge> tag requires that the sub-layout be constructed to fit in the parent layout; for example, you cannot use a layout designed for a LinearLayout in a hierarchy containing a FrameLayout (technically this isn't prevented, but it doesn't make much sense to do it).

VIEWSTUBS

While the <include> tag makes it easy to separate your UI into reusable components, you may find that your included layouts are rarely used. Layouts such as progress and error bars need to be available, but they are not shown during normal usage. When included in your layout, these UI elements are still inflated, taking CPU cycles and memory even if they are not shown. Luckily, Android provides an abstraction to solve this problem.

The ViewStub class is an invisible view that takes no space in your layout. Like the <include> tag, the ViewStub references an external layout that will be added to your UI. However, unlike what happens with the <include> tag, the referenced layout is not inflated until you specifically request it to be inflated. With a ViewStub, the optional parts of your layout are available if you should need them, but they are invisible otherwise, which speeds up the drawing of your UI.

Here is a simple ViewStub layout that is similar to the previous include example:

```
<ViewStub
    android:id="@+id/view_stub"
    android:layout_width="match_parent"
    android:layout_height="wrap_content"
    android:inflatedId="@+id/sub"
    android:layout="@layout/sub" />
```

VIEW **VISIBILITY**

Android views have three possible visibility states, each with a different effect on your layout:

- `View.VISIBLE`: The view is visible to the user and takes up space in the layout.
- `View.INVISIBLE`: The view is not visible to the user, but continues to take space in the layout.
- `View.GONE`: The view is not visible to the user and consumes no space in the layout.

Visibility can also effect layout performance. A view with visibility set to GONE will not be included in the layout and drawing process.

To inflate the external layout referenced by your `ViewStub`, you can either inflate it yourself or change its visibility:

```
// Inflate by changing the visibility of the ViewStub
((ViewStub) findViewById(R.id.view_stub)).setVisibility(View.VISIBLE);
// or by calling inflate
View v = ((ViewStub) findViewById(R.id.view_stub)).inflate();
```

The `android:id` attribute is not applied to the sub-layout (as it is when using the `<include>` tag). Since you need to manually inflate the `ViewStub`, you have to be able to reference its ID, but you can still set the ID of the inflated sub-layout using the `android:inflatedId` attribute. Similarly, the `android:layout_*` attributes can be overridden by setting the attributes on the `ViewStub`.

ABSTRACTING STYLES AND THEMES

In addition to abstracting the layout of your UI, you can also abstract the styling of the UI. Just as you can separate layout from design in websites using Cascading Style Sheets, you can use Android's styles and themes to separate the design of your views from their content. This allows you to quickly change the look of your app without updating dozens of individual layout files.

STYLES

Throughout this book, you have applied appearance-altering attributes to your views. This is convenient, but it quickly becomes tedious when you have larger layouts. Android provides the `style` attribute, which allows you to quickly apply a new set of attributes to your views.

Styles are defined in an XML file and are applied to views by using the `style` attribute. For example, rather than writing this:

```
<TextView
    android:layout_width="match_parent"
    android:layout_height="wrap_content"
    android:textColor="#FF0000"
    android:text="@string/hello" />
```

...you can move the highlighted attributes into a style and place the style in an XML file in the `res/values` folder. This file can have any name, and you can have multiple separate style files. For example, imagine a style file named `styles.xml`. In this file is a `<resources>` tag with a series of `<style>` elements. Here is a style named `RedText`:

```
<?xml version="1.0" encoding="utf-8"?>
<resources>
    <style name="RedText" >
        <item name="android:layout_width">match_parent</item>
        <item name="android:layout_height">wrap_content</item>
        <item name="android:textColor">#FF0000</item>
    </style>
</resources>
```

Each attribute is listed as an `<item>` element. The `RedText` style specifies that the `android:textColor` attribute will be set to red, the `android:layout_width` attribute to `match_parent`, and the `android:layout_height` attribute to `wrap_content`.

Now you can write the following, replacing the text view attributes with a single `style` attribute referencing the new style:

```
<TextView
    style="@style/RedText"
    android:text="@string/hello" />
```

Note that the `style` attribute has no `android:` prefix. By using the `<style>` tag, you can quickly make changes to the look of your app without updating all the layout files.

Styles can inherit from other styles by adding the `parent` attribute to the `<style>` tag. Here is a new style that inherits from the system-default text appearance:

```
<style name="GreenText" parent="@android:style/TextAppearance">
    <item name="android:textColor">#00FF00</item>
</style>
```

The Android platform's default styles are available in the `R.style` class. When referencing them in XML, you use the `@android:` prefix. Eclipse will autocomplete these attributes for you. By making styles inherit from the platform-default styles, you will ensure that your app looks like a native Android application.

TIP: Attributes that are declared in a style but that aren't applicable to a view will simply be ignored by that view. For example, a `LinearLayout` does not display text and so does not accept the `android:text` attribute. If a style containing the `android:text` attribute is applied to a `LinearLayout`, the `android:text` attribute will be ignored when the other styles are applied.

When styles inherit from your own styles, a shortcut is available that doesn't require the parent tag: You just include the parent style in the new style name, separated with periods. For example, you could create a new style named `RedText.Small` that inherits from `RedText`:

```
<style name="RedText.Small" >
    <item name="android:textSize">8dip</item>
</style>
```

The TimeTracker app's detail text views could still use a little more styling.

1. Create a `styles.xml` file in the `res/values` folder, and create the following styles:

```
<?xml version="1.0" encoding="utf-8"?>
<resources>
    <style name="detail_name">
        <item name="android:gravity">right|bottom</item>
        <item name="android:textAppearance">?android:
        → attr/textAppearanceSmall</item>
        <item name="android:layout_marginRight">3dp</item>
    </style>
    <style name="detail_text">
        <item name="android:gravity">left|bottom</item>
        <item name="android:textAppearance">?android:
        → attr/textAppearanceLarge</item>
    </style>
    <style name="custom_button">
        <item name="android:layout_marginRight">3dp</item>
        <item name="android:layout_marginLeft">3dp</item>
    </style>
</resources>
```

These styles will be applied to the name and text fields of the `detail_item.xml` layout. The `custom_button` style adds some margins from the edges of the screen and will be applied to all the buttons in the app.

2. Open the `detail_item.xml` file, and set the style of the two `TextViews` to the new styles defined in `styles.xml`:

```
<TextView
    android:id="@+id/name"
    style="@style/detail_name"
    android:layout_width="0dp"
    android:layout_height="wrap_content"
    android:layout_weight="1"
    android:text="@string/detail_name" />
<TextView
    android:id="@+id/text"
    style="@style/detail_text"
    android:layout_width="0dp"
    android:layout_height="wrap_content"
    android:layout_weight="3"
    android:text="@string/text" />
```

3. Apply the new button style to all the buttons in the app. Here is the style applied to the Edit button in `task_detail.xml`:

```
<Button
    android:id="@+id/edit"
    style="@style/custom_button"
    android:layout_width="match_parent"
    android:layout_height="wrap_content"
    android:text="@string/edit" >
</Button>
```

Like all resources, styles can be applied based on the device hardware configuration. By creating different style files and placing them in the appropriate resource folder, you can create different appearances for your app on different devices.

THEMES

Styles applied to a view apply only to that view and not to the children of that view. Even if you apply the style to a `ViewGroup` such as a `LinearLayout`, the style will only apply to that view. To apply the style to the child views, you would need to set the `style` attribute for each of those children.

It's possible to apply a style to all the views of an activity or application without specifying the `style` attribute of all the views. You do this by applying the `android:theme` attribute to the `<activity>` or `<application>` elements of your application manifest. This is known as a theme. Here is an example:

```
<activity
    android:name=".ExampleActivity"
    android:theme="@android:style/Theme.Holo" >
</activity>
```

The Holo theme, which is the default theme for all applications targeted at Android 3.0 and higher, will be applied to all elements of this activity.

USING **FRAGMENTS**

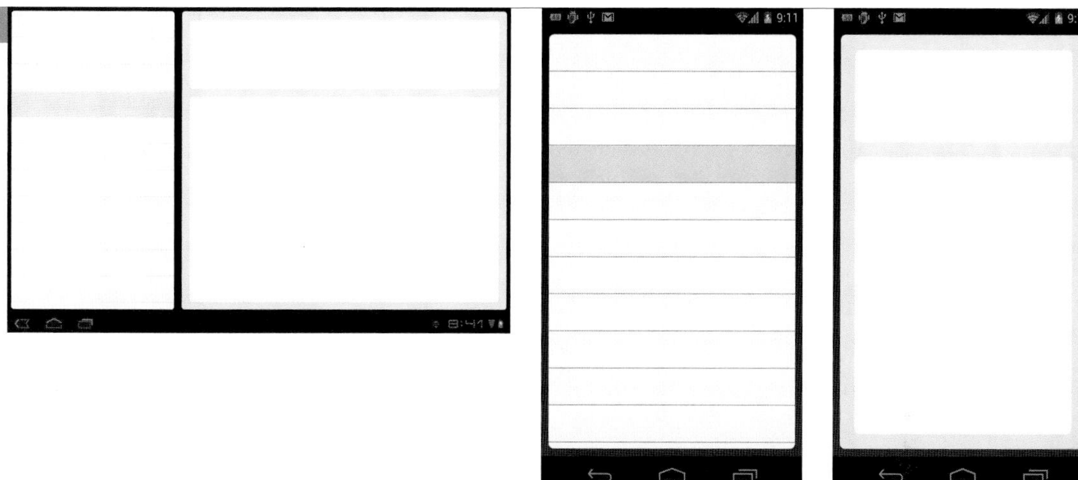

When Android made the jump from phones to tablets, Google had to redesign the architecture of applications because Android's existing UI elements were insufficient to create the type of information-rich interfaces required by tablets. To address this issue, Google introduced the fragments framework in Android 3.0. Fragments provide a method for decomposing your UI into its constituent parts so that each may be presented in a manner that is right for the device it's running on (**Figure 5.1**). On a phone, the list view would consume the whole screen, and tapping an item would take the user to a new screen presenting content. But on a tablet, the list view is simply a part of the display, with the content being displayed simultaneously. As you can see in Figure 5.1, the list view and the content are each contained in a fragment.

FIGURE 5.1 Fragments allow you to divide your UI into logical pieces and display them differently for each device. Left: Two fragments are displayed at once on a tablet device. Selecting a list item will change the content displayed. Center: The list fragment takes the entire display on a phone. Right: The detail fragment showing content is reached by selecting an item from the list fragment on the phone.

Fragments are the future of building interfaces on Android. They allow you to provide simple UI elements and arbitrarily combine them into new forms. Android now uses them extensively, and you should strive to do the same in your own applications. The key to using fragments is to understand how they differ from and interact with activities.

LAYOUT

Adding a fragment to your layout requires a simple XML element:

```
<FrameLayout xmlns:android=http://schemas.android.com/
→ apk/res/android
    android:layout_width="match_parent"
    → android:layout_height="match_parent">
    <fragment class="com.example.ExampleFragment"
        android:id="@+id/example"
        android:layout_width="match_parent"
        → android:layout_height="match_parent" />
</FrameLayout>
```

Note that the `<fragment>` tag is lowercase and has a `class` attribute. This attribute must reference a fully qualified Java class that extends the `Fragment` class. The `class` attribute is not required, however; when it is left out, you need to add the fragment at runtime using the `FragmentManager`. The `FragmentManager` is the interface for working with fragments in Java code—you use it to find, add, remove, and replace fragments. You'll see more examples of the `FragmentManager` shortly.

FRAGMENT LIFE CYCLE

Fragments always run within the context of an existing activity. The life cycle of a fragment is similar to that of an activity, but with a few added callbacks that handle events such as attaching to the host activity. **Table 5.1** summarizes the life cycle callbacks of fragments and how they correspond to activity callbacks.

You only need to override the `onCreateView` method of a fragment to display its UI. Here is an example fragment that shows a simple `TextView`:

```
public class SimpleTextFragment extends Fragment {
    @Override
    public View onCreateView(LayoutInflater inflater,
    → ViewGroup container,
        Bundle savedInstanceState) {
        TextView tv = new TextView(getActivity());
```

```
        tv.setText("Hello Fragment!");
        return tv;
    }
}
```

TABLE 5.1 Fragment Life Cycle

ACTIVITY CALLBACK	FRAGMENT CALLBACK	DESCRIPTION
onCreate	onAttach	Called when the fragment is first associated with an activity.
	onCreate	Called to initialize the fragment. Note that the host activity may not have finished its onCreate call.
	onCreateView	Called to create the view hierarchy of the fragment. This method should return the inflated layout for the fragment. Note that it is not required that the fragment have a UI component.
	onActivityCreated	Called when the host activity has finished its onCreate callback. Used for any fragment initialization that requires the host activity to be initialized.
onStart	onStart	Called when the fragment is visible to the user. Generally called at the same time the host activity's onStart method is called.
onResume	onResume	Called when the fragment is visible to the user and actively running. Generally called at the same time the host activity's onResume method is called.
onPause	onPause	Called when the fragment is no longer interacting with the user, either because the activity is paused or the fragment is being replaced. Generally called at the same time the host activity's onPause method is called.
onStop	onStop	Called when the fragment is no longer visible to the user, either because the host activity is stopped or the fragment is being replaced. Generally called at the same time the host activity's onStop method is called.
onDestroy	onDestroyView	Called when the view returned by onCreateView is detached from the fragment.
	onDestroy	Called when the fragment is no longer used. You should clean up any remaining states here.
	onDetach	Called when the fragment is no longer attached to its host activity.

Android contains a few convenience fragments for displaying common views like lists and web content. These fragments take care of creating their views for you. When using them, you will not need to override the onCreateView method.

It should be easy to refactor the TimeTracker app to use fragments:

1. Create a new class called TaskListFragment that extends ListFragment. The only method you need to override is the onCreateView method:

```
@Override
public View onCreateView(LayoutInflater inflater,
→ ViewGroup container,
        Bundle savedInstanceState) {
    return inflater.inflate(R.layout.task_list, null);
}
```

   This just returns the existing task_list.xml layout as the view for the fragment.

TIP: Fragments must have a default no-argument constructor. The default constructor is used by the system to instantiate fragments when their host activities are re-created. Failing to provide a default constructor will not generate an error, but it will result in unexpected behavior in your application. If you need to pass arguments to your fragments at construction, it's recommended you use the setArguments method.

2. Create another fragment called TimerFragment that extends Fragment. This will contain all the setup of the button views that was previously done in TimeTrackerActivity, along with the new setNameAndText method. Remove them from TimeTrackerActivity:

```
public class TimerFragment extends Fragment {
    @Override
    public View onCreateView(LayoutInflater inflater,
    → ViewGroup container, Bundle savedInstanceState) {
        return inflater.inflate(R.layout.task_detail, null);
    }
```

```
private void setNameAndText(View v, int nameId,
→ String value) {
    TextView name = (TextView) v.findViewById(R.id.name);
    TextView text = (TextView) v.findViewById(R.id.text);
    String s = getResources().getString(nameId);
    name.setText(s);
    text.setText(value);
}
@Override
public void onActivityCreated(Bundle savedInstanceState) {
    super.onActivityCreated(savedInstanceState);
    TimeTrackerActivity activity = (TimeTrackerActivity)
    → getActivity();
    // Initialize the timer
    TextView counter = (TextView)
    → activity.findViewById(R.id.counter);
    counter.setText(DateUtils.formatElapsedTime(0));
    Button startButton = (Button)
    → activity.findViewById(R.id.start_stop);
    startButton.setOnClickListener(activity);
    Button editButton = (Button)
    → activity.findViewById(R.id.edit);
    editButton.setOnClickListener(activity);
    View v = activity.findViewById(R.id.task_name);
    String text = getResources().getString
    → (R.string.task_name);
    setNameAndText(v, R.string.detail_name, text);
    v = activity.findViewById(R.id.task_date);
    text = DateUtils.formatDateTime(activity, date,
    → TimeTrackerActivity.DATE_FLAGS);
```

```
            setNameAndText(v, R.string.detail_date, text);
            v = activity.findViewById(R.id.task_desc);
            text = getResources().getString(R.string.description);
            setNameAndText(v, R.string.detail_desc, text);
        }
    }
```

3. The layout used by TimeTrackerActivity is just the new TimerFragment. Save this in the main.xml file:

```
<?xml version="1.0" encoding="utf-8"?>
<FrameLayout xmlns:android="http://schemas.android.com/
→ apk/res/android"
    android:layout_width="fill_parent"
    android:layout_height="fill_parent" >
    <fragment
        android:id="@+id/timer_fragment"
        android:layout_width="match_parent"
        android:layout_height="match_parent"
        class="com.example.TimerFragment" />
</FrameLayout>
```

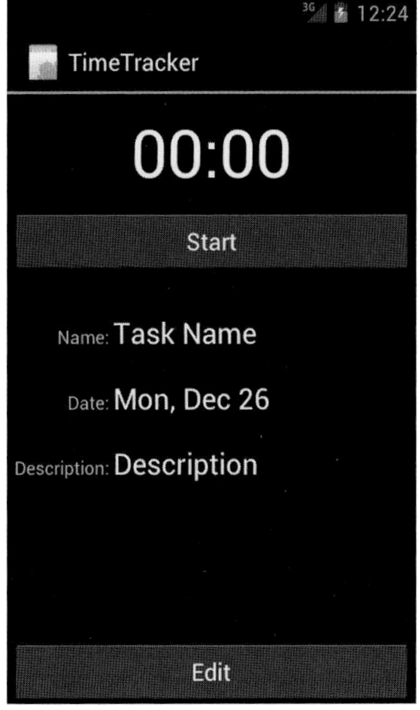

FIGURE 5.2 The timer layout of the TimeTracker app

You should now have an app that looks like **Figure 5.2**. You won't yet be able to access the timer list, but in the next chapter you will add some navigation so that you can quickly switch between the task list and the timer.

FRAGMENT TRANSACTIONS

Because multiple fragments can be displayed onscreen at once, it's possible to add and remove them without switching activities. For example, the content portion of your app (represented by a fragment) can be replaced with a different fragment when the user selects a different item from a list fragment. This allows you to create dynamic interfaces that change content as the user interacts with them.

To make changes to the existing fragments in your UI, you must encapsulate them within a transaction. A fragment transaction, which is similar to a database transaction, batches all the operations that will affect the fragments (like adding or removing fragments and transitions) and performs them at the same time. Transactions are performed using the `FragmentManager`:

```
FragmentManager fm = getFragmentManager()
FragmentTransaction ft = fm.beginTransaction();
ExampleFragment fragment = new ExampleFragment();
ft.add(R.id.fragment_container, fragment);
ft.commit();
```

Here, a new fragment is added to the UI, placed in the view, and given the ID `fragment_container`. The `FragmentManager` also provides the interface for retrieving the existing fragments in your layout. Fragments can be referenced by their ID or by a tag string:

```
fm.findFragmentById(R.id.frag);
fm.findFragmentByTag("tag");
```

NOTE: Fragments can be added to or removed from your layouts only when the activity is in the resumed state.

FRAGMENT BACK STACK

Like activities, fragments can have a back stack. However, you have direct control over which fragments are added to the stack and when they are added. Before committing a transaction, you can add the transaction to the back stack. Here is an example:

```
FragmentManager fm = getFragmentManager()
FragmentTransaction ft = fm.beginTransaction();
ExampleFragment fragment = new ExampleFragment();
ft.add(R.id.fragment_container, fragment);
ft.addToBackStack(null); // takes a string name argument,
→ not used here
ft.commit();
```

Later, when the user presses the Back button, the fragment transaction will be reversed. This actually reverses all the steps of the transaction, including any transitions.

You also have the option of popping transactions off the back stack yourself by calling the `FragmentManager.popBackStack()` method, which simply pops the last transaction off the back stack; it takes `not` parameters. Using `popBackStack` gives you more control over how your UI behaves, rather than just relying on the forward and backward paradigm.

WRAPPING **UP**

In this chapter, you learned the basics of abstracting and componentizing your UI. By breaking a complex layout into components and altering a few key layout files, you can quickly change the look and feel of your UI. You also learned the basics of Android's powerful fragments framework. Fragments allow you to abstract your app into functional components and then combine them to create complex layouts appropriate for phones, tablets, and televisions. Here are the highlights:

- You can include one layout in another by using the `<include>` and `<merge>` tags.
- Rarely used layouts can slow down the drawing of your UI. For those situations, use a `ViewStub`.
- You can change the look and feel of your entire app by creating and applying a theme to your activities.
- You should use fragments to break an app into separate, reusable components.
- Changes to the displayed fragments must be performed in a fragment transaction.

INTRODUCING THE ACTION BAR

FIGURE 6.1 The action bar running on Android 4.01. Shown are a single action item, the overflow menu, and the drop-down that appears after tapping the overflow menu.

Starting with version 3, Android gained a major new UI paradigm called the action bar (**Figure 6.1**). The action bar sits at the top of the screen and contains the app name, the app icon, navigation elements (such as tabs), and a series of buttons for quick actions. Using this native UI element, Android developers can quickly add functionality to their apps and create a platform-consistent user interface.

TIP: The action bar is automatically added to your app if it's using one of the Holo themes. `Theme.Holo` is the default for all apps with a target SDK version of 11 or higher (Android version 3.0).

ACTION ITEMS

The action bar replaces the traditional menu found on pre-3.0 versions of Android. Instead of a hidden set of options revealed by pressing the menu button, menu options are presented as buttons on the action bar. Not all menu options can fit, of course, so by default menu options are placed in an overflow menu that appears at the end of the action bar. Tapping the overflow menu drops down a list revealing the remaining options. When developing an app, the developer chooses which options should be shown as actions on the action bar.

The buttons visible on the action bar are called action items. They represent options defined in the menu.xml file (you learned how to create menus in Chapter 3). There is a new option that controls whether the menu option is presented as an action item or is pushed into the overflow group: the android:showAsAction attribute. Setting this attribute to always will make the menu item always appear on the action bar, but this is discouraged, as there may not be room for all menu items on devices with smaller screens. In that situation, the action items will be presented as a horizontally scrolling list. For this reason, it's recommended you set the android:showAsAction attribute to ifRoom, which will display the menu item as an action item only if there is enough room on the display. On smaller screens, the actions will be collapsed into the overflow menu.

Here is an example menu file with a single item:

```
<?xml version="1.0" encoding="utf-8"?>
<menu xmlns:android="http://schemas.android.com/apk/res/android" >
    <item
        android:id="@+id/search"
        android:title="Search"
        android:icon="@android:drawable/ic_menu_search"
        android:showAsAction="ifRoom|withText"
    />
</menu>
```

In this example, a search menu item will be displayed as an action item. Note that the android:showAsAction attribute also has the withText option set—this declares that both the icon and the title text of the menu item will be displayed in the action bar. The action items are added to the action bar automatically when you inflate your menu:

```
@Override
public boolean onCreateOptionsMenu(Menu menu) {
    MenuInflater inflater = getMenuInflater();
    inflater.inflate(R.menu.menu, menu);
    return true;
}
```

SPLIT ACTION **BAR**

Android 4.0 introduced a new option for the action bar: the split action bar. In this mode, the action bar is split between the top and bottom of the screen, with navigational elements at the top and action items at the bottom (**Figure 6.2**). This mode is found throughout Google's applications, including in the Gmail app.

FIGURE 6.2 A split action bar with tabs

To enable this, add an `android:uiOptions` attribute to the `<application>` or `<activity>` elements in the `AndroidManifest.xml` file, and set it to `splitActionBarWhenNarrow`. Here's an example, enabling a split action bar on an activity:

```
<activity
    android:name=".SampleActivity"
    android:uiOptions="splitActionBarWhenNarrow" >
</activity>
```

On narrow-screen devices, the action bar will now show the action items in a bar along the bottom of the screen. On larger devices, like tablets, the actions will continue to be displayed at the top of the screen. Note that you can safely include the `android:uiOptions` attribute in your manifest for older versions of Android—unknown manifest attributes will be ignored by the system.

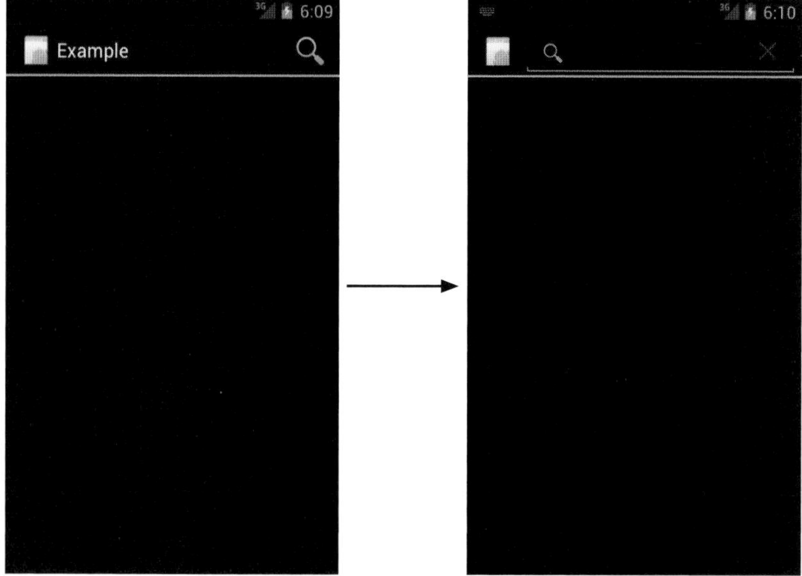

FIGURE 6.3 The search icon expands into a search action view.

The overflow menu will be added to the action bar if none of the menu items are action items.

> **NOTE:** The action bar API is not available on Android versions before 3.0. If you want to use the action bar in older versions of Android, you will have to create your own layout and populate it with action items. Alternatively, you can use the open-source library ActionBarSherlock (http://actionbarsherlock.com).

ACTION VIEWS

The action bar is more than just a row of buttons. It can also display interactive widgets called action views, which provide enhanced functionality beyond just a tappable button. A good example is the search widget: By default, a search icon is displayed; when the user presses the icon, a search widget appears, providing an area where the user can type a query (**Figure 6.3**). You will see this used throughout Android apps to provide rich functionality beyond simple option selection.

Take a look at the code for the action view shown in Figure 6.3. To make this action item into an action view, add the `android:actionViewClass` attribute and set it to the desired view:

```
<?xml version="1.0" encoding="utf-8"?>
<menu xmlns:android="http://schemas.android.com/apk/res/android" >
    <item
        android:id="@+id/search"
        android:title="Search"
        android:icon="@android:drawable/ic_menu_search"
        android:showAsAction="ifRoom|collapseActionView"
        android:actionViewClass="android.widget.SearchView"
    />
</menu>
```

Here, the search icon will activate the Android-provided SearchView widget, which displays a text-entry box. Note that the android:showAsAction attribute has a new setting: collapseActionView. This attribute is new to Android 4.0 and will collapse the action view into just an action item. Otherwise, the search widget would consume space on the action bar even when not in use.

THE ACTIONPROVIDER CLASS

Action views provide a richer widget set for the action bar, but they still use the default event handling. The ActionProvider class allows you to create an action bar component with a custom layout and custom event handling beyond the standard button press. You can optionally create a submenu, which can be triggered from both the action bar and the overflow menu. Here is an example action provider:

```
<?xml version="1.0" encoding="utf-8"?>
<menu xmlns:android="http://schemas.android.com/apk/res/android">
    <item android:id="@+id/share"
        android:title="@string/share"
        android:showAsAction="ifRoom"
        android:actionProviderClass="android.widget.
        → ShareActionProvider" />
</menu>
```

FIGURE 6.4 The `ShareActionProvider` class is easier to use than the standard sharing intent.

In this example, the new `ShareActionProvider` is used to create a sharing interaction that is simpler than the standard sharing intent. Rather than creating a pop-up dialog window, the `ShareActionProvider` creates a short drop-down list of just the most-used sharing applications (**Figure 6.4**). This is possible using the `ActionProvider`'s support for custom layouts and events. `ActionProvider` is a new class available in Android 4.0, so you will need to ensure that your app functionality does not rely on it if compatibility with earlier versions of Android is important.

The action bar is a great way to quickly add functionality to your application while maintaining a native platform look and feel. It provides a unified interface for the common interaction patterns found on Android. And as you will soon see, the action bar also provides basic navigation to your application.

NAVIGATING YOUR APP

In mobile applications, speed is essential. Users expect to navigate your application quickly and won't wait for needless animations or screen changes. Using activities, you can add multiple screens to your app, but switching between them is not particularly fast. The solution to this problem is to add a navigation element like tabs to your UI. Tabs allow the user to quickly navigate between multiple screens of your app with a single tap.

ACTION BAR NAVIGATION

The action bar is the preferred way to add a tabbed interface to your UI (Figure 6.2 shows an example of the action bar with tabs). A tabbed action bar is especially useful when combined with the split navigation mode, and you can create this slick interface with just a few lines of code. There are two primary types of action bar navigation: tabs and lists.

TAB NAVIGATION MODE

To create a tabbed interface, you set the navigation mode for the action bar in the onCreate method of your activity:

```
public void onCreate(Bundle bundle) {
    super.onCreate(bundle);
    final ActionBar bar = getActionBar();
    bar.setNavigationMode(ActionBar.NAVIGATION_MODE_TABS);
}
```

You then just have to add the tabs and their listeners to the action bar:

```
Tab t = bar.newTab();
t.setText("Tab Text");
t.setTabListener(this);
bar.addTab(bar.newTab()
```

In this example, this is passed to the setTabListener method, indicating that the activity implements the ActionBar.TabListener interface. This interface is used to provide implementations for the tab-handling callbacks. In the activity, you implement the logic to swap fragments in your UI. The TabListener interface requires three callbacks to be implemented:

```
public void onTabSelected(ActionBar.Tab tab, FragmentTransaction ft) {
    // Called when a tab is selected
    ft.replace(R.id.content, fragment, null);
}
public void onTabUnselected(ActionBar.Tab tab, FragmentTransaction ft) {
    // Called when current tab is no longer selected
    ft.remove(fragment);
}
public void onTabReselected(ActionBar.Tab tab, FragmentTransaction ft) {
    // Called when a tab is already selected and user presses it again
}
```

In this example, the content view is replaced with a new fragment when the users selects a tab, and that fragment is removed when the tab is no longer selected.

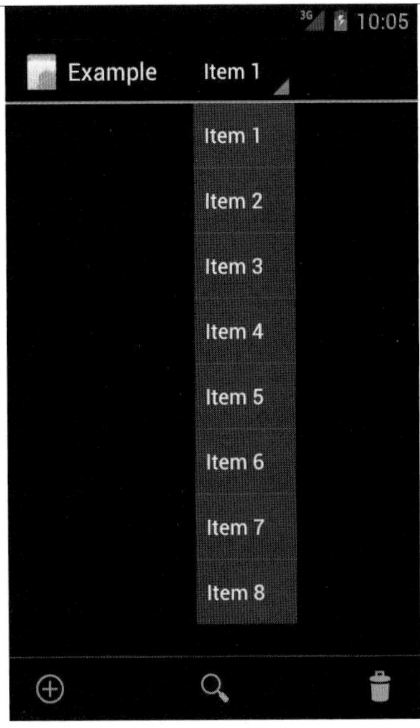

FIGURE 6.5 List navigation mode displays a drop-down list instead of tabs.

LIST NAVIGATION MODE

An alternative to the tabbed interface is the drop-down list interface (**Figure 6.5**). This is a good choice when the number of possible navigation options is too large to make tabs practical. You enable list navigation by setting the navigation mode on the ActionBar:

```
final ActionBar bar = getActionBar();
bar.setNavigationMode(ActionBar.NAVIGATION_MODE_LIST);
bar.setListNavigationCallbacks(mSpinnerAdapter, this);
```

You will need to supply both a SpinnerAdapter to bind data to the list and an implementation of the OnNavigationListener interface to handle callbacks triggered when a list item is selected. You will learn more about data binding later in this chapter.

TABWIDGET

The action bar is convenient for adding tabs to the top of your app. But if you need to add tabs to a sub-view of your app (for example, a sidebar in a tablet app), you can create a tab-style interface by using a `TabWidget`. `TabWidgets` are also used for adding tabbed interfaces to apps written for Android versions prior to 3.0, since the action bar is not available on those versions.

> **NOTE:** Prior to Android 3.0, you would use a `TabActivity` class to set up tabbed interfaces. This class is now deprecated, and you should write your own handlers for tabs.

To implement tabs using a `TabWidget`, you need both a `TabWidget` and a `TabHost`. `TabHost` is a container that you set as the root of your layout hierarchy. Inside it, you place a `FrameLayout` and a `TabWidget`. The `TabWidget` is the switchable list of labeled tabs. Typically you would arrange the `FrameLayout` and the `TabWidget` inside a `LinearLayout`, but you're not required to. Unfortunately, this style of tabs is not completely compatible with the fragments API and requires some hacks to integrate with fragments.

Here is an example implementation of a tab layout:

```
<TabHost
    xmlns:android=http://schemas.android.com/apk/res/android
    android:id="@android:id/tabhost"
    android:layout_width="match_parent"
    android:layout_height="match_parent">
    <LinearLayout
        android:orientation="vertical"
        android:layout_width="match_parent"
        android:layout_height="match_parent" >
        <TabWidget
            android:id="@android:id/tabs"
            android:orientation="horizontal"
```

```
            android:layout_width="match_parent"
            android:layout_height="wrap_content"
            android:layout_weight="0"/>
        <FrameLayout
            android:id="@android:id/tabcontent"
            android:layout_width="0dp"
            android:layout_height="0dp"
            android:layout_weight="0"/>
        <FrameLayout
            android:id="@+id/realtabcontent"
            android:layout_width="match_parent"
            android:layout_height="0dp"
            android:layout_weight="1"/>
    </LinearLayout>
</TabHost>
```

Note that the IDs of the TabHost and TabWidget are system IDs—the tab classes require this to properly function. When the user changes tabs, the system will find the FrameLayout with ID android:id/tabcontent and change its content. However, those APIs are deprecated, and you should use fragments to swap the layouts in your UI. To handle this, you set the size of the tabcontent layout as 0 and instead place all your content in a second FrameLayout (this example uses the ID realtabcontent).

TIP: You should still place a FrameLayout with ID android:id/tabcontent in your layout to prevent errors.

To add the tabs to your layout, you define them in the onCreate method of your activity:

```
mTabHost = (TabHost) findViewById(android.R.id.tabhost);
mTabHost.setup();
mTabHost.setOnTabChangedListener(new TabHost.OnTabChangeListener() {
    @Override
    public void onTabChanged(String tabId) {
        // View-switching code goes here
    }
});
mTabHost.addTab(mTabHost.newTabSpec("first").setIndicator("First").
→ setContent(new DummyTabFactory(this)));
mTabHost.addTab(mTabHost.newTabSpec("second").
→ setIndicator("Second").setContent(new DummyTabFactory(this)));
mTabHost.addTab(mTabHost.newTabSpec("third").setIndicator("Third").
→ setContent(new DummyTabFactory(this)));
```

You are required to call setup on the TabHost before you add any tabs to it. You register a listener for changes in the active tab. The onTabChanged method will be called every time the user presses one of the tabs. You then add the tabs to the TabHost.

Finally, notice the DummyTabFactory. This is another hack that enables you to use fragments with the TabWidget. The following example has a simple implementation that just returns a 0-sized view to match the API required by the TabContentFactory interface:

```
public static class DummyTabFactory implements
→ TabHost.TabContentFactory {
    private final Context mContext;
    public DummyTabFactory(Context context) {
        mContext = context;
    }
```

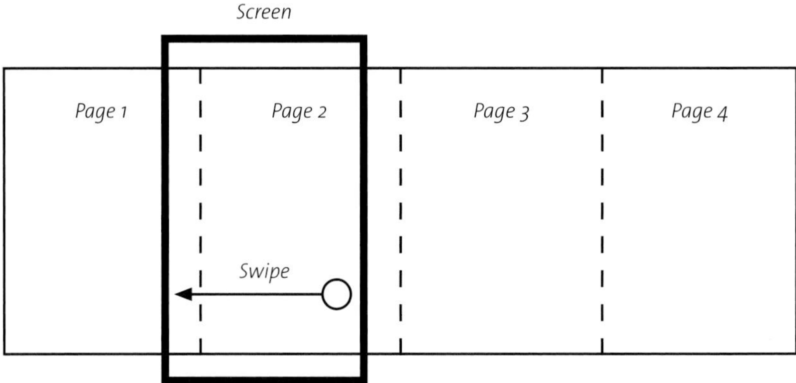

FIGURE 6.6 In this illustration of ViewPager behavior, new pages are accessed by swiping left and right.

```
    @Override
    public View createTabContent(String tag) {
        View v = new View(mContext);
        v.setMinimumWidth(0);
        v.setMinimumHeight(0);
        return v;
    }
}
```

You can now implement the logic in onTabChanged to swap in a new layout (using fragments) when the user presses a tab.

VIEWPAGER

When Google released Android 3.0, they also released the compatibility library—a collection of classes that brings the new APIs to older platforms. In addition, the compatibility library allows Google to ship new classes that they don't yet want to add to the official Android release. The compatibility library contains one such class named the ViewPager. The ViewPager is similar to TabHost, but in the ViewPager—instead of pressing labeled tabs to switch views—the user drags the entire display to the left or right to switch pages (**Figure 6.6**). This is the same behavior used by the Android home screen to switch "pages." This new behavior is available to any application that implements the ViewPager class.

ViewPager uses fragments to change the displayed content. To use the ViewPager, follow these steps:

1. Include the compatibility library JAR (Java Archive) in your application's lib/ folder.

2. Create a layout containing the ViewPager tag. ViewPager is a ViewGroup, so you can use it as the root element of the layout:

   ```
   <?xml version="1.0" encoding="utf-8"?>
   <android.support.v4.view.ViewPager
       xmlns:android="http://schemas.android.com/apk/res/android"
       android:id="@+id/pager"
       android:layout_width="match_parent"
       android:layout_height="match_parent" />
   ```

3. Create a new class that extends the FragmentPagerAdapter class available in the compatibility library. You will have to use the compatibility library version of all classes.

   ```
   public class SamplePagerAdapter extends FragmentPagerAdapter {
       public SamplePagerAdapter(android.support.v4.app.
       → FragmentManager fm) {
           super(fm);
       }
   }
   ```

4. Override the getCount and getItem methods. The getCount method should return the total number of fragments in the pager; the getItem method returns the fragment at the specified position. These methods will be called as the user scrolls through the pages. Adjacent fragments are acquired before they are visible so that the UI can display them while the user is paging.

   ```
   @Override
   public int getCount() {
       return 3;
   }
   ```

```
@Override
public Fragment getItem(int position) {
    return SimpleTextFragment.newInstance(position);
}
```

5. For this example, create a simple fragment that just displays a line of text:

```
public class SimpleTextFragment extends Fragment {
    private int mPosition;
    public static SimpleTextFragment newInstance(int position) {
        SimpleTextFragment frag = new SimpleTextFragment();
        frag.mPosition = position;
        return frag;
    }
    @Override
    public View onCreateView(LayoutInflater inflater, ViewGroup
    → container, Bundle savedInstanceState) {
        TextView tv = new TextView(getActivity());
        tv.setText("Page " + mPosition);
        return tv;
    }
}
```

TIP: Google has begun to use the paging-style interface throughout the built-in Android applications. You should consider adding support for this interface paradigm in your own application to achieve consistency with the platform.

LOADING DATA INTO VIEWS

In Chapter 2, you learned about list views and how you bind data to the list. The ListView class is actually an implementation of the more general AdapterView. Adapter views are used to display data that is not known until runtime; these take the form of lists, spinners, grids, or anything else where a series of similar elements is displayed. To bind the data to the display, you use the Adapter class. The adapter takes data from a data source, inflates and configures the item views, and then loads the data into the adapter view. The data source is typically an array or a database cursor. You will use adapters and adapter views throughout your Android applications.

BASIC DATA BINDING

The easiest way to bind data to a view is to use one of the premade adapter classes. SimpleAdapter is available for mapping static data defined in an array. SimpleCursorAdapter allows you to easily bind data from a database query. Both of these adapters require a few parameters that map the underlying data to the item view layout. Here is a simple example:

```
SimpleCursorAdapter adapter = new SimpleCursorAdapter(this,
    android.R.layout.simple_list_item1,
    cursor,
    new String[] {TITLE},
    new int[] {android.R.id.text1});
setListAdapter(adapter);
```

Here, a SimpleCursorAdapter is created that binds data to the built-in simple_list_item1 layout. This layout displays a single row of text and is used to display a single row in a ListView. The two arrays provided map the columns of the database cursor to the IDs of views in the layout. Note that you're not constrained to using one of the Android system layouts; you can supply your own layouts, as long as the column and ID arrays match the cursor data and layout. Once the adapter has been created, it's bound to the AdapterVIew (a ListView, in this example) that will display the data to the user.

THE ADAPTER CLASS

Simple adapters work well when you have just a few views, but more complex data requires a custom adapter. To create a custom adapter, you override the `Adapter` class (or one of its subclasses) and implement the `getView` method. This method is called for each element of data and should return the fully inflated view for the data. Android is intelligent about loading the data, and it only loads as much as is needed to display onscreen. In addition, the view containers are recycled as the data is swapped. That way, the view will only consume the memory required to display what the user sees onscreen.

NOTE: Some subclasses of `Adapter` already implement the `getView` method for you. For example, `CursorAdapter` implements `getView` and requires that you instead implement `newView` and `bindView`. Be sure to read the documentation on your superclass adapter before creating your own.

You saw an example adapter in Chapter 2 when you implemented a list view. In that example, you created an adapter that extended `ArrayAdapter` to display in a list. The TimeTracker app will use a database for storing tasks, so you'll need to implement a new adapter that extends `CursorAdapter`. This is also a good time to learn about an important optimization that you can use in your adapters.

THE VIEWHOLDER PATTERN

Creating smoothly scrolling lists requires that you optimize the time spent in the `getView` method. If you do too many allocations, it can cause stutters when the garbage collector runs and collects memory. Additionally, expensive operations like view inflation will slow down the drawing of your list. The `ViewHolder` pattern provides a way to optimize your adapters.

Here is the new adapter for the TimeTracker app, using the `ViewHolder` pattern:

```
public class TimeListAdapter extends CursorAdapter {
    private static class ViewHolder {
        int nameIndex;
        int timeIndex;
        TextView name;
        TextView time;
    }
    public TimeListAdapter(Context context, Cursor c, int flags) {
        super(context, c, flags);
    }
    @Override
    public void bindView(View view, Context context, Cursor cursor) {
        ViewHolder holder = (ViewHolder) view.getTag();
        holder.name.setText(cursor.getString(holder.nameIndex));
        holder.time.setText(cursor.getString(holder.timeIndex));
    }
    @Override
    public View newView(Context context, Cursor cursor, ViewGroup
    → parent) {
        View view = LayoutInflater.from(context).inflate
        → (R.layout.time_row, null);
        ViewHolder holder = new ViewHolder();
        holder.name = (TextView) view.findViewById(R.id.task_name);
        holder.time = (TextView) view.findViewById(R.id.task_time);
```

```
        holder.nameIndex = cursor.getColumnIndexOrThrow
        ➥ (TaskProvider.Task.NAME);
        holder.timeIndex = cursor.getColumnIndexOrThrow
        ➥ (TaskProvider.Task.DATE);
        view.setTag(holder);
        return view;
    }
}
```

This adapter extends CursorAdapter, so it needs to override the newView and bindView methods. The important thing to note is that the inflate and findViewById calls occur only when newView is called. After that, you simply retrieve the existing sub-views from the row view itself. This works because the rows of the list are recycled as you scroll. Once the system has enough rows inflated, it will stop calling newView to inflate a new row, and instead start reusing the existing views. Helpfully, the View class contains a setTag method that allows you to store an arbitrary object within the view. This is a simple pattern you can use in your adapters to greatly improve performance with little effort.

Now that you've seen how to efficiently bind data to your views, you just have to get the data. But long-running operations, like database queries, can't be performed on the main thread. So how do you get the data to bind in the first place? That's where loaders come in.

LOADERS

Before version 3.0, Android required a complex set of method calls to query the database asynchronously and retrieve a cursor. Android 3.0 introduced loaders to make loading, watching, and re-querying data a much simpler task. Loaders automate the grunt work of querying your database and returning usable data to your app. They also monitor their data source for changes and will call into your app when something changes. You should absolutely be using loaders in your application, because they will greatly simplify your data binding code, and thanks to the compatibility library, you can use loaders with Android versions earlier than 3.0.

The basic use of a loader requires three steps:

1. Get a reference to a `LoaderManager` by calling `getLoaderManager()`. If running on a version earlier than Android 3.0, your activity will have to extend `FragmentActivity` from the compatibility library.

2. Initialize the loader by calling `initLoader`. The `initLoader` method takes three arguments: a unique integer ID for the loader, an optional bundle of arguments, and a `LoaderManager.LoaderCallbacks` implementation. In the TimeTracker app, the activity itself implements the callbacks:

   ```
   getLoaderManager().initLoader(0, null, this);
   ```

   The loader ID is used only within the context of your app. It is needed to distinguish between loaders when using the same `LoaderManager` callbacks for more than one loader.

3. Implement the `LoaderCallbacks`, providing data for the loader and actions to take when the data changes.

   ```
   public Loader<Cursor> onCreateLoader(int id, Bundle args) {
       Uri uri = CONTENT_URI;
       return new CursorLoader(getActivity(), uri, null, null,
       ➥ null, null);
   }
   public void onLoadFinished(Loader<Cursor> loader, Cursor data) {
       mAdapter.swapCursor(data);
   }
   public void onLoadReset(Loader<Cursor> loader) {
       mAdapter.swapCursor(null);
   }
   ```

The `CursorLoader` in this example will query a database using a static `URI` and query parameters (`null` in this case results in the default data being returned). When `onLoadFinished` is called, it swaps the new cursor into the adapter that will then trigger the view to be updated. In the case that the data is reset, the adapter is configured with null data, clearing the display.

WRAPPING UP

This chapter introduced Android's new action bar view, a simplified bar that provides quick actions for Android applications. You learned about the options for adding navigation to your app, including the `ViewPager`, which is used extensively throughout the Android 4 release. The TimeTracker app has really come together now that you're loading data from a database into the UI. In this chapter, you learned that

- The action bar replaces Android's menu button and provides a unified look across applications.
- You can use an action view to provide a search interface that is integrated into the action bar.
- The action bar provides a simple tabbed browsing interface you can easily add to your app.
- The `ViewPager` class, available in the compatibility library, creates a paging-style interface.
- You can use loaders to asynchronously query and load data into your UI.

7

ANDROID **WIDGETS**

The Android home screen is more than just a collection of application launchers. It's a user-configurable dashboard that contains a mix of quick-launch shortcuts and easily accessible information. Android apps can create mini applications called widgets, which contain a subset of the full functionality of an app. This chapter covers the basics of widgets. Along the way, you'll learn that widgets can be embedded in any application, though they are typically embedded in the home screen; that `RemoteViews` allow apps to create a full layout hierarchy and send it to other processes that can inflate and display it; and that widgets can display dynamic collections of data from sources such as databases.

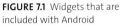

CREATING A BASIC WIDGET

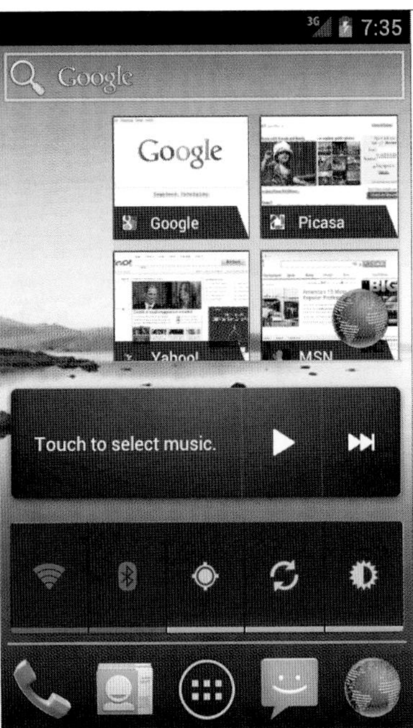

FIGURE 7.1 Widgets that are included with Android

An Android widget is a small window into the functionality of a full application. They can be used to display status information, such as the current weather or the number of unread messages, and they can provide quick access to commonly used controls like the Play/Pause button on a music player. Widgets are embedded in other applications, though they are typically only embedded in the Launcher application. The Launcher app is the starting screen, or home screen, for an Android device. **Figure 7.1** shows an example home screen with a few widgets.

TIP: Google provides an app widget template pack to assist you in creating visually stunning widgets. It includes pre-built 9-patch graphics, XML layouts, and Adobe Photoshop templates. You can download the template pack at http://developer.android.com/guide/practices/ui_guidelines/widget_design.html.

DECLARING THE WIDGET

The TimeTracker app needs a quick way for users to start and stop the timer. A widget is perfect for providing this control. Like activities and services, widgets must be declared in your application manifest.

Add the following to the TimeTracker manifest:

```
<receiver android:name=".TimerWidgetProvider" >
    <intent-filter>
        <action android:name="android.appwidget.action.
        ➥ APPWIDGET_UPDATE" />
    </intent-filter>
    <meta-data
        android:name="android.appwidget.provider"
        android:resource="@xml/time_tracker_appwidget_info" />
</receiver>
```

This code declares an AppWidgetProvider class (more on that in a bit) and gives it a name. In this case, it's TimerWidgetProvider. Notice that the XML element is a <receiver>. This declares it as a BroadcastReceiver, similar to the one you used for communicating between the TimerService and the TimeTrackerActivity. The AppWidgetProvider class is really just a BroadcastReceiver. You'll learn more about the AppWidgetProvider class in a little bit, but just know that you have to specify the <intent-filter> and that it should filter on the android.appwidget.action.APPWIDGET_UPDATE broadcast. You also need to declare the <meta-data> element that specifies the AppWidgetProviderInfo XML file.

THE APPWIDGETPROVIDERINFO XML

Every widget that your app provides must have a corresponding AppWidgetProviderInfo XML file. This file contains all the metadata that the system needs to create and maintain your widget: size, update interval, preview image, layout, and so on. This file should be placed in the res/xml directory in your project.

1. Open the TimeTracker app, and create a folder named xml in the res/ directory.

2. In this folder, create a file named timer_appwidget_info.xml.

FIGURE 7.2 The timer widget you will build for the TimeTracker app

3. Enter the following code in the file:

```
<appwidget-provider xmlns:android="http://schemas.android.com/
→ apk/res/android"
    android:minWidth="110dp"
    android:minHeight="40dp"
    android:updatePeriodMillis="86400000"
    android:previewImage="@drawable/icon"
    android:initialLayout="@layout/timer_widget"
    android:resizeMode="horizontal|vertical">
</appwidget-provider>
```

This should be self-explanatory. The `<appwidget-provider>` element defines a series of metadata for the widget. Every widget you create should have a different provider info file. **Table 7.1** summarizes the available options.

You will also need to create the layout used by the widget. For the TimeTracker, the widget will show a simple box with the time and a Start/Stop button (**Figure 7.2**).

TABLE 7.1 AppWidgetProviderInfo Options

OPTION	DESCRIPTION
minHeight, minWidth	The default width and height that your widget will be given when created. Note that the widget may be given more space than requested. This should be in units of dp. Use the formula (70 x *n*) – 30, where *n* is the number of cells your widget needs. (See the sidebar "How to Calculate Widget Size" for more info.)
minResizeHeight, minResizeWidth	The absolute minimum height and width that your widget can be resized to. If greater than minWidth and minHeight, this is ignored.
label	The label the user will see when selecting a widget.
icon	The icon the user will see when selecting a widget.
updatePeriodMillis	The interval, in milliseconds, at which the widget should be updated. If this is not specified, the AppWidgetManager will update your widget once every 30 minutes by default.
previewImage	The image that is displayed to the user when selecting a widget. This is used only on Android 3.0 and above.
initialLayout	The XML layout file used by your widget. Note that the final widget layout may change if the user resizes it.
resizeMode	Set this to allow users to resize your widget. Valid values are NONE, VERTICAL, HORIZONTAL, or BOTH. The default is NONE.
configure	Optional attribute that declares the app widget configuration activity.
autoAdvanceViewId	Used with a collection widget, this specifies the view ID that should be auto-advanced by the widget's host.

4. Create a shape drawable named **`widget_background.xml`** for the widget background, and place it in the `res/drawable` folder. This will simply be a box with rounded corners and a little transparency:

```
<?xml version="1.0" encoding="utf-8"?>
<shape xmlns:android="http://schemas.android.com/
→ apk/res/android"
    android:shape="rectangle" >
    <solid android:color="#80000000" />
    <corners android:radius="4dp" />
</shape>
```

TIP: You can create transparent colors on Android by adding two significant digits to the color code. In this case, the transparency value is 80. A value of 00 is fully transparent, and a value of FF is fully opaque.

5. Create a new layout file named `timer_widget.xml`, and place it in the `res/layout` folder. Use the built-in play image for the Start/Stop button:

```
<?xml version="1.0" encoding="utf-8"?>
<LinearLayout xmlns:android="http://schemas.android.com/
→ apk/res/android"
    android:layout_width="match_parent"
    android:layout_height="match_parent"
    android:orientation="horizontal"
    android:background="@drawable/widget_background" >
    <TextView
        android:id="@+id/counter"
        android:layout_width="0dp"
```

```
        android:layout_height="match_parent"
        android:layout_weight="1"
        android:gravity="center"
        android:text="00:00"
        android:singleLine="true"
        android:textAppearance=
        → "?android:attr/textAppearanceLarge" />
    <ImageView
        android:id="@+id/start_stop"
        android:layout_width="0dp"
        android:layout_height="match_parent"
        android:layout_weight="1"
        android:scaleType="center"
        android:src="@android:drawable/ic_media_play" />
</LinearLayout>
```

You have now completed all the layout work for the widget.

TIP: The Android emulator contains an application called Widget Preview, which can be used to capture an image preview for your widget. Just install your app on the emulator, run Widget Preview, configure your widget, and save the image. The image will be available in the emulator's `sdcard/Download/` folder.

HOW TO **CALCULATE** WIDGET **SIZE**

The Android home screen is divided into cells arranged in a grid. Generally, phones have home screens with a 4 by 4 grid, and tablets have home screens with an 8 by 7 grid, but device manufacturers may create home screens with grids of any size.

Here are some tips to ensure that your widgets function properly:

- Widgets will expand to the grid size that contains them. So if the cell size is 10dp by 10dp and your widget requests a size of 15dp by 15dp, it will consume 4 cells on the grid (2 high and 2 wide).
- The minimum size of a widget is 1 cell.
- To calculate the size of your widget, use the formula (70 x *n*) – 30, where *n* is the desired number of cells. So, if you want your widget to be 4 cells wide, set the `minWidth` attribute to (70 x 4) – 30 = (280) – 30 = 250dp.
- Widgets should not extend to the edges of their containers; they should have padding such that there is space around the visible part of the widget. Android 4.0 adds padding to the widget layout for you, but you should add some padding for previous versions of Android. Unlike normal layouts, you cannot use resource qualifiers for widget layouts. To create padding for a widget layout only on pre-4.0 devices, use `dimens` or different drawable resources.
- For maximum compatibility, never make a widget that requires more than 4 by 4 cells.

THE APPWIDGETPROVIDER CLASS

The AppWidgetProvider class is the primary interface to your widgets. It is responsible for defining the layout of the widget and providing all updates to it. It provides callbacks that are triggered at different points in the life cycle of a widget. By implementing these callbacks, you can control the behavior of your widgets. **Table 7.2** shows the callback methods and when they are called.

TABLE 7.2 AppWidgetProvider Methods

METHOD	DESCRIPTION
onUpdate	Called when the AppWidgetManager updates the widget. Also called the first time a widget is added, but only if you do not have a configuration activity set. This is the most important method to implement.
onDeleted	Called every time a widget is deleted from the host.
onEnabled	Called the first time a widget is created, but not for subsequent widget creations. Use this to perform a one-time initialization, such as instantiating database cursors that all app widgets can share.
onDisabled	Called when the last instance of a widget is deleted. Use this to clean up any operations performed in onEnabled.
onReceive	The standard BroadcastReceiver onReceive callback. This is called every time a broadcast that is relevant to an app widget is received. You normally don't need to implement this.

1. For the TimeTracker app, create a new class named **TimerWidgetProvider** that extends AppWidgetProvider:

```
public class TimerWidgetProvider extends AppWidgetProvider {
    @Override
    public void onUpdate(Context context, AppWidgetManager
    → appWidgetManager, int[] appWidgetIds) {
    }
}
```

The most important method to override is onUpdate. This is called every time a new widget is added to the home screen. It's also called when the system updates your widget, based on the updatePeriodMillis attribute you specified. You'll learn about how to implement this method shortly.

AppWidgetProvider is actually a subclass of BroadcastReceiver. Specifically, it receives the APPWIDGET_UPDATE broadcasts and generates the widget life cycle callbacks. This is just a convenience for you. You could create your own BroadcastReceiver and handle those updates yourself. In fact, you can override the onReceive method of AppWidgetProvider to handle broadcasts other than just the app widget broadcasts. The TimeTracker app can take advantage of this to update the widget whenever a timing event is broadcast.

2. Open TimeTrackerActivity and add some new static strings:

```
public class TimeTrackerActivity extends FragmentActivity
→ implements OnClickListener, ServiceConnection,
→ ViewPager.OnPageChangeListener, TaskListener {
    public static final String ACTION_TIME_UPDATE =
    → "com.example.ActionTimeUpdate";
    public static final String ACTION_TIMER_FINISHED =
    → "com.example.ActionTimerFinished";
    public static final String ACTION_TIMER_STOPPED =
    → "com.example.ActionTimerStopped";
    ...
```

3. Add a new TIMER_STOPPED broadcast to the TimerService that is broadcast when the timer is stopped:

```
public void stopTimer() {
    mHandler.removeMessages(0);
    stopSelf();
    mNM.cancel(TIMER_NOTIFICATION);
    updateTask();
    // Broadcast timer stopped
```

```
    Intent intent = new Intent(TimeTrackerActivity.
    → ACTION_TIMER_STOPPED);
    intent.putExtra("time", mTime);
    sendBroadcast(intent);
    }
```

4. Also in TimerService, update the onStartCommand method to stop the timer if it is already running:

```
@Override
public int onStartCommand(Intent intent, int flags,
→ int startId) {
    if (isTimerRunning()) {
        stopTimer();
        return START_STICKY;
    }
    ...
```

5. Add the three timer-related broadcasts to the <intent-filter> of the TimerWidgetProvider:

```
<receiver android:name=".TimerWidgetProvider" >
    <intent-filter>
        <action android:name="android.appwidget.action.
        → APPWIDGET_UPDATE" />
        <action android:name="com.example.ActionTimeUpdate" />
        <action android:name="com.example.ActionTimerFinished" />
        <action android:name="com.example.ActionTimerStopped" />
    </intent-filter>
    <meta-data
        android:name="android.appwidget.provider"
        android:resource="@xml/time_tracker_appwidget_info" />
        </receiver>
```

6. Implement the onReceive method. You will create the missing updateWidgetTime method in the next section. Don't forget to call the superclass onReceive at the end, or the widget updates will not be received:

```
@Override
    public void onReceive(Context context, Intent intent) {
        String action = intent.getAction();
        if (TimeTrackerActivity.ACTION_TIME_UPDATE.
        → equals(action)) {
            Bundle extras = intent.getExtras();
            long time = extras.getLong("time");
            updateWidgetTime(context, time, true);
            return;
        } else if (TimeTrackerActivity.ACTION_TIMER_FINISHED.
        → equals(action) ||
                TimeTrackerActivity.ACTION_TIMER_STOPPED.
                → equals(action)) {
            Bundle extras = intent.getExtras();
            long time = extras.getLong("time");
            updateWidgetTime(context, time, false);
            return;
        }
        super.onReceive(context, intent);
    }
```

REMOTE VIEWS

All Android applications run in a sandbox that prevents them from interfering with other apps or with the system. However, widgets run as part of another application (the Launcher, in this case). How does Android handle this case? By using a new class called `RemoteViews`.

The `RemoteViews` class is not actually a view. It's a `Parcelable` object that contains all the information necessary to inflate the view hierarchy of the widget. It can then be sent to other applications via an intent. Those applications can inflate this new view hierarchy in their own processes. This is all done with no interaction among the apps other than the basic data types allowed by the `Parcelable` interface. This maintains the separation between application processes while allowing one application to create a view hierarchy in another application. You can think of this as similar to how HTML is transferred across the Internet and then displayed (inflated) on your computer.

NOTE: `Parcelable` **is similar to the standard Java Serializable interface. However,** `Parcelable` **requires that you implement the serialization of classes yourself. This makes it faster and more efficient than using the standard Serializable interface.**

The `RemoteViews` object doesn't actually contain a view hierarchy, but rather contains the necessary information to create one. Since the views don't exist, the `RemoteViews` object doesn't allow direct manipulation of the view attributes. Instead, you set view attributes using methods of the `RemoteViews` object itself, supplying the ID of the view to be updated.

Add the rest of the `TimerWidgetProvider` implementation.

1. Implement the `onUpdate` method. Set a `PendingIntent` to be sent when the Start/Stop button is pressed:

```
@Override
    public void onUpdate(Context context, AppWidgetManager
    → appWidgetManager, int[] appWidgetIds) {
       Intent intent = new Intent(context,
       → TimerService.class);
```

```
    PendingIntent pi = PendingIntent.getService
    → (context, 0, intent, 0);
    RemoteViews views = new RemoteViews
    → (context.getPackageName(), R.layout.timer_widget);
    views.setOnClickPendingIntent(R.id.start_stop, pi);
    appWidgetManager.updateAppWidget(appWidgetIds, views);
}
```

This method simply creates a new `PendingIntent` that will send an `Intent` to the `TimerService`. This triggers the starting and stopping of the timer. Note that the `setOnClickPendingIntent` takes the view ID as the first parameter. Remember that a remote process inflates the views in a `RemoteViews` object, so you cannot set the fields directly. Finally, you update the widgets by calling `updateAppWidget` on the `AppWidgetManager`.

2. Implement the `updateWidgetTime` method. This method simply updates the displayed time and chooses the appropriate image for the button, based on whether the timer is running:

```
private void updateWidgetTime(Context context, long time,
→ boolean isRunning) {
    AppWidgetManager manager = AppWidgetManager.
    → getInstance(context);
    int[] ids = manager.getAppWidgetIds(new
    → ComponentName(context, TimerWidgetProvider.class));
    RemoteViews views = new RemoteViews
    → (context.getPackageName(), R.layout.timer_widget);
    views.setTextViewText(R.id.counter,
    → DateUtils.formatElapsedTime(time/1000));
    views.setImageViewResource(R.id.start_stop,
            isRunning ? android.R.drawable.ic_media_pause
            → : android.R.drawable.ic_media_play);
    manager.updateAppWidget(ids, views);
}
```

The images used here are the platform-default images for a Play button and a Pause button.

Now you should have a working widget for the TimeTracker app. You can use this to start and stop the timer.

NOTE: Because `RemoteViews` must be parceled before they are used, they do not support the full set of views on the Android platform. Check the Android documentation on widgets for the full list of supported classes.

APP WIDGET CONFIGURATION ACTIVITY

You can optionally create an activity to configure your widgets. When the user adds a widget to the home screen, the activity will launch. The contents of the activity are up to you; there are no special classes to extend or interfaces to implement. In the activity, it is your responsibility to update the widget based on the user's input.

Here are the steps you need to take to create a widget configuration activity:

1. Add the configuration activity to the widget's provider info XML file:

```
<appwidget-provider xmlns:android=http://schemas.android.com/
→ apk/res/android

    ...

    android:configure="com.example.android.
    → ExampleAppWidgetConfigure" >

</appwidget-provider>
```

2. Create an activity with an `<intent-filter>` for the `APPWIDGET_CONFIGURE` broadcast:

```
<activity android:name=".ExampleWidgetConfigurationActivity">

    <intent-filter>

        <action android:name="android.appwidget.action.
        → APPWIDGET_CONFIGURE"/>

    </intent-filter>

</activity>
```

3. Implement the activity that will configure the widget. In the activity onCreate method, the widget ID is available as an extra in the intent used to start the activity:

```
Intent intent = getIntent();
Bundle extras = intent.getExtras();
if (extras != null) {
    widgetId = extras.getInt(AppWidgetManager.
    ➥ EXTRA_APPWIDGET_ID, -1);
}
```

4. Set the widget configuration as you normally would—by calling AppWidgetManager.updateAppWidget(). You must return a result code from the activity to inform the host of the success or failure of the configuration:

```
Intent resultValue = new Intent();
resultValue.putExtra(AppWidgetManager.EXTRA_APPWIDGET_ID,
➥ mAppWidgetId);
setResult(RESULT_OK, resultValue);
finish();
```

5. Set the result to RESULT_CANCELED in onCreate, before anything else happens, to cancel the creation of the widget if the user backs out of the activity.

```
@Override
public void onCreate(Bundle bundle) {
    super.onCreate(bundle);
    Intent resultValue = new Intent();
    resultValue.putExtra(AppWidgetManager.EXTRA_APPWIDGET_ID,
    ➥ mAppWidgetId);
    setResult(RESULT_CANCELED, resultValue);
    ...
```

Remember that when you use a widget configuration activity, the onUpdate method of the AppWidgetProvider class is not called when the app is added. It is the responsibility of your activity to perform initial setup of the new widget instance.

NOTE: You must return the EXTRA_APPWIDGET_INFO extra when your widget configuration activity finishes. If you fail to do so, your widget may not initialize properly. For this reason, always set the extra in your activity onCreate method.

CREATING A COLLECTION WIDGET

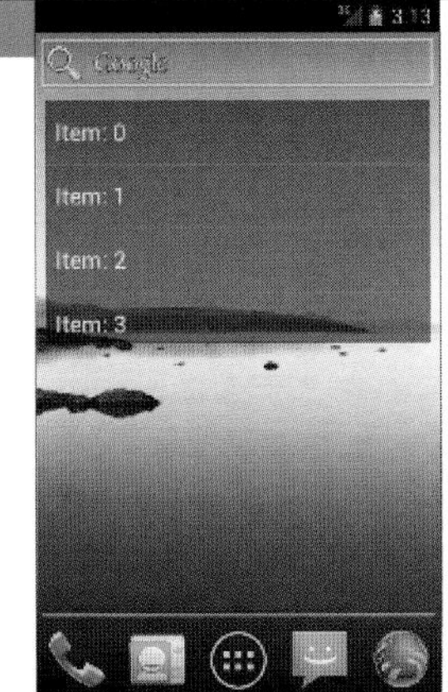

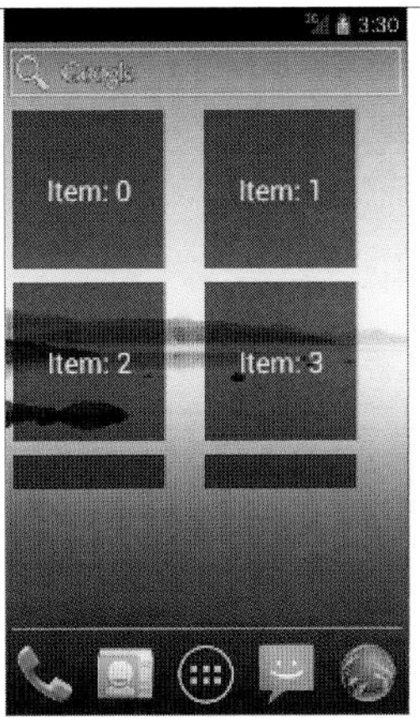

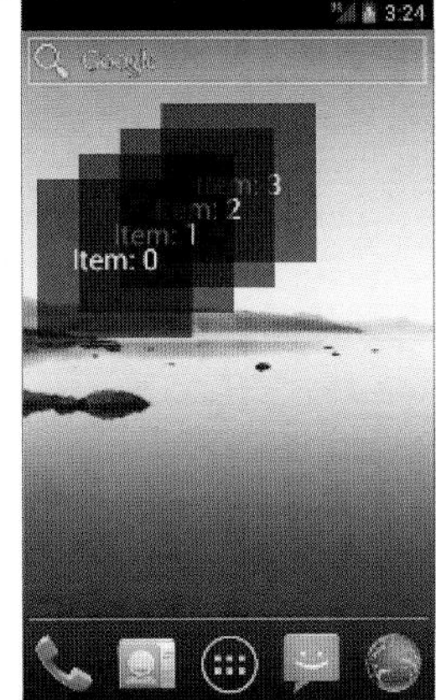

FIGURE 7.3 The view types available to display in a collection widget. From left to right: a `ListView`, a `GridView`, a `StackView`, and an `AdapterViewFlipper`.

Android 3.0 introduced a new type of widget that can display a collection of data provided by a remote data source such as a `ContentProvider`. The widget itself displays this data in a list, grid, stack, or picture frame. Creating one of these widgets is exactly like creating a standard widget but requires a new `RemoteViewsService` and `RemoteViewsFactory` to supply the collection data.

CREATING THE LAYOUT

The layout for a collection widget should contain a collection view, as well as a `TextView` that displays when the collection is empty. The collection view can be one of the following:

- `ListView`. A vertically scrolling list of items.
- `GridView`. A vertically scrolling grid of items.
- `StackView`. A stack of cards the user can flip through.
- `AdapterViewFlipper`. A picture frame-style widget. Only a single view is visible at a time, and views are auto-advanced.

Figure 7.3 shows the four types of collection widgets.

Here is an example layout that uses a ListView:

```
<?xml version="1.0" encoding="utf-8"?>
<FrameLayout xmlns:android="http://schemas.android.com/
→ apk/res/android"
    android:layout_width="match_parent"
    android:layout_height="match_parent"
    android:background="#80000000">
    <ListView
        android:id="@+id/list_view"
        android:layout_width="match_parent"
        android:layout_height="match_parent"/>
    <TextView
        android:id="@+id/empty_view"
        android:layout_width="match_parent"
        android:layout_height="match_parent"
        android:gravity="center"
        android:text="Empty List" />
</FrameLayout>
```

The ListView and the TextView are contained inside a FrameLayout so that the TextView can be displayed when there is no data. Each item displayed by the widget will need a layout as well. Since this example uses a ListView, you can just use the standard android.R.layout.simple_list_item_1 layout.

TIP: The empty view must be a sibling of the collection view in your widget layout.

CREATING THE SERVICE

To provide data to the widget, you create a service that the widget's hosting application can query. This service should extend the RemoteViewsService class and implement the onGetViewFactory method, which returns an instance of a RemoteViewsService.RemoteViewsFactory to act as the interface between the service and the widget. In fact, the service only exists to create the factory that the host application uses to display the widget.

The RemoteViewsFactory provides the data for the collection widget. The interface mirrors that of the Adapter class and uses the same semantics. Here is a sample implementation of both the RemoteViewsService and the RemoteViewsFactory:

```
public class ExampleWidgetService extends RemoteViewsService {

    public class ExampleRemoteViewsFactory implements
    → RemoteViewsService.RemoteViewsFactory {

        Context mContext;

        public ExampleRemoteViewsFactory(Context context) {

            mContext = context;

        }

        @Override

        public int getCount() {

            return 10;

        }

        @Override

        public RemoteViews getViewAt(int position) {

            RemoteViews views = new RemoteViews(mContext.
            → getPackageName(), android.R.layout.
            → simple_list_item_1);

            views.setTextViewText(R.id.text1, "Item: " + position);

            return views;

        }
```

```
    // Other methods omitted for brevity
    }
    @Override
    public RemoteViewsFactory onGetViewFactory(Intent intent) {
        return new ExampleRemoteViewsFactory
        → (this.getApplicationContext());
    }
}
```

The factory is used by the host activity to retrieve the data to display. The `getViewAt` method is where the `RemoteViews` object is returned. Here, the standard list item layout is used when populating the `ListView`; note that this example returns ten results. Finally, the widget must be set up to use the service in the `AppWidgetProvider`:

```
public class ExampleWidgetProvider extends AppWidgetProvider {
    @Override
    public void onUpdate(Context context, AppWidgetManager
    → appWidgetManager, int[] appWidgetIds) {
        Intent intent = new Intent(context,
        → ExampleWidgetService.class);
        RemoteViews views = new RemoteViews
        → (context.getPackageName(), R.layout.widget_layout);
        views.setRemoteAdapter(R.id.list_view, intent);
        views.setEmptyView(R.id.list_view, R.id.empty_view);
        appWidgetManager.updateAppWidget(appWidgetIds, views);
        super.onUpdate(context, appWidgetManager, appWidgetIds);
    }
}
```

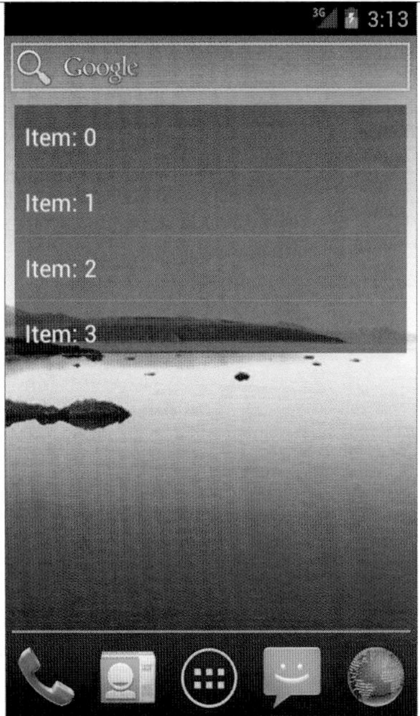

FIGURE 7.4 The `ListView` widget

When the `onUpdate` method of the `AppWidgetProvider` is called, it should return the view for the entire widget. When using a collection widget, you call the `setRemoteAdapter` method to set the ID of the collection view and pass it an `Intent` for the service that will populate the collection. You can optionally set a view ID to display when the collection is empty by using the `setEmptyView` method.

NOTE: Unlike most callbacks on Android, the `onDataSetChanged` and `getViewAt` methods of `RemoteViewsFactory` do not run on the UI thread. You are free to perform synchronous, long-running operations in those methods. Also, if the `getViewAt` method takes a long time, the loading view returned by `getLoadingView` will be shown until it finishes.

You should now be able to run the example and create a widget similar to the one shown in **Figure 7.4**.

WRAPPING UP

Android widgets provide a convenient method by which apps can present data to the user without the need to load the full application. This is a powerful addition to your application's feature set. Using widgets, users can quickly find the information they need without needless device interaction. This chapter covered the basics of creating widgets on Android. Along the way, you learned that

- An `AppWidgetProvider` is really just a `BroadcastReceiver` that handles the widget update broadcasts for you.
- The `RemoteViews` class allows widgets to be created and updated by other processes in Android.
- The `AppWidgetProviderInfo` XML file is used to configure the widget and its behavior.
- Collection widgets display data from a service using an adapter-like class named `RemoteViewsFactory`.

PART 3

ADVANCED
UI DEVELOPMENT

8

HANDLING **GESTURES**

The basic Android UI toolkit provides the most common interaction gestures you will need in your application: taps, long presses, and swipes. But sometimes the built-in gestures aren't sufficient for your application or are not available on the view you're using. For those cases, Android provides the ability to create custom gestures. This chapter introduces the basics of detecting and responding to gestures. Along the way, you'll learn that all views have an `onTouchEvent` method you can use to intercept touch events; that the `MotionEvent` class is the low-level interface to the touchscreen inputs; that you should use `GestureDetector` and its subclasses to enable the most common gestures; and that you can enable pinch-to-zoom functionality by using the `ScaleGestureDetector`.

LISTENING TO TOUCH EVENTS

The most basic form of gesture recognition is the touch event. Touch events are the lowest level of user interaction with the touchscreen. Events include putting a finger on the screen, sliding a finger along the screen, and lifting a finger off the screen. Each of these represents a discrete touch event. There are two ways you can listen for these events: by registering an `OnTouchListener` on a view and implementing the `onTouchEvent` method, or by implementing your own view and overriding its `onTouchEvent` method. These methods are called with a `MotionEvent` object containing information about the event.

Here is a simple example class that overrides `View` and implements the `onTouchEvent` method:

1. Create a class named `TouchExample` that extends `View`:

```
public class TouchExample extends View {
    public TouchExample(Context context) {
        super(context);
    }
}
```

2. Add some fields for position coordinates and some pre-computed color and font size values. Create a new `Paint` object to store the text color and size:

```
public class TouchExample extends View {
    private Paint mPaint;
    private float mFontSize;
    private float dx;
    private float dy;
    public TouchExample(Context context) {
        super(context);
        mFontSize = 16 * getResources().getDisplayMetrics().
        → density;
        mPaint = new Paint();
```

```
        mPaint.setColor(Color.WHITE);
        mPaint.setTextSize(mFontSize);
    }
}
```

3. Override the onDraw method, and use the dx and dy values to set the position of the text:

   ```
   @Override
   protected void onDraw(Canvas canvas) {
       super.onDraw(canvas);
       String text = "Hello World!";
       canvas.drawText(text, dx, dy, mPaint);
   }
   ```

   Here, the text is drawn onto the canvas at the specified position, using the Paint object.

4. Now override the onTouchEvent method, set the *x* and *y* coordinates based on the input MotionEvent object, and finish by invalidating the view:

   ```
   @Override
   public boolean onTouchEvent(MotionEvent event) {
       dx = event.getX();
       dy = event.getY();
       invalidate();
       return true;
   }
   ```

TIP: When overriding the onTouchEvent method, you should return true to consume the event and prevent the base class from handling it. Otherwise, you will receive only the ACTION_DOWN events and no others.

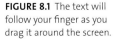

FIGURE 8.1 The text will follow your finger as you drag it around the screen.

5. Finally, create an activity that uses your new view as its content:

```
public class GestureActivity extends Activity {
    @Override
    public void onCreate(Bundle savedInstanceState) {
        super.onCreate(savedInstanceState);
        TouchExample view = new TouchExample(this);
        setContentView(view);
    }
}
```

When you run this app, you should now see the text "Hello World!" follow your finger around the screen (**Figure 8.1**). This simple example shows how you can listen to, and take action based on, the user's touch input. But the example only handles a single finger. How would you handle a multi-touch screen?

MULTI-TOUCH EVENTS

The `MotionEvent` object actually contains information on multiple events. Each finger the user puts on the screen is tracked and referred to as a pointer. By default, the `getX()` and `getY()` methods return the default pointer. But all the other pointers are available, accessible via the `getX(int)` and `getY(int)` methods. The input parameter is the index of the pointer. The primary pointer, the first one to touch the screen, is index 0. The total number of pointers is available by calling the `getPointerCount()` method. The index of a pointer can change, so each pointer is also assigned an ID.

For example, if the user places a single finger on the screen, that finger is assigned pointer index 0 and ID 0. Now when they place a second finger on the screen, that new pointer is assigned index 1 and ID 1. If the user were to lift up their first finger, the second pointer would become index 0 but would retain ID 1. It's the only pointer present; hence, it is the first pointer in the array of pointers. However, the pointer ID is consistent across touches. So if the user were to place their first finger on the screen again, that finger would again be assigned ID 0 and would once again become index 0.

NOTE: **For efficiency, Android batches touch events into a single call to `onTouchEvent`. In addition to containing multiple pointer events, the `MotionEvent` object also contains a recent history for each event. You can access these times by using the `getHistoricalX` and `getHistoricalY` calls.**

In addition to containing the pointers, the MotionEvent object also contains an action parameter that describes what event has occurred. **Table 8.1** summarizes the list of events relevant to touchscreen interfaces. This is not an exhaustive list. There are many more events for handling different interface types, such as keyboards, mice, TVs, and game controllers. You should refer to the Android documentation for a full list.

TABLE 8.1 MotionEvent Actions

ACTION	DESCRIPTION
ACTION_DOWN	The user has placed a finger on the screen in a single place. This is the first touch event and is known as the primary pointer. This pointer will have index 0.
ACTION_POINTER_DOWN	The user has placed a non-primary finger on the screen. The pointer index is greater than 0.
ACTION_POINTER_UP	A single finger has been removed from the screen, but not the finger corresponding to the primary pointer.
ACTION_MOVE	The user is sliding a finger across the screen.
ACTION_UP	The user has stopped touching the screen and has lifted all fingers away from it.
ACTION_CANCEL	Sent by the touchscreen framework when the current set of touch events should be canceled. This occurs if the hardware has generated a spurious touch or if a parent view has stolen the touch event.

The earlier example always uses pointer index 0 to place and move the text. If you place a finger on the screen, the text will follow it. Try altering the example to show each touch pointer index and ID:

1. Add both a new class to hold the pointer data and an array to store the pointers. For this example, you only need to track five points. Initialize the array with Pointer objects. You can remove the dx and dy fields:

```
final static int MAX_POINTERS = 5;
private Pointer[] mPointers = new Pointer[MAX_POINTERS];
class Pointer {
```

```
        float x = 0;
        float y = 0;
        int index = -1;
        int id = -1;
    }
    public TouchExample(Context context) {
        for (int i = 0; i<MAX_POINTERS; i++) {
            mPointers[i] = new Pointer();
        }
        ...
```

2. Update the onTouchEvent method to track each finger that is placed on the screen. Set the pointer data when the first touch occurs and while the user swipes their finger across the screen:

```
@Override
public boolean onTouchEvent(MotionEvent event) {
    int pointerCount = Math.min(event.getPointerCount(),
    → MAX_POINTERS);
    switch (event.getAction() & MotionEvent.ACTION_MASK) {
    case MotionEvent.ACTION_DOWN:
    case MotionEvent.ACTION_POINTER_DOWN:
    case MotionEvent.ACTION_MOVE:
        // Clear previous pointers
        for (int id = 0; id<MAX_POINTERS id++)
            mPointers[id].index = -1;
        // Now fill in the current pointers
        for (int i = 0; i<pointerCount i++) {
            int id = event.getPointerId(i);
            Pointer pointer = mPointers[id];
```

```
                pointer.index = i;
                pointer.id = id;
                pointer.x = event.getX(i);
                pointer.y = event.getY(i);
            }
            invalidate();
            break;
        case MotionEvent.ACTION_CANCEL:
            for (int i = 0; i<pointerCount i++) {
                int id = event.getPointerId(i);
                mPointers[id].index = -1;
            }
            invalidate();
            break;
    }
    return true;
}
```

3. Update the onDraw method to display the index and ID of each pointer:

```
@Override
protected void onDraw(Canvas canvas) {
    super.onDraw(canvas);
    for (Pointer p : mPointers) {
        if (p.index != -1) {
            String text = "Index: " + p.index + " ID: " + p.id;
            canvas.drawText(text, p.x, p.y, mPaint);
        }
    }
}
```

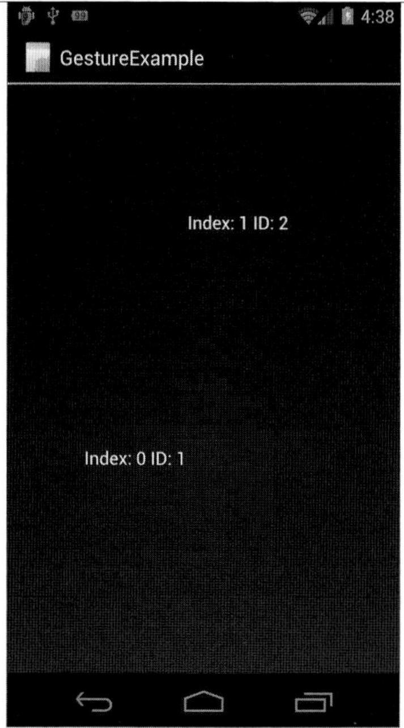

FIGURE 8.2 The index and ID of each pointer will be displayed as you place your fingers on the screen.

Now as you press each finger on the screen, you will see text showing the index and ID of each pointer (**Figure 8.2**). Experiment with touching multiple fingers at once and then lifting them off the screen. Observe how the ID remains consistent, but the index changes.

NOTE: You should always handle the `ACTION_CANCEL` event, because the touch system may erroneously report touches and cancel them later. This will also happen when a parent view steals the touch event. For example, if your view is inside a `ListView`, then the list may steal the touch event once it has detected that the user is actually scrolling the list.

RESPONDING TO GESTURES

Touch events provide a very low-level interface to the touchscreen that can be difficult to interpret. Often what you really need is the ability to recognize certain gestures the user makes on the screen. For that, Android provides convenience classes that detect gestures for you.

GESTUREDETECTOR

To detect gestures, you create an instance of the GestureDetector class and send it all touch events your view receives. You register an OnGestureListener with the GestureDetector to receive callbacks when gestures are detected. This interface has callbacks for the most common gestures you will need: taps, double taps, swipes, and flings.

Modify the example to zoom the text when you double-tap the screen:

1. Add a scale field to the View. You will use this to scale the text size:

```
public class TouchExample extends View {
    private float mScale = 1.0f;
    ...
```

2. Create the gesture listener that will zoom the text. In this case, extend the SimpleOnGestureListener, which provides stub implementations for the callback methods. Override the onDoubleTap method to listen for double-tap gestures:

```
public class ZoomGesture extends GestureDetector.
→ SimpleOnGestureListener {
    private boolean normal = true;
    @Override
    public boolean onDoubleTap(MotionEvent e) {
        mScale = normal ? 3f : 1f;
        mPaint.setTextSize(mScale*mFontSize);
        normal = !normal;
```

```
            invalidate();
            return true;
        }
    }
```

The listener simply alternates the scale factor based on the Boolean `normal` value and updates the text size. When finished, it invalidates the view to force it to redraw.

3. Add a `GestureDetector` field and instantiate it in the view constructor, initializing it with the `ZoomGesture` listener you created:

    ```
    private GestureDetector mGestureDetector;
    public TouchExample(Context context) {
        super(context);
        mGestureDetector = new GestureDetector(context,
        → new ZoomGesture());
        ...
    ```

4. You must call the `onTouchEvent` method of the gesture detector in the `onTouchEvent` method of the view:

    ```
    @Override
    public boolean onTouchEvent(MotionEvent event) {
        mGestureDetector.onTouchEvent(event);
        ...
    ```

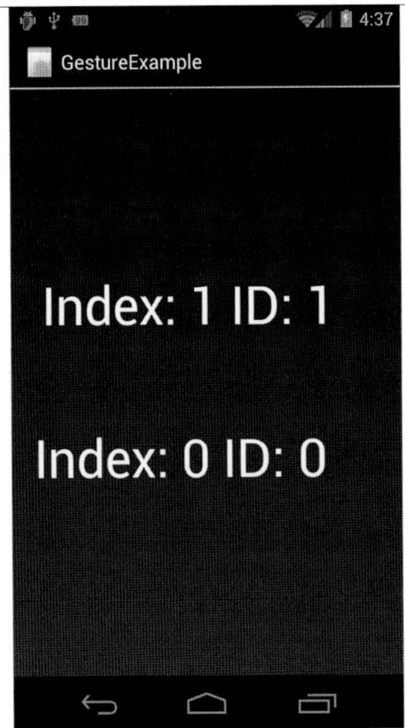

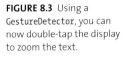

FIGURE 8.3 Using a GestureDetector, you can now double-tap the display to zoom the text.

Now when you run the app, double-tapping the screen will zoom the text (**Figure 8.3**). Double-tap again and the text will return to its original size. This example shows how easy it is add simple gesture detection to your app. Adding a similar double-tap gesture to the TimeTracker app will make starting and stopping the timer a snap. Go ahead and register an `onTouchListener` on the timer text view and add a double-tap gesture that acts exactly like a press of the Start/Stop button.

The `GestureDetector` makes working with gestures a snap, but it is missing one important and very frequent gesture: pinch to zoom. For that reason, Android 2.2 added the `ScaleGestureDetector`.

SCALEGESTUREDETECTOR

The `ScaleGestureDetector` class functions exactly like the standard `GestureDetector`, but it provides gesture recognition for two-fingered motions. Callbacks are available for accessing the distance between two pointers, the scale change between the current and previous pointers, and the focal point of two pointers. The most common use for this is the pinch-to-zoom feature, where a user presses two fingers on the screen and expands them to zoom in to a view. Google Maps provides a good example of this interaction pattern.

Implementing the pinch-to-zoom gesture requires that you implement the OnScaleGestureListener, which is similar to the GestureListener. The pinch-to-zoom implementation uses the onScale method to detect pinching and spreading motions, and it uses those motions to alter the displayed views. Here is a simple example:

1. Create a new class called ScaleGesture that extends the SimpleOnScaleGestureListener:

```
public class ScaleGesture extends
→ ScaleGestureDetector.SimpleOnScaleGestureListener {
    @Override
    public boolean onScale(ScaleGestureDetector detector) {
        mScale *= detector.getScaleFactor();
        mPaint.setTextSize(mScale*mFontSize);
        invalidate();
        return true;
    }
}
```

2. To use this gesture in the example app, you need to add the ScaleGestureDetector to the view onCreate method:

```
private GestureDetector mGestureDetector;
private ScaleGestureDetector mScaleGestureDetector;
public TouchExample(Context context) {
    super(context);
    mGestureDetector = new GestureDetector(context,
    → new ZoomGesture());
    mScaleGestureDetector = new ScaleGestureDetector(context,
    → new ScaleGesture());
    ...
```

3. Remember to call the onTouchEvent method of the OnScaleGestureListener in the onTouchEvent method of the view:

```
@Override
public boolean onTouchEvent(MotionEvent event) {
    mGestureDetector.onTouchEvent(event);
    mScaleGestureDetector.onTouchEvent(event);
    ...
```

Now, in addition to being able to double-tap to zoom, you can pinch to zoom as well. With ScaleGestureDetector and GestureDetector, you will be able to handle all the common touchscreen interaction that users will expect.

CUSTOM **GESTURES**

You are not limited to the predefined gestures provided by the Android framework—you are free to implement your own gesture detection. Follow the example of the existing gesture detectors; the source code is available at http://source.android.com/.

There is another option for implementing custom gestures that doesn't require custom detection code. The Android emulator contains an app called Gestures Builder that lets you create gesture patterns by drawing on the screen with your mouse. These patterns are saved in a file that you can bundle with your app. By loading this gestures file at runtime, you can register to receive a callback when the user performs the gesture.

This custom gesture functionality is available through the `android.gesture` package. While this library has limited use, it can be a convenient way to add a completely custom gesture to your application.

WRAPPING UP

This chapter introduced the basics of touch events and gesture handling. You learned how to intercept touchscreen events, what actions correspond to those events, and how to detect higher-order touch events like gestures. Along the way, you learned that

- The `View.onTouchEvent` method is called when a user touches that view.
- Each touch point on a multi-touch screen is called a pointer.
- `MotionEvent` objects contain all touch pointers and their recent history.
- The `GestureDetector` class provides a simple way to add gesture support to your app.
- You can use the `ScaleGestureDetector` class to detect pinch-to-zoom gestures.

9

ANIMATION

Animation helps users understand the functionality of your app without the need for explicit instruction. Android provides a few animation APIs with different use cases. Drawable and view animations offer the best compatibility, but they only operate on views. Starting with Android 3.0, the property animation framework is the preferred method for creating animations. This framework removes the limitations of view animations and can animate any object, not just views.

In this chapter, you'll learn that you can use drawable animations to create sprite-style animation; that the view animation framework provides compatibility for older versions of Android, but that it can be used only on views; that the `ObjectAnimator` is used to change the properties of an object over time; that interpolators change the rate at which an animation is applied, creating a more natural animation; and that the `ViewPropertyAnimator` lets you animate views using a series of chainable method calls.

CREATING **DRAWABLE ANIMATIONS**

The simplest animations on Android display a series of drawables in sequence. This is known as *drawable animation*. To create a drawable animation, you create an XML file that lists the drawables that are part of the animation. Android will then display these drawables in sequence, creating the animation. You define attributes for the duration and for whether the animation should loop or just run a single time.

Here is a simple example that creates an animated ball:

1. Create three simple shape drawables. Use the `android:shape` attribute to make the circles: one black, one gray, and one white. Here is the white circle:

```
<?xml version="1.0" encoding="utf-8"?>
<shape xmlns:android="http://schemas.android.com/
→ apk/res/android"
    android:shape="oval" >
    <solid android:color="#FFFFFF"/>
    <size android:height="100dp" android:width="100dp" />
</shape>
```

2. Now create the drawable animation. This will be a one-shot animation, meaning it will run once and then stop. Set the animation duration to 250 milliseconds:

```
<?xml version="1.0" encoding="utf-8"?>
<animation-list xmlns:android="http://schemas.android.com/
→ apk/res/android"
    android:visible="true" android:oneshot="true">
    <item android:drawable="@drawable/white_circle"
    → android:duration="250" />
    <item android:drawable="@drawable/gray_circle"
    → android:duration="250" />
    <item android:drawable="@drawable/black_circle"
    → android:duration="250" />
</animation-list>
```

The `android:visible` attribute specifies that the animated drawable will be visible before the animation starts.

3. Create a simple layout that contains just an ImageView with its source set to the animation:

```
<?xml version="1.0" encoding="utf-8"?>
<ImageView xmlns:android="http://schemas.android.com/
→ apk/res/android"
    android:id="@+id/image_view"
    android:layout_width="match_parent"
    android:layout_height="match_parent"
    android:scaleType="center"
    android:src="@drawable/animation" />
```

4. Create the activity, and set its content view to the layout. Set a touch listener on the image view to start the animation when the user taps it. Because the animation is a one-shot, you need to call stop() before start() for subsequent taps:

```
public class AnimationExampleActivity extends Activity {
    @Override
    public void onCreate(Bundle savedInstanceState) {
        super.onCreate(savedInstanceState);
        setContentView(R.layout.main);
        ImageView iv = (ImageView)
        → findViewById(R.id.image_view);
        iv.setOnTouchListener(new OnTouchListener() {
            @Override
            public boolean onTouch(View v, MotionEvent event) {
                ImageView iv = (ImageView) v;
                AnimationDrawable ad = (AnimationDrawable)
                → iv.getDrawable();
                ad.stop();
                ad.start();
```

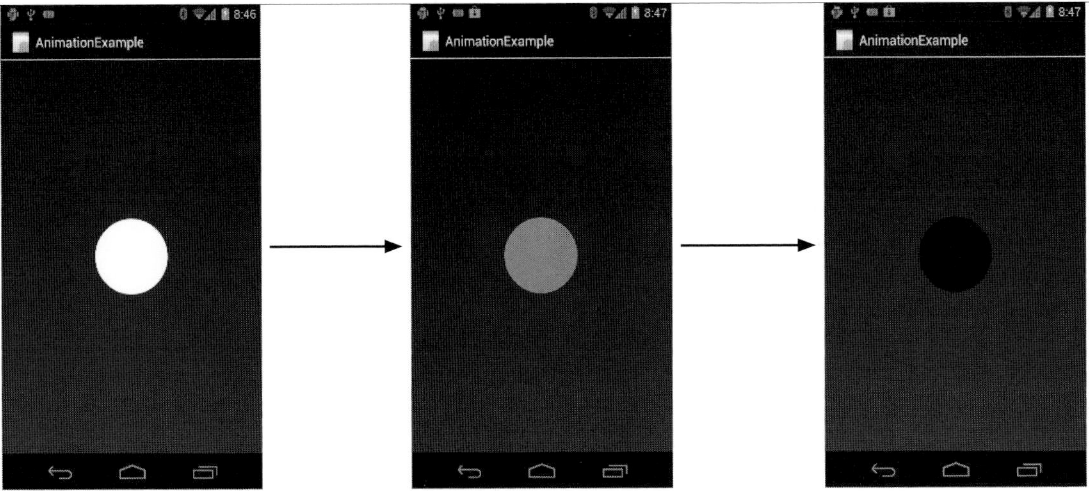

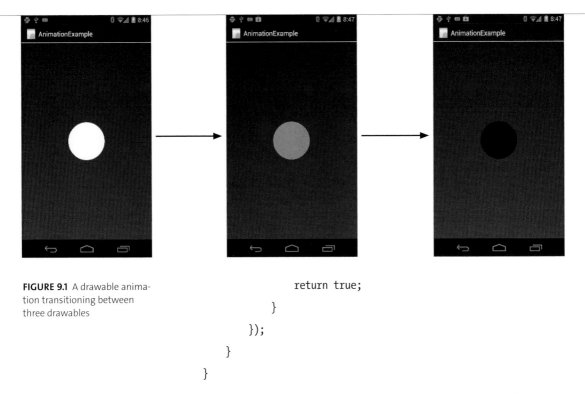

FIGURE 9.1 A drawable animation transitioning between three drawables

```
                return true;
            }
        });
    }
}
```

5. Run the app, and tap the screen to see the circle animating as the system swaps between each drawable (**Figure 9.1**).

This simple method is very fast to set up and works well when you want a sprite-type animation.

CREATING **VIEW ANIMATIONS**

The primary method of creating animations prior to Android 3.0 was the view animation system. View animation provides a series of built-in animation operations that generate in-between, or tween, views. You supply the starting and ending values, and the animation framework will transform the displayed view. This system is simple to implement, but it has a few drawbacks. First, it's limited to operating on `View` objects. If you want to animate something that is not a view, you'll need to do so yourself. Second, it operates only on a default set of properties; it does not affect other properties. Finally, view animation alters only how the view is drawn, not where it is positioned. Importantly, the rectangular hit area of views is not moved during a view animation—a common bug found in animation code. You need to alter the view after the animation is finished to update its position.

These limitations led to the deprecation of the view animation framework in Android 3.0 and later. However, there are still a large number of pre-3.0 devices in use, so when possible you should use the view animation framework for maximum app compatibility.

DEFINING ANIMATIONS

Like most UI code in Android, animations can be defined either in code or in XML. It's preferred to use XML, however, because it is easier to create complex animations and is easily reusable. View animations defined in XML are placed in the `res/anim/` folder. The basic structure of an animation is similar to that of a view. These are the available options for view animation:

- `translate`, which moves a view
- `scale`, which changes the size of a view
- `rotate`, which rotates a view
- `alpha`, which changes the transparency of a view

Here is a simple example animation that moves (translates) a view:

```
<?xml version="1.0" encoding="utf-8"?>
<translate xmlns:android="http://schemas.android.com/
→ apk/res/android"
    android:duration="500"
    android:toYDelta="25%"
    android:toXDelta="25%" />
```

This should look familiar from other Android XML formats. The attributes here set the duration and the ending position of the animation. The position is specified as a percentage of the view size—this animation will move the view down and to the right. Duration is always expressed in milliseconds. Position can be specified as a percentage of the view size, as a percentage of the parent view size, or in pixel values (with no units). This same animation can be created in Java code as follows:

```
TranslateAnimation anim =
    new TranslateAnimation(
        TranslateAnimation.RELATIVE_TO_SELF, 0.0f,
        TranslateAnimation.RELATIVE_TO_SELF, 0.25f,
        TranslateAnimation.RELATIVE_TO_SELF, 0.0f,
        TranslateAnimation.RELATIVE_TO_SELF, 0.25f);
anim.setDuration(500);
```

Animations can be grouped into sets, with several animations occurring simultaneously. Here is the same example, but this time grouped in a set with another animation that changes the transparency of the view:

```
<?xml version="1.0" encoding="utf-8"?>
<set xmlns:android="http://schemas.android.com/apk/res/android">
    <translate
        android:duration="500"
        android:toYDelta="25%"
        android:toXDelta="25%" />
```

```
    <alpha
        android:duration="500"
        android:fromAlpha="1.0"
        android:toAlpha="0.0" />
</set>
```

This animation will cause the view to be moved down and to the right, while simultaneously fading out. The `fromAlpha` and `toAlpha` attributes define the beginning and ending alpha transparency, where 1.0 is fully opaque and 0.0 is fully transparent.

In the example, the animations occur simultaneously, but that is not required. You can have them occur in sequence, or partially overlapping, by defining the `android:startOffset` attribute. Set this to a value in milliseconds to have the animation wait until that time offset before starting. Here is the same example again, but this time with the alpha animation beginning after the translate has finished:

```
<?xml version="1.0" encoding="utf-8"?>
<set xmlns:android="http://schemas.android.com/apk/res/android">
    <translate
        android:duration="500"
        android:toYDelta="25%"
        android:toXDelta="25%" />
    <alpha
        android:duration="500"
        android:startOffset=500"
        android:fromAlpha="1.0"
        android:toAlpha="0.0" />
</set>
```

You can use this attribute to make several animations occur in sequence. In addition, you can nest animation sets to create animations that are even more complex. Check the Android documentation for the full list of animation options.

USING INTERPOLATORS

An important aspect of animation is how it is applied over time. By default, animations occur in a linear fashion, meaning that they are applied evenly over the duration of the animation. However, this often *feels* wrong to users. To address this, you use what's called an interpolator to change how the animation is applied.

Android supports several different interpolators: accelerate, decelerate, overshoot, bounce, and many more. Applying these interpolators is as simple as adding an attribute to your animation tags:

```
<translate xmlns:android="http://schemas.android.com/
→ apk/res/android"
    android:duration="500"
    android:toYDelta="50%"
    android:toXDelta="50%"
    android:interpolator="@android:anim/accelerate_interpolator" />
```

Now when you run the animation, it will start slowly and accelerate until it reaches the end of the duration.

USING ANIMATIONS

To use an animation in your application, you have to apply it to a view and run it. You do this by calling the `startAnimation` method on the view, passing it the animation you want to run:

```
TextView tv = (TextView) findViewById(R.id.text);
Animation animation = AnimationUtils.loadAnimation(this, R.anim.slide);
tv.startAnimation(animation);
```

This animation will now cause the `TextView` to animate down and to the right. However, once the animation is finished, the view will return to its previous position. Remember that view animation alters only how the view is drawn, not the actual view object itself. When the animation is finished, the view is drawn once again and appears to return to its previous position, because it never really moved at all. To address this, you can use an `AnimationListener` to change the view once its animation has finished. Here is an example that listens for the end of the animation and makes the view invisible when finished:

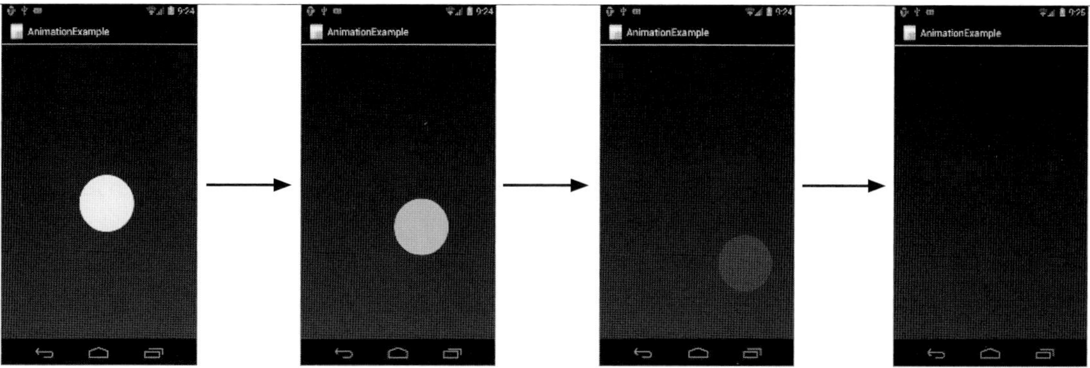

FIGURE 9.2 In this view animation, the circle animates from the center to the bottom right while fading out.

```
final TextView tv = (TextView) findViewById(R.id.text1);
Animation animation = AnimationUtils.loadAnimation(this, R.anim.slide);
animation.setAnimationListener(new AnimationListener() {
    @Override
    public void onAnimationStart(Animation animation) {}
    @Override
    public void onAnimationRepeat(Animation animation) {}
    @Override
    public void onAnimationEnd(Animation animation) {
        tv.setVisibility(View.INVISIBLE);
    }
});
tv.startAnimation(animation);
```

Using this example, you should be able to create an animation similar to **Figure 9.2**.

TIP: As an alternative to using an `AnimationListener`, you can set the `fillAfter` attribute of your animation to `true`. This will cause the result of the animation to persist after it finishes. However, keep in mind that only the display of the view will change. If you expect the user to tap your view, you'll need to use an animation listener to actually move it.

ADDING A CLOCK-FLIPPING ANIMATION TO THE TIMETRACKER

Since the TimeTracker app is being built to support Android 2.2, you'll use view animation to create a clock-flipping animation for the time counter. To do this, you'll need to first create a new layout for the counter, then define a few animations, and finally add the logic to the app to properly change each digit. The counter will use two separate `TextViews` for each digit. The animation can then slide one out and the other in while fading them to create a nice flipping effect.

1. Create a layout called `digit.xml` that will contain the two `TextViews`, and set one to be invisible by default:

```
<?xml version="1.0" encoding="utf-8"?>
<FrameLayout xmlns:android="http://schemas.android.com/
→ apk/res/android"
    android:layout_width="match_parent"
    android:layout_height="match_parent" >
    <TextView
        android:id="@+id/text1"
        android:layout_width="wrap_content"
        android:layout_height="wrap_content"
        android:layout_gravity="center"
        android:text="0"
        android:textSize="50sp" />
    <TextView
        android:id="@+id/text2"
        android:layout_width="wrap_content"
        android:layout_height="wrap_content"
        android:layout_gravity="center"
        android:text="1"
        android:textSize="50sp"
        android:visibility="invisible" />
</FrameLayout>
```

2. Create a new layout for the counter itself, and name it `counter.xml`. It will include multiple instances of the digit layout, separated by colons. Everything is arranged in a horizontal `LinearLayout`:

```
<?xml version="1.0" encoding="utf-8"?>
<LinearLayout xmlns:android="http://schemas.android.com/
→ apk/res/android"
    android:id="@+id/counter"
    android:layout_width="match_parent"
    android:layout_height="match_parent"
    android:gravity="center_horizontal" >
    <include android:id="@+id/hour1" layout=
    → "@layout/digit" android:layout_width="wrap_content"
    → android:layout_height="wrap_content"/>
    <include android:id="@+id/hour2" layout=
    → "@layout/digit" android:layout_width="wrap_content"
    → android:layout_height="wrap_content"/>
    <TextView
        android:layout_width="wrap_content"
        android:layout_height="wrap_content"
        android:text=":"
        android:textSize="50sp"
        android:gravity="bottom"/>
    <include android:id="@+id/minute1" layout=
    → "@layout/digit" android:layout_width="wrap_content"
    → android:layout_height="wrap_content"/>
    <include android:id="@+id/minute2" layout=
    → "@layout/digit" android:layout_width="wrap_content"
    → android:layout_height="wrap_content"/>
    <TextView
        android:layout_width="wrap_content"
        android:layout_height="wrap_content"
```

```
        android:text=":"
        android:textSize="50sp"
        android:gravity="bottom"/>
    <include android:id="@+id/second1" layout=
    ➥ "@layout/digit" android:layout_width="wrap_content"
    ➥ android:layout_height="wrap_content"/>
    <include android:id="@+id/second2" layout=
    ➥ "@layout/digit" android:layout_width="wrap_content"
    ➥ android:layout_height="wrap_content"/>
</LinearLayout>
```

3. Add the logic to set the time and trigger the animations. Start by calculating the hours, minutes, and seconds:

```
long hours = 0;
long minutes = 0;
long seconds = 0;
if (time > 3600*1000) {
    hours = time/(3600*1000);
    time -= hours*3600*1000;
}
if (time > 60*1000) {
    minutes = time/(60*1000);
    time -= minutes*60*1000;
    seconds = time/1000;
if (time > 1000) {
    seconds = time/1000;
    time -= seconds*1000;
}
```

4. Animate each digit:

```
animateDigit(R.id.minute2, minutes%10);
animateDigit(R.id.minute1, minutes/10);
animateDigit(R.id.hour2, hours%10);
animateDigit(R.id.hour1, hours/10);
animateDigit(R.id.second2, seconds%10);
animateDigit(R.id.second1, seconds/10);
```

5. Create the `animateDigit` function; this function takes a digit layout ID and a value, and it sets the digit while animating the transition. Next, prevent the animation from running if a previous animation has not finished. Then create an animation listener that sets the proper digit value once the animation is complete:

```
private void animateDigit(final int id, final long value) {
    final View v = findViewById(id);
    final TextView text1 = (TextView)
    → v.findViewById(R.id.text1);
    final TextView text2 = (TextView)
    → v.findViewById(R.id.text2 );
    boolean running = false;
    if (text1.getAnimation() != null)
            running = !text1.getAnimation().hasEnded();
    if (Long.parseLong(text1.getText().toString()) ==
    → value || running) return;
    Animation animation = AnimationUtils.loadAnimation
    → (this, R.anim.slide_out);
    animation.setAnimationListener(new AnimationListener() {
        @Override
        public void onAnimationStart(Animation animation) {
        }
```

```
        @Override
        public void onAnimationRepeat(Animation animation) {
        }
        @Override
        public void onAnimationEnd(Animation animation) {
            text1.setText("" + value);
        }
    });
    text1.startAnimation(animation);
    animation = AnimationUtils.loadAnimation
    → (this, R.anim.slide_in);
    text2.startAnimation(animation);
    text2.setText("" + value);
}
```

NOTE: This code could be made more efficient by performing the view lookups at activity creation time and caching them for later use. You could also use a single animation listener, rather than creating one on every animation. However, for the TimeTracker app, this code is sufficient.

6. Create the sliding animations for the two text views. These should be familiar by now. Here is the slide *in* animation:

```
<?xml version="1.0" encoding="utf-8"?>
<set xmlns:android="http://schemas.android.com/
→ apk/res/android"
    android:interpolator="@android:anim/
    → accelerate_interpolator" >
    <translate
        android:duration="250"
        android:fromYDelta="-50%" />
    <alpha
```

FIGURE 9.3 The clock-flipping animation for the TimeTracker app

```
        android:duration="250"
        android:fromAlpha="0.0"
        android:toAlpha="1.0" />
</set>
```

And the slide *out* animation:

```
<?xml version="1.0" encoding="utf-8"?>
<set xmlns:android="http://schemas.android.com/
→ apk/res/android"
    android:interpolator="@android:anim/
    → accelerate_interpolator" >
    <translate
        android:duration="250"
        android:toYDelta="50%" />
    <alpha
        android:duration="250"
        android:fromAlpha="1.0"
        android:toAlpha="0.0" />
</set>
```

7. Run TimeTracker, and you will now see a nice animated clock (**Figure 9.3**).

As you can see, working with view animations is quite simple. However, the limitations of view animations required a reworking of the Android animation system. For 3.0 and later devices, it's recommended you use the property animation framework.

CREATING **PROPERTY ANIMATIONS**

Android 3.0 introduced an animation framework called property animation. This framework allows you to change any object, not just views, and it actually changes an object's values, not just the way it is drawn. It may seem strange to animate something that is not a view; after all, views are what the user sees. But you can think of property animation as a framework for changing any value over time. Generally, these values will cause some animation on the screen, but this is not strictly necessary. Property animation is very powerful and can make some animations much easier.

VALUEANIMATOR

The base class for all property animation is `ValueAnimator`. This class takes a starting value, an ending value, and a duration, and it calculates a new value at each time step of an animation; the time steps are determined by the speed of the animation thread. The `ValueAnimator` requires an `Interpolator` and a `TypeEvaluator` to compute the property values. Here is a brief explanation of each class:

- `ValueAnimator`. This is the base class for all animators. At each frame of animation, it calculates the percentage of the animation that is completed, based on the animation's starting time and duration. It then calls the `Interpolator` and `TypeEvaluator` to calculate the new property values.
- `Interpolator`. Like view animation, property animation allows you to set different interpolators that define how the animated property changes over time. After the `ValueAnimator` determines the percentage progress of the animation, it passes that value to the interpolator to determine the amount of change that should be applied to the property value. The default interpolator is an accelerate-decelerate interpolator.
- `TypeEvaluator`. Because the property animation system can operate on any type of value, it requires a `TypeEvaluator` class to convert between a float progress value and the appropriate value for the type of the property. The framework supplies evaluators for floats, integers, and color values. For other types, you will have to implement your own subclass of `TypeEvaluator`.

A simple example will demonstrate how `ValueAnimator` works:

```
ValueAnimator animation = ValueAnimator.ofFloat(0f, 1f);
animation.setDuration(250);
animation.start();
```

Here, an animation is created and set to run for a duration of 250 milliseconds, starting at a floating point value of 0 and stopping at the value 1. The interpolator is the default accelerate-decelerate interpolator. Notice the `ofFloat` method? That method specifies that the values are floats and that a float `TypeEvaluator` should be used. There are also `ofInt` and `ofObject` methods for creating animations with integers and generic `Object` properties. In the case of objects, you will need to supply a custom `TypeEvaluator` for the `ValueAnimator` to produce correct output.

This code does not yet do anything useful, because the values computed by the `ValueAnimator` are not used. You can register an `AnimatorListener` and a `ViewAnimator.AnimatorUpdateListener` to listen for animation events and make updates accordingly. However, Android provides a convenience implementation of `ValueAnimator` called `ObjectAnimator` that performs updates for you.

THE OBJECTANIMATOR CLASS

`ObjectAnimator`, a subclass of `ValueAnimator`, sets the value of an object for you. Its API is similar to that of `ValueAnimator`, but it has default implementations for the callbacks that will update an object's property. Here is a simple example that updates the alpha transparency of a view:

```
View view = findViewById(R.id.my_view);
ObjectAnimator animation = ObjectAnimator.ofFloat(view, "alpha",
→ 0f, 1f);
animation.setDuration(250);
animation.start();
```

Note that the API requires two new additions: the object to update and the property that should be updated. In this case, the `ObjectAnimator` will update the alpha transparency of the view from completely transparent to completely opaque. There are a few conditions the object must meet in order for this to work:

- The object must have a camel-case style setter method for the property, of the form `set<propertyName>()`. If your object does not have a setter, consider creating a wrapper class that implements such a setter.
- The `ofFloat`, `ofInt`, and `ofObject` methods have an alternate form that requires only the ending value. If you wish to use this short form, then your object must have a getter method that the `ObjectAnimator` can use to retrieve the starting value. This method must be a camel-case style getter of the form `get<propertyName>()`.
- The getter and setter must operate on the same value type that you supply for the animator. So, if the getter and setter use integers, you must use the `ofInt` method when creating the `ObjectAnimator`.

If you follow those rules, you can animate any object. For some properties of views, you may need to call invalidate on the view to force it to redraw. By default, most of the view properties will do this for you. See the Android documentation for the full API requirements.

NOTE: When setting the property value, be sure to use the camel-case version of the property. While the `ObjectAnimator` will set the initial letter to the correct case, any other letters will need to be properly cased. For example, to call `setTranslationX`, you would supply the string `"translationX"`. In addition, the `ObjectAnimator` uses reflection internally to set the properties of objects. This can be resource intensive, so be mindful of animation performance.

THE PROPERTY CLASS

In the example, the string alpha was used to specify that the alpha property of the view should be modified. This allows you to set any property of an object. However, it can sometimes lead to programming errors if the string does not match an actual property of the object. To make this easier, Android 4.0 introduced the Property class to ensure that the correct properties of an object are updated. Here is the same example, but this time using the ALPHA property of View:

```
View view = findViewById(R.id.my_view);
ObjectAnimator animation = ObjectAnimator.ofFloat(view, View.ALPHA,
→ 0f, 1f);
animation.setDuration(250);
animation.start();
```

As you can see, this allows you to statically check the property matches before deploying your code. You can create your own Property implementations to achieve type correctness when animating your objects.

ANIMATOR SETS

Property animations can be grouped into sets, just like view animations. To create a set, you instantiate an AnimatorSet object and add animations to it. The AnimatorSet object has several methods for defining how animations are grouped. Here is a simple example that demonstrates the basics:

```
View v = findViewById(R.id.test);
AnimatorSet set = new AnimatorSet();
ObjectAnimator alpha = ObjectAnimator.ofFloat(v, View.ALPHA, 0f);
ObjectAnimator slide = ObjectAnimator.ofFloat(v, View.TRANSLATION_Y,
→ 100f);
ObjectAnimator scale = ObjectAnimator.ofFloat(v, View.SCALE_X, 2f);
set.play(alpha).with(slide).after(scale);
set.setDuration(1000);
set.start();
```

The play method schedules an animation to run and returns an AnimatorSet.Builder object. The builder provides a simple declarative API that allows you to schedule animations using natural language. In this example, the view will first scale to become twice as large, then simultaneously slide down and fade away. The entire animation will take 3 seconds. You can also supply another AnimatorSet object to create more-complex animations with multiple different sets running sequentially or in parallel.

TIP: The `setDuration` method of `AnimatorSet` applies the supplied value to all animators contained within that set. It does not set the total duration of the entire sequence of animations.

It's possible to create very complex animation sequences using AnimatorSet. However, as you will see later, using ViewPropertyAnimator is an even easier way to animate view classes.

PROPERTY ANIMATIONS IN XML

You are not limited to creating property animations in code. Like view animations, property animations can be defined using XML, allowing for easy reuse of common animations. When you write property animations in XML, you should place the files in the res/animator/ directory. This is not strictly necessary, but it will help you separate view animations from property animations. It is also required for the Eclipse ADT plugin to properly locate your property animations.

Here is an example animation set, containing the same three animations from before:

```
<?xml version="1.0" encoding="utf-8"?>
<set xmlns:android="http://schemas.android.com/apk/res/android"
    android:ordering="sequentially" >
    <objectAnimator
        android:duration="1000"
        android:propertyName="scaleX"
        android:valueTo="2"
        android:valueType="floatType" />
    <set>
```

```
        <objectAnimator
            android:duration="1000"
            android:propertyName="translationY"
            android:valueTo="100"
            android:valueType="floatType" />
        <objectAnimator
            android:duration="1000"
            android:propertyName="alpha"
            android:valueTo="0"
            android:valueType="floatType" />
    </set>
</set>
```

This is very similar to the XML for view animations, but the attributes are a little different. First, you must supply the property name that you wish the animation to update; if the property doesn't exist on the object, then the animation does nothing. Next, you must supply a value type; in this case, they are all floats. Finally, just as with a view animation, you supply the duration and ending value. To load and use this animation, add the following code:

```
TextView tv = (TextView) findViewById(R.layout.text);
AnimatorSet set = (AnimatorSet) AnimatorInflater.loadAnimator(this,
→ R.animator.animation);
set.setTarget(tv);
set.start();
```

You can also define the ordering of the animations in a set. Set the optional `android:ordering` property to `sequential` to play the animations one after the other, rather than simultaneously.

TIP: If there is any mistake in your animation XML, such as an incorrect property name or an attribute that does not exist, the animation simply does nothing. If you're having trouble getting the animation to run, double-check all the attributes.

HARDWARE **ACCELERATION**

Android 3.0 added better support for drawing 2D graphics using hardware acceleration. Previous versions of Android used more software operations for graphics rendering. To add hardware acceleration support to your application, add the `android:hardwareAccelerated="true"` attribute to the `<application>` tag in your application manifest. All applications targeting API level 14 or above have this setting turned on by default.

In addition to enabling application-wide acceleration, you can also enable (or disable) accelerated rendering at the activity or view level. Adding hardware acceleration to a view can increase the performance of your animations. For example, when using an `ObjectAnimator`, you can turn on acceleration to get an extra boost of performance. You will need to disable it when finished, however, to free graphics memory:

```
view.setLayerType(View.LAYER_TYPE_HARDWARE, null);
ObjectAnimator anim = ObjectAnimator.ofFloat(view, "alpha", 1f);
anim.addListener(new AnimatorListenerAdapter() {
    @Override
    public void onAnimationEnd(Animator animation) {
        view.setLayerType(View.LAYER_TYPE_NONE, null);
    }
});
anim.start();
```

While hardware acceleration is generally not necessary, consider enabling it if you have complex views or experience animation performance issues.

VIEWPROPERTYANIMATOR

ObjectAnimator is very powerful, but its ability to apply to any object requires that it have a rather verbose API. Since the common case is animating a single view, Android provides a convenience class to do just that: ViewPropertyAnimator. This class has a very concise API that enables the chaining of multiple animation API calls on a single line. In addition, because it is constrained to just views, it provides some modest performance improvements over the ObjectAnimator class.

To use a ViewPropertyAnimator, you call the animate() method on a view, which returns a ViewPropertyAnimator instance. This class provides methods for updating the common view properties, such as position, transparency, and size. In addition, each of the ViewPropertyAnimator methods returns itself, so you can chain multiple API calls together. Here is a simple example that moves a view and changes the alpha level:

```
TextView tv = (TextView) findViewById(R.id.text);
tv.animate().x(200).y(200).alpha(0f);
```

This code will move the text view to position 200 x 200 on the display, while changing the alpha from its current value to 0. Note that it never calls start. By default, the ViewPropertyAnimator is started immediately. Setting a start offset will delay the beginning of the animation.

The expressive nature of the ViewPropertyAnimator API makes it very powerful. Consider using it to create animations when you are dealing only with views and common view properties.

LAYOUTTRANSITION

A common animation you may wish to use is animating the adding and removing of views in a layout. This animation is so common that Google created a simple class to automate these animations for you. Called the `LayoutTransition`, it can be added to any `ViewGroup` to animate changes to that `ViewGroup` layout. You set the `LayoutTransition` by calling `setLayoutTransition` on the `ViewGroup` object:

```
ViewGroup vg = (ViewGroup) findViewById(R.id.relative_layout);
vg.setLayoutTransition(new LayoutTransition());
```

Alternatively, you can use layout transitions with a simple one-line XML change:

```
<FrameLayout xmlns:android="http://schemas.android.com/
→ apk/res/android"
    android:layout_width="match_parent"
    android:layout_height="match_parent"
    android:animateLayoutChanges="true" >
</LinearLayout>
```

With the `android:animateLayoutChanges` attribute, changes to the `ViewGroup` will be animated using the default `LayoutTransition` animation. You can optionally use a custom animation by calling the `setAnimation` method of `LayoutTransition` and passing it an `Animator` and flags specifying that the animator applies to views being added, removed, or changed. `LayoutTransition` is a simple way to add animations to your app with almost no effort.

WRAPPING UP

This chapter covered the basics of animation on Android. There are currently three animation frameworks: drawable animation, view animation, and property animation. Drawable animations are simple to implement but require a different image for each frame of animation. View animations can be used only on views and have been deprecated in favor of property animations. Property animations are very powerful and allow you to apply time-based functions to any object. In this chapter, you learned that

- Drawable animations create sprite-style animated graphics by rapidly switching images.
- You should define your animations using XML for easy reusability.
- Android supplies several interpolators that alter how your animation is applied over time.
- You can use the `ObjectAnimator` class to animate properties of any object.
- The `ViewPropertyAnimator` class provides a very compact API for animating `View` objects.
- You can animate changes to your layout by adding the `android:animateLayoutChanges` attribute to your layout view groups.

10

CREATING CUSTOM VIEWS

The Android view framework provides a rich visual toolkit with which to create your application UI. However, you may find that the functionality you need is not available in the stock views. For those cases, Android allows you to create a custom view that will better match your needs. In this chapter, you will learn that Android draws views in two passes, a measure phase and a layout phase; that you should override the `onMeasure` and `onDraw` methods when creating a custom view; that using custom view attributes requires that you declare a new XML namespace for those attributes; and that compound views combine multiple views into a custom component.

UNDERSTANDING HOW ANDROID DRAWS VIEWS

Before learning how to create custom views, you should understand how Android draws the display. As you learned earlier in the book, the Android UI is arranged in a hierarchy. This hierarchy consists of the system elements, such as the notification bar and the navigation bar, and the current activity view hierarchy. When an activity is brought to the foreground, the system requests the root node of that activity and then draws the view hierarchy on the display. You set the root node of the activity when you call `setContentView`. The activity layout consumes everything between the notification and action bars at the top and the navigation bar at the bottom (if present).

The region of the display that is being drawn is flagged as invalid. Anything that intersects with the invalid region needs to be redrawn. The system does this when it draws an activity, but you can force this to happen by calling `invalidate()` on a view. Once the view has been drawn, it is marked as valid.

Drawing takes place in two passes. In the first pass, the root of the hierarchy is asked to measure itself. The root then measures each of its child views. Each child view, in turn, measures its child views. In this way, the size of each view in the view hierarchy is measured. At each level, a parent view may give its child views a specific size or may request that the child set its own size.

Once the measuring phase is complete, the system performs the layout of the view hierarchy. It walks down the layout tree in a predetermined order, drawing each view onto a bitmap. Parent views are drawn first, and then the child views are drawn on top of them. Once layout is complete, the drawing system draws the bitmap to the screen to display it to the user.

CREATING A CUSTOM VIEW

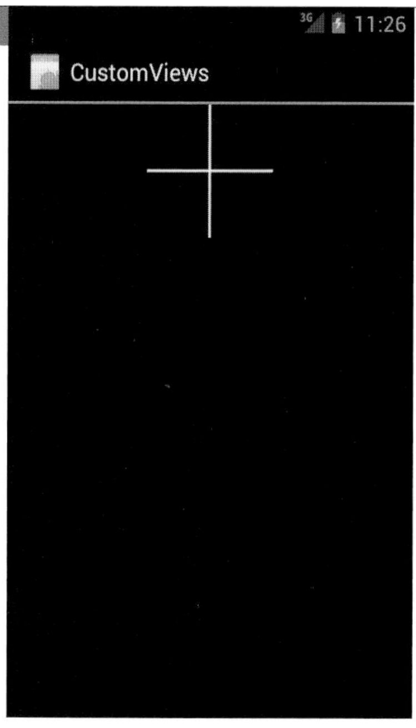

FIGURE 10.1 A simple custom view displaying two lines that form a cross

Creating your custom UI components starts with extending a view class. You can extend the base `View` class for maximum configurability, or you can start with one of the existing view classes and add the functionality you need. Which choice you should make depends on your application needs. The basic implementation is the same either way: extend the view and override the appropriate methods, adding your customized code along the way.

This only applies to static views or low-performance 2D graphics. If you want to create 3D graphics or complex animations, you should extend `SurfaceView` or use either RenderScript or OpenGL. See Chapter 11 for more details on advanced graphics.

To learn how to create custom views, you're going to create a simple custom view that displays two lines in the shape of a cross (**Figure 10.1**). To start, create a new class called `CrossView` that extends the `View` class:

```
public class CrossView extends View {
    public CrossView(Context context, AttributeSet attrs) {
        super(context, attrs);
    }
}
```

Note that the constructor takes both a `Context` and an `AttributeSet` object. The `Context` provides the interface to the application resources and system services that are needed to properly inflate the view and attach it to your activity. The `AttributeSet` is required to pass XML parameters to your view. You'll learn more about this when you learn how to create custom XML attributes. You should generally call through to the superclass in your overridden methods to perform the initial setup of your view. With this done, there are two basic methods you will likely want to override: `onMeasure` and `onDraw`.

ONMEASURE

The `onMeasure` method is called by the system to determine the size of the view and its children. It's passed two integers that are actually `MeasureSpecs`. A `MeasureSpec` is just a combination of a mode flag and an integer size value. It's implemented as an integer to reduce unneeded object allocations. The mode tells the view how it should calculate its size. These are the possible modes:

- `UNSPECIFIED`. The parent view has placed no constraints on this view; it can be any size it wants.
- `AT_MOST`. The view can be any size less than or equal to the `MeasureSpec` size.
- `EXACTLY`. The view will be exactly the `MeasureSpec` size regardless of what it requests.

When you create a custom view and override the `onMeasure` method, it is your job to properly handle each of these cases. In addition, the measuring contract dictates that you call the `setMeasuredDimensions` method with the determined integer size values. If you fail to do this, an `IllegalStateException` will be thrown.

1. Override the onMeasure method of ExampleCustomView:

```
@Override
protected void onMeasure(int widthMeasureSpec,
→ int heightMeasureSpec) {
    setMeasuredDimension(calculateMeasure(widthMeasureSpec),
    → calculateMeasure(heightMeasureSpec));
}
```

   Remember, you are required to call setMeasuredDimension with the calculated width and height values. Here, the code is using the same function for width and height.

2. Implement the code for calculating the measurements. Start by adding a default size for the view:

```
private static final int DEFAULT_SIZE = 100;
private int calculateMeasure(int measureSpec) {
    int result = (int) (DEFAULT_SIZE *
    → getResources().getDisplayMetrics().density);
}
```

   Because the pixel density of devices varies, you must calculate the actual pixel value using the display density.

TIP: Your onMeasure method may be called multiple times as the view system and your parent view calculate their layout. For example, a parent view may call each of its children's onMeasure methods with UNSPECIFIED dimensions to gather their desired sizes, then again after calculating the total space available. Your view may be asked to recalculate its height and width if all the child views will not fit in the parent.

3. Retrieve the mode and size from the MeasureSpec:

```
private int calculateMeasure(int measureSpec) {
    int result = (int) (DEFAULT_SIZE *
    → getResources().getDisplayMetrics().density);
    int specMode = MeasureSpec.getMode(measureSpec);
    int specSize = MeasureSpec.getSize(measureSpec);
}
```

4. Select the size based on the mode:

```
private int calculateMeasure(int measureSpec) {
    int result = (int) (DEFAULT_SIZE *
    → getResources().getDisplayMetrics().density);
    int specMode = MeasureSpec.getMode(measureSpec);
    int specSize = MeasureSpec.getSize(measureSpec);
    if (specMode == MeasureSpec.EXACTLY) {
        result = specSize;
    } else if (specMode == MeasureSpec.AT_MOST) {
        result = Math.min(result, specSize);
    }
    return result;
}
```

If the mode is set to EXACTLY, then the input size will be used. If the mode is set to AT_MOST, then the smaller of the DEFAULT_SIZE and the input size will be used. Otherwise, the DEFAULT_SIZE for the view will be used.

RESOURCES

When you compile your Android application, the SDK doesn't just blindly copy your application resources into the APK. Instead, it compiles them into an efficient binary format to reduce their size and improve lookup performance. To access the resources at runtime, you use a `Resources` object. You retrieve a `Resources` object by calling `getResources()` from your application context. The `Resources` object provides methods that take the compiled integer IDs for your resources and return the resource with the proper type.

ONDRAW

The `onDraw` method is called when the view should draw its content. It is passed a `Canvas` object, which holds the underlying bitmap for the view. The `Canvas` provides methods to do the basic drawing operations you use to build your view, and it performs those drawing operations on its internal bitmap.

To perform the actual drawing, you can call one of the `Canvas` draw methods or use a drawing primitive. Android provides several drawing primitives to construct your UI: rectangles, ovals, paths, text, and bitmaps. You will also need a `Paint` object to hold the styling that will be applied to the drawing. It handles things like color and text size.

1. Create a `Paint` object to hold the styling for the cross:

```
private Paint mPaint;
public CrossView(Context context, AttributeSet attrs) {
    super(context);
    mPaint = new Paint();
    mPaint.setAntiAlias(true);
    mPaint.setColor(0xFFFFFFFF);
}
```

TIP: Views also have a `draw` method that is called by their parents to request the view be drawn. This method handles basic drawing steps like setting up the canvas and drawing the background. You should avoid overriding this method and instead override the `onDraw` method.

2. Override the onDraw method. All calls to draw on the canvas should be bounded by corresponding save() and restore() calls:

```
@Override
protected void onDraw(Canvas canvas) {
    super.onDraw(canvas);
    canvas.save();
    // Code goes here
    canvas.restore();
}
```

3. To make your drawing code simpler, scale the canvas based on the size of the view. Doing this allows you to draw using simple floats between 0 and 1 without carrying around dimensions:

```
@Override
protected void onDraw(Canvas canvas) {
    super.onDraw(canvas);
    canvas.save();
    int scale = getWidth();
    canvas.scale(scale, scale);
    canvas.restore()
}
```

4. To draw the two lines of the cross, you'll use the drawLines method of Canvas:

```
float[] mPoints = {
    0.5f, 0f, 0.5f, 1f,
    0f, 0.5f, 1f, 0.5f};
@Override
protected void onDraw(Canvas canvas) {
    super.onDraw(canvas);
    canvas.save();
    int scale = getWidth();
```

```
        canvas.scale(scale, scale);
        canvas.drawLines(mPoints, mPaint);
        canvas.restore();
    }
```

The drawLines method takes an array containing the lines to draw (two *x*-coordinates and two *y*-coordinates per line endpoint) and a Paint object that it uses to draw the lines on the canvas. By scaling the canvas, you are able to specify all your dimensions using fractional float values.

5. Create an activity to display your view:

```
public class CustomViewsActivity extends Activity {
    @Override
    public void onCreate(Bundle savedInstanceState) {
        super.onCreate(savedInstanceState);
        setContentView(R.layout.main);
    }
}
```

6. Open the main.xml file and add the CrossView:

```
<?xml version="1.0" encoding="utf-8"?>
<LinearLayout xmlns:android="http://schemas.android.com/
→ apk/res/android"
    android:layout_width="fill_parent"
    android:layout_height="fill_parent"
    android:orientation="vertical"
    android:gravity="center_horizontal" >
    <com.example.CrossView
        android:layout_width="wrap_content"
        android:layout_height="wrap_content" />
</LinearLayout>
```

INNER **CLASSES**

When using custom views in your layouts, you generally use the class name as the element tag name. However, this won't work if your custom view is an inner class of another Java class, because the required $ character is not valid in Android's XML layout. For example, if you were to make `CrossView` an inner class of `CustomViewsActivity`, then the layout would not compile. In that case, you would need to use the `class` attribute to set the fully qualified view name:

```
<view
    class="com.example.CustomViewsActivity$CrossView"
    android:layout_width="wrap_content"
    android:layout_height="wrap_content"/>
```

Note that this uses the lowercase (`view`) rather than the capitalized (`View`) element. This signifies that it's a generic view and that the class definition can be found in the `class` attribute.

When using custom views in XML, you must use the full package name to inform the system which view class should be inflated.

7. Run the application, and you should see a cross shape similar to the one in Figure 10.1.

ADDING CUSTOM ATTRIBUTES TO YOUR CUSTOM VIEWS

Now that you have your custom view, you'll want to make it configurable to use throughout your UI. Adding methods to the class for setting attributes is standard Java practice, but how do you add attributes in the XML layout? To accomplish that, you'll first need to declare the attributes, then add a new namespace to your XML layouts, and finally handle the `AttributeSet` object that gets passed to your custom views constructor.

DECLARING THE ATTRIBUTES

The first step in creating custom attributes is to declare them. Custom attributes are declared using a new XML resource element: `<declare-styleable>`. These elements should be defined in a file named `attrs.xml` and placed in the `res/values/` directory.

Create this file now to declare the `CrossView` attributes:

```
<?xml version="1.0" encoding="utf-8"?>
<resources>
    <declare-styleable name="cross">
        <attr name="android:color" />
        <attr name="rotation" format="string" />
    </declare-styleable>
</resources>
```

The first thing to note is that the `<declare-styleable>` element has a `name` attribute. You use this to reference the styles in your code. Each custom attribute is declared using an `<attr>` element. The `<attr>` element itself has two attributes: `name` and `format`. The attribute `name` is used to reference custom attributes in XML. The attribute `format` is the data type. In this example, one of the default system attributes is used. In that case, you don't need to declare the format, as it is already defined by Android.

Every attribute with a format can be declared only once. This example works because it uses the existing `android:color` format. If you tried to use a different format, the project would not build. If you want to reuse the same attribute for multiple custom styles, declare it under the `<resources>` tag and include a format; then declare it inside each `<declare-styleable>` element without a format. Here is an example:

```
<?xml version="1.0" encoding="utf-8"?>
<resources>
    <attr name="test" format="string" />
    <declare-styleable name="foo">
        <attr name="test" />
    </declare-styleable>
    <declare-styleable name="bar">
        <attr name="test" />
    </declare-styleable>
</resources>
```

TIP: There is no real documentation on the possible attribute format types. The best documentation is the Android source code for the `android.R.styleable.attr.xml` file and the `android.content.res.TypedArray` class. Current formats include reference, string, color, dimension, Boolean, integer, float, fraction, enum, and flag.

You can create custom attributes with predefined values that are similar to the built-in attributes like `wrap_content` and `match_parent`. To do that, you declare the values using `<enum>` or `<flag>` elements:

```
<attr name="enum_attr">
    <enum name="value1" value="1" />
    <enum name="value2" value="2" />
</attr>
<attr name="flag_attr">
    <flag name="flag1" value="0x01" />
    <flag name="flag2" value="0x02" />
</attr>
```

Enums and flags are required to be integers. The difference between them is that the `flag` attributes can be combined using a bitwise `OR` operation. Use flags when you want the option to combine multiple attribute values:

```
<com.example.Foo example:flag_attr="flag1|flag2" />
```

USING ATTRIBUTES IN XML

To use the new attributes in your XML code, you first must declare the namespace for the view. Recall that in all your layouts, the enclosing `ViewGroup` always has an XML namespace attribute:

```
<?xml version="1.0" encoding="utf-8"?>
<LinearLayout xmlns:android="http://schemas.android.com/
→ apk/res/android"
    android:layout_width="fill_parent"
    android:layout_height="fill_parent"
    android:orientation="vertical" >
</LinearLayout>
```

This namespace declares that all attributes that begin with the keyword `android:` can be found in the `android` package. To use custom attributes, you declare a new namespace with a new package. This prevents your custom attributes from colliding with system attributes that may be defined in later versions of Android.

Add a new namespace for the `CrossView` attributes:

```
<?xml version="1.0" encoding="utf-8"?>
<LinearLayout xmlns:android="http://schemas.android.com/
→ apk/res/android"
    xmlns:example="http://schemas.android.com/apk/res/com.example"
    android:layout_width="fill_parent"
    android:layout_height="fill_parent"
    android:orientation="vertical"
    android:gravity="center_horizontal" >
</LinearLayout>
```

This declares that all attributes that begin with example: will reference a view in the com.example package. (You can choose any prefix you want; it's not necessary to use example.)

Now you can create a new layout file with more than one cross, each with different attributes:

```
<?xml version="1.0" encoding="utf-8"?>
<LinearLayout xmlns:android="http://schemas.android.com/
→ apk/res/android"
    xmlns:example="http://schemas.android.com/apk/res/com.example"
    android:layout_width="fill_parent"
    android:layout_height="fill_parent"
    android:orientation="vertical"
    android:gravity="center_horizontal" >
    <com.example.CrossView
        android:layout_width="wrap_content"
        android:layout_height="wrap_content" />
    <com.example.CrossView
        android:layout_width="wrap_content"
        android:layout_height="wrap_content"
        example:rotation="30"
        android:color="#0000FF" />
    <com.example.CrossView
        android:layout_width="wrap_content"
        android:layout_height="wrap_content"
        example:rotation="45"
        android:color="#FFFF00" />
</LinearLayout>
```

This creates three crosses that are arranged vertically in a row. The second cross is rotated 30 degrees and is blue. The third cross is rotated 45 degrees and is yellow.

USING ATTRIBUTES IN CODE

Now that you have the attributes defined, you need to create a constructor to use them. Remember the `AttributeSet` object you were passed in the constructor of your custom view:

```
public CrossView(Context context, AttributeSet attrs) {
    super(context, attrs);
    ...
```

The `AttributeSet` object is passed to your view by the system when it is instantiated. This object contains all the attributes declared by the XML layout, but it stores them in a more efficient binary format. Use it to retrieve the attribute values and set them on your view.

1. Update the `CrossView` constructor to query the `AttributeSet` object for the new rotation and color attributes:

```
public CrossView(Context context, AttributeSet attrs) {
    super(context);
    mPaint = new Paint();
    mPaint.setAntiAlias(true);
    mPaint.setColor(0xFFFFFFFF);
    TypedArray arr = getContext().obtainStyledAttributes
    → (attrs, R.styleable.cross);
    int color = arr.getColor(R.styleable.cross_android_color,
    → Color.WHITE);
    float rotation = arr.getFloat(R.styleable.cross_rotation,
    → 0f);
    // Remember to call this when finished
    arr.recycle();
    setColor(color);
    setRotation(rotation);
}
```

Here, the obtainStyleAttributes method is used to create a TypedArray, which is a convenience class for accessing the values stored in an AttributeSet. This class performs caching internally, so always call recycle when you are finished using it. Also, note that you access your custom attributes using a combination of the <declare-styleable> name and the <attr> name.

2. Add a rotation field and update the onDraw method to rotate the canvas:

```
float mRotation;
@Override
protected void onDraw(Canvas canvas) {
    super.onDraw(canvas);
    canvas.save();
    int scale = getWidth();
    canvas.scale(scale, scale);
    canvas.rotate(mRotation);
    canvas.drawLines(mPoints, mPaint);
    canvas.restore();
}
```

3. Add two new setters on the view. These are called by the constructor:

```
public void setColor(int color) {
    mPaint.setColor(color);
}
public void setRotation(float degrees) {
    mRotation = degrees;
}
```

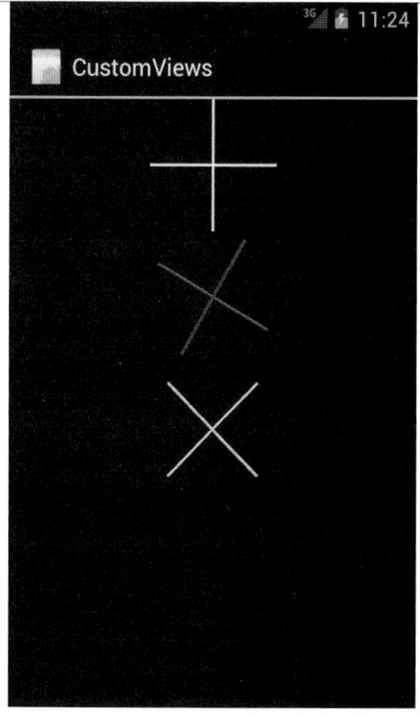

FIGURE 10.2 Custom attributes are used to rotate and change the color of `CrossView`.

Now when you run the app, you should see three crosses with different colors and rotations (**Figure 10.2**).

CREATING COMPOUND COMPONENTS

Creating a custom view by extending the View class gives you the most control over your custom view. However, you will often need something simpler, such as adding functionality to an existing view. It is much easier to create a custom component by extending one of the built-in Android views and expanding its functionality. By leveraging the built-in view code, you can focus on adding enhanced functionality. A simple way to do this is by creating a new view that combines several existing views. This is called a compound component.

CREATING A COMPOUND COMPONENT

Compound components have two primary advantages over custom views. First, they leverage the existing view group classes to create the layout for you. And second, you won't need to override the onMeasure and onDraw methods.

1. Create a new layout file named toggle_text.xml, and place it in the res/layout/ folder:

```
<?xml version="1.0" encoding="utf-8"?>
<LinearLayout xmlns:android="http://schemas.android.com/
→ apk/res/android"
    android:layout_width="match_parent"
    android:layout_height="match_parent"
    android:orientation="horizontal" >
    <ToggleButton
        android:id="@+id/toggle_button"
        android:layout_width="wrap_content"
        android:layout_height="wrap_content"
        android:text="ToggleButton" />
    <EditText
        android:id="@+id/edit_text"
        android:layout_width="0dp"
        android:layout_height="wrap_content"
        android:layout_weight="1" >
```

```
        <requestFocus />
    </EditText>
</LinearLayout>
```

This is simply a horizontal LinearLayout with a ToggleButton and an EditText.

2. Create a new class that extends LinearLayout. Use the LayoutInflater system service to inflate the layout you just created:

```
public class ToggleText extends LinearLayout {
    public ToggleText(Context context, AttributeSet attrs) {
        super(context, attrs);
        LayoutInflater inflater = (LayoutInflater) context.
        → getSystemService(Context.LAYOUT_INFLATER_SERVICE);
        View view = inflater.inflate(R.layout.toggle_text,
        → this);
    }
}
```

Note that you are passing in this as the parent ViewGroup for the inflated layout.

3. Add the custom functionality for your compound view. Add a listener for changes in the selected state of the toggle button, and set the enabled state of the EditText accordingly:

```
public class ToggleText extends LinearLayout
→ implements OnCheckedChangeListener {
    EditText mTextView;
    public ToggleText(Context context, AttributeSet attrs) {
        super(context, attrs);
        LayoutInflater inflater = (LayoutInflater) context.
        → getSystemService(Context.LAYOUT_INFLATER_SERVICE);
        View view = inflater.inflate(R.layout.toggle_text,
        → this);
```

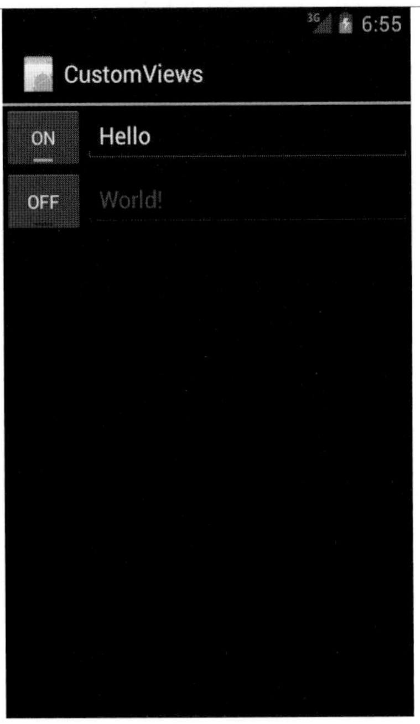

FIGURE 10.3 A compound view that combines a `ToggleButton` with an `EditText`. The `EditText` is disabled when the `ToggleButton` is unchecked.

```
        mTextView = (EditText) view.findViewById
        → (R.id.edit_text);
        ToggleButton toggle = (ToggleButton)
        → view.findViewById(R.id.toggle_button);
        toggle.setChecked(true);
        toggle.setOnCheckedChangeListener(this);
    }
    @Override
    public void onCheckedChanged(CompoundButton buttonView,
    → boolean isChecked) {
        mTextView.setEnabled(isChecked);
    }
}
```

You can now use the new compound component in layouts, and the toggle button will change the enabled state of the `EditText` (**Figure 10.3**).

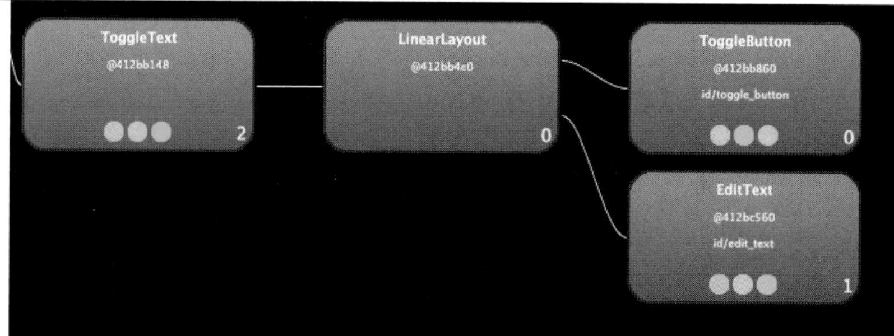

FIGURE 10.4 The ToggleButton has an unnecessary LinearLayout as its child.

OPTIMIZING THE LAYOUT

If you use the Hierarchy Viewer tool to look at the layout hierarchy for the ToggleButton you just created, you will see something like **Figure 10.4**. Notice that the ToggleButton class has a single child element: the LinearLayout. But ToggleButton itself is a LinearLayout, so this is an unnecessary level in your hierarchy. To remove it, open the toggle_text.xml file and change the LinearLayout element to a merge element:

```
<?xml version="1.0" encoding="utf-8"?>
<merge xmlns:android="http://schemas.android.com/apk/res/android"
    android:layout_width="match_parent"
    android:layout_height="match_parent"
    android:orientation="horizontal" >
    <ToggleButton
        android:id="@+id/toggle_button"
```

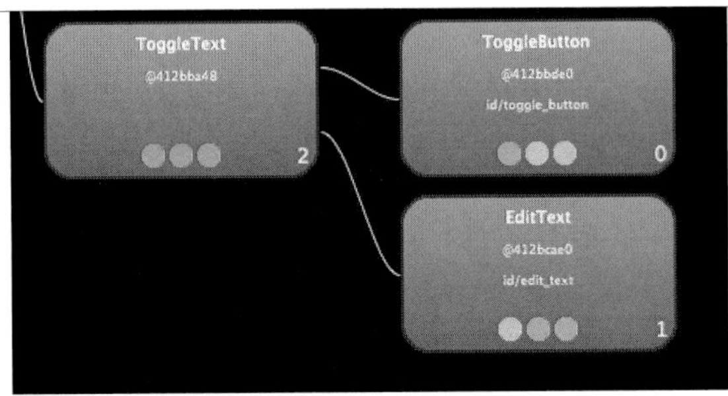

FIGURE 10.5 With the <merge> element, the hierarchy of the ToggleButton view is flatter and more efficient.

```
        android:layout_width="wrap_content"
        android:layout_height="wrap_content"
        android:text="ToggleButton" />
    <EditText
        android:id="@+id/edit_text"
        android:layout_width="0dp"
        android:layout_height="wrap_content"
        android:layout_weight="1" >
        <requestFocus />
    </EditText>
</merge>
```

Now when you view the ToggleButton in the Hierarchy Viewer, the unnecessary LinearLayout will be gone (**Figure 10.5**).

WRAPPING UP

Creating custom views gives you greater control over the look and functionality of your application. Android allows you to extend the built-in view classes, leveraging the existing drawing code while adding your own functionality. And by adding custom attributes, you can use your new views in XML layout files for easy UI development. In this chapter, you learned that

- You create a completely custom view by extending `View` and overloading the `onMeasure` and `onDraw` methods.
- You use custom attributes of a view by declaring the XML namespace for those attributes.
- Compound components let you easily build custom views out of existing components but that you must remember to merge the layout with your `ViewGroup`.

11

CREATING ADVANCED GRAPHICS

The Android view framework is convenient for creating complex layouts. However, this convenience comes at the cost of performance. When performance is critical, Android provides several more-robust graphics capabilities with increasing levels of difficulty. In this chapter, you will learn that the `SurfaceView` and `TextureView` classes use the standard `Canvas` object combined with a separate rendering thread to achieve better performance than standard views; that the new RenderScript framework can be used to create architecture-independent graphics rendering; and that OpenGL is available for serious graphics work and games.

The easiest way to increase drawing performance is by moving your performance-critical drawing operations onto a separate thread. However, as you learned earlier, all drawing operations must take place on the UI thread or an exception will be thrown. For this reason, Android provides the `SurfaceView` class. This class allows you to achieve better performance by executing your drawing code outside the normal UI thread. By drawing in a separate thread, you can rapidly update graphics without waiting for the rest of the view hierarchy to finish drawing.

IMPLEMENTING SURFACEVIEW

The `SurfaceView` exists outside the normal view hierarchy. It actually exists behind the normal window and is made visible by punching a hole through the view layout in your app. The `SurfaceView` can then be updated independently of the rest of your views without waiting for the UI thread.

To use a `SurfaceView`, you'll need to create a new view that extends the `SurfaceView` class. In addition, you should implement the `SurfaceView.Callback` interface and provide implementations of the required callbacks:

1. Create a new `ExampleSurfaceView` class that extends `SurfaceView` and implements `SurfaceView.Callback`:

```
public class ExampleSurfaceView extends SurfaceView implements
→ SurfaceHolder.Callback {
}
```

2. You need to initialize the superclass, so create a constructor that takes a `Context` object. You should also set up the callback here:

```
public ExampleSurfaceView(Context context) {
    super(context);
    SurfaceHolder holder = getHolder();
    holder.addCallback(this);
}
```

3. Now implement the callbacks. The first, `surfaceCreated`, is called when the surface view is ready to be used. You should start your drawing code here:

```
@Override
public void surfaceCreated(SurfaceHolder holder) {
    // Called when the surface view is first created.
    → Start your drawing here.
}
```

4. The surfaceChanged method is called when the view dimensions change, typically when the device is rotated:

```
@Override
public void surfaceChanged(SurfaceHolder holder, int format,
→ int width,
        int height) {
    // Called when the surface view dimensions change.
    → Typically called when the device is rotated.
}
```

5. The surfaceDestroyed method is called when the view is being destroyed. You should clean up any threads and drawing code here:

```
@Override
public void surfaceDestroyed(SurfaceHolder holder) {
    // Called when the surface is destroyed. Clean up any
    → threads here.
}
```

DRAWING TO A SURFACEVIEW

Unlike a normal view, all drawing to a SurfaceView takes place on a separate thread. To draw on a SurfaceView, you must call the lockCanvas method of SurfaceHolder, which returns a Canvas object. The lockCanvas method prevents the SurfaceView from updating the underlying surface until you call the corresponding unlockCanvasAndPost method. This eliminates the need for synchronization around writing to the surface (though you still need to synchronize fields between your threads). You should wrap all your drawing to a SurfaceView in lockCanvas and unlockCanvasAndPost blocks.

The example doesn't do anything yet, so you'll need to change things to draw something. The whole reason to make a SurfaceView is to enable continuous drawing using a separate thread, so create a new thread and use it to animate a triangle. At the same time, update the background color of the SurfaceView based on the user's touch.

NOTE: **There is no guarantee that the surface will be unchanged the next time you call** lockCanvas. **You should not rely on using the canvas returned by** lockCanvas() **to hold drawing state.**

1. Create a new class named DrawingThread that extends Thread and calls the onDraw method of the view. This thread will run every 20 milliseconds (for 50 fps) and will update an angle field for the rotation of the triangle. Remember to synchronize the drawing:

```
private class DrawingThread extends Thread {
    boolean keepRunning = true;
    @Override
    public void run() {
        Canvas c;
        while (keepRunning) {
            c = null;
            try {
                c = mSurfaceHolder.lockCanvas();
                synchronized (mSurfaceHolder) {
                    mAngle += 1;
                    onDraw(c);
                }
            } finally {
                if (c != null)
                    mSurfaceHolder.unlockCanvasAndPost(c);
            }
            // Run the draw loop at 50 fps
            try {
```

```
                Thread.sleep(20);
            } catch (InterruptedException e) {}
        }
    }
}
```

2. Add some fields to your view for the RGB colors, the triangle, and the new thread:

```
DrawingThread mThread;
int mRed = 0;
int mGreen = 0;
int mBlue = 127;
float[] mVertices = new float[6];
int[] mColors = {
    0xFFFFFFFF, 0xFFFFFFFF, 0xFFFFFFFF,
    0xFFFFFFFF, 0xFFFFFFFF, 0xFFFFFFFF};
Paint mPaint = new Paint();
float mAngle = 0;
float mCenterX = 0;
float mCenterY = 0;
public ExampleSurfaceView(Context context) {
    super(context);
    mSurfaceHolder = getHolder();
    mSurfaceHolder.addCallback(this);
    mThread = new DrawingThread();
    mPaint.setColor(0xFFFFFFFF);
    Paint.setStyle(Paint.Style.FILL);
}
```

The triangle is defined using lines, called vertices. The triangle will be filled with color based on the `mColors` array.

3. Update the surfaceCreated and surfaceDestroyed methods to start and stop the thread:

```
@Override
public void surfaceCreated(SurfaceHolder holder) {
    mThread.keepRunning = true;
    mThread.start();
}
@Override
public void surfaceDestroyed(SurfaceHolder holder) {
    mThread.keepRunning = false;
    boolean retry = true;
    while (retry) {
        try {
            mThread.join();
            retry = false;
        } catch (InterruptedException e) {}
    }
}
```

4. Update the surfaceChanged method to create the vertices of the triangle, using the supplied width and height values:

```
@Override
public void surfaceChanged(SurfaceHolder holder, int format,
→ int width, int height) {
    mVertices[0] = width/2;
    mVertices[1] = height/2;
    mVertices[2] = width/2 + width/5;
    mVertices[3] = height/2 + width/5;
    mVertices[4] = width/2;
    mVertices[5] = height/2 + width/5;
```

```
    mCenterX = width/2 + width/10;
    mCenterY = height/2 + width/10;
    }
```

The vertices define the edges of the triangle. The center values define the pivot point around which the triangle will rotate.

5. Override the onDraw method of your view. Update the color and draw the triangle:

```
@Override
protected void onDraw(Canvas canvas) {
    canvas.drawRGB(mRed, mGreen, mBlue);
    canvas.rotate(mAngle, mCenterX, mCenterY);
    canvas.drawVertices(Canvas.VertexMode.TRIANGLES, 6,
    → mVertices, 0, null, 0, mColors, 0, null, 0, 0, mPaint);
}
```

6. Implement the onTouchEvent method and update the color as you slide your finger across the screen. Note the synchronization on the changing of the color values:

```
@Override
public boolean onTouchEvent(MotionEvent event) {
    switch (event.getAction()) {
    case MotionEvent.ACTION_DOWN:
    case MotionEvent.ACTION_MOVE:
        synchronized(mSurfaceHolder) {
            mRed = (int) (255*event.getX()/getWidth());
            mGreen = (int) (255*event.getY()/getHeight());
        }
        return true;
    }
    return super.onTouchEvent(event);
}
```

FIGURE 11.1 A rotating triangle drawn by a `SurfaceView`. Sliding your finger across the screen should change the color.

Run the example and you should see a slowly rotating triangle (**Figure 11.1**). Sliding your finger around the screen will change the background color.

THE `TextureView` CLASS

The `SurfaceView` class lets you improve performance by moving the drawing onto a separate thread. But this comes with some significant drawbacks. In particular, because `SurfaceView` exists outside the normal view system, it can't be transformed the way a normal view can. You can't move, scale, or rotate a surface view. In addition, `SurfaceView` doesn't support transparency effects using `setAlpha`.

To address these shortcomings, Android 4.0 introduced `TextureView`. A texture view is essentially the same as a surface view, but it behaves as a normal view and supports normal view operations. You can use a texture view to display a content stream such as video camera preview, while also transforming it using the View API.

`TextureView` requires hardware acceleration and, because it is more flexible than `SurfaceView`, incurs a performance hit. You would not want to use it for running a full-screen game, for example. However, if you are developing on Android 4.0 and need to transform a high-performance canvas view, consider using `TextureView`.

USING **RENDERSCRIPT**

RenderScript is a language, API, and runtime used to write high-performance code on Android. Introduced in Android 3.0, RenderScript includes both graphics APIs and computing APIs similar to CUDA or OpenCL. It is architecture-independent, so there is no need to customize your code for different CPU or GPU processors. RenderScript optimizes your running code by selecting the appropriate processor and number of cores at runtime. As a fallback, RenderScript will run all operations on the CPU if the appropriate GPU is unavailable. This section covers the basics of using RenderScript with a simple example.

NOTE: RenderScript relies on OpenGL ES 2.0 APIs that are not available in the emulator. To run the RenderScript code example, you will need an Android device.

THE RENDERSCRIPT FILE

RenderScript uses a syntax based on the C99 standard of the C programming language. This makes it immediately familiar to anyone who has developed in C. Here is a simple RenderScript file example that will rotate a triangle onscreen and set the background color:

```
#pragma version(1)
#pragma rs java_package_name(com.example);
#include "rs_graphics.rsh"
// Background color is a 4-part float
float4 bgColor;
// Triangle mesh
rs_mesh gTriangle;
// Rotation float
float gRotation;
void init() {
    // Initialize background color to black
    bgColor = (float4) { 0.0f, 0.0f, 0.0f, 1.0f };
    gRotation = 0.0f;
}
```

```
int root() {
    // Set background color
    rsgClearColor(bgColor.x, bgColor.y, bgColor.z, bgColor.w);
    // Load matrix for translate and rotate
    rs_matrix4x4 matrix;
    rsMatrixLoadIdentity(&matrix);
    rsMatrixTranslate(&matrix, 300.0f, 300.0f, 0.0f);
    rsMatrixRotate(&matrix, gRotation, 0.0f, 0.0f, 1.0f);
    rsgProgramVertexLoadModelMatrix(&matrix);
    // Draw the triangle mesh
    rsgDrawMesh(gTriangle);
    // Animate rotation
    gRotation += 1.0f;
    // Run every 20 milliseconds
    return 20;
}
```

This code should be saved in a file called `example.rs` in your Android project's `src/` directory. The first two lines declare the RenderScript version and the Java package that contains the Java code that will use the RenderScript. A graphics library, `rs_graphics.rsh`, is included. The `init()` and `root()` methods are special to RenderScript. `init` is called when the script is first loaded. The `root` function is like the `main` function in a standard C application; it will be called each time the script runs. The number returned from `root()` requests the interval in milliseconds at which the script should be called. Here, it is requested that the code be called every 20 milliseconds. It does not guarantee that the code will be called that often, however, only that the system will attempt to call the script that often.

TIP: **The full native RenderScript API is available in the Android SDK. Navigate to** `<sdk_root>/platforms/android-11/renderscript`**, and find the header files in the** `include/` **and** `clang-include/` **directories.**

The rest of the root method contains the graphics drawing code, which should be self-explanatory. The color is set, and then a matrix is used to translate the surface and rotate it. The triangle is represented by an rs_mesh that will be set from the Java class. Finally, the rotation of the triangle is updated every time root runs.

THE JAVA API

Once the RenderScript file is saved in your src/ directory, the Android build tools will generate a reflected Java file you can use in your application. This file is given the name ScriptC_your_renderscript_file_name and extends the ScriptC class. To use the RenderScript you just created, you'll need to build a view that extends the RSSurfaceView class:

1. Create a new class named ExampleView that extends RSSurfaceView:

```
public class ExampleView extends RSSurfaceView {
    public ExampleView(Context context) {
        super(context);
    }
}
```

2. Initialize the RenderScript Java objects. You first must create a RenderScriptGL object, passing it a SurfaceConfig. The RenderScriptGL object ties the output of the RenderScript to the display via the root() method:

```
public class ExampleView extends RSSurfaceView {
    private RenderScriptGL mRS;
    private ScriptC_example mScript;
    public ExampleView(Context context) {
        super(context);
        final RenderScriptGL.SurfaceConfig sc =
        → new SurfaceConfig();
        mRS = createRenderScriptGL(sc);
        mScript = new ScriptC_example(mRS, getResources(),
        → R.raw.example);
        buildTriangle();
```

```
        mRS.bindRootScript(mScript);
    }
}
```

Once the RenderScriptGL object is created, you can instantiate the ScriptC object that contains the interface to your RenderScript file. Finally, you must call the bindRootScript method to set your RenderScript as the handler for calls to render the surface. You will implement the buildTriangle() method shortly.

3. Create a simple activity that uses your new view as its content:

```
public class RenderScriptExampleActivity extends Activity {
    @Override
    public void onCreate(Bundle savedInstanceState) {
        super.onCreate(savedInstanceState);
        setContentView(new ExampleView(this));
    }
}
```

4. The reflected Java API lets you set variables in your RenderScript using auto-generated setters. A setter for the bgColor variable has already been created and can be used to change the background color. Add some interactivity by updating the graphics when you touch the screen. Override the onTouchEvent method, and call the set_bgColor method:

```
@Override
public boolean onTouchEvent(MotionEvent event) {
    switch (event.getAction()) {
    case MotionEvent.ACTION_DOWN:
    case MotionEvent.ACTION_MOVE:
        float x = event.getX()/getWidth();
        float y = event.getY()/getHeight();
        Float4 color = new Float4(x, y, 0.5f, 1.0f);
```

```
            mScript.set_bgColor(color);
            return true;
        }
        return super.onTouchEvent(event);
    }
```

5. Finally, create the `buildTriangle()` method, which will define the triangle that your RenderScript will draw:

```
public void buildTriangle() {
    Mesh.TriangleMeshBuilder triangles =
    → new Mesh.TriangleMeshBuilder(mRS, 2,
    → Mesh.TriangleMeshBuilder.COLOR);
    triangles.addVertex(0.f, -75.0f);
    triangles.addVertex(-150.0f, 75.0f);
    triangles.addVertex(150.0f, 75.0f);
    triangles.addTriangle(0, 1, 2);
    Mesh mesh = triangles.create(true);
    mScript.set_gTriangle(mesh);
}
```

The `TriangleMeshBuilder` is used to create a triangle and draw it on the screen. You add each vertex and then call the `addTriangle` method to build the triangle out of the specified vertex calls. In this case, the last three vertices are used. Finally, you create the mesh and pass it to the RenderScript.

When you run this, you will see a slowly rotating triangle, just as in the `SurfaceView` example. The background color will change as you slide your finger across the screen. Each call to the `set_bgColor` method updates the `bgColor` variable. The `root()` method is called every 20 milliseconds and updates the background color and the triangle. It also updates the rotation angle by 1 degree. Try it out by loading the app on a device and sliding your finger across the screen.

This simple example only scratches the surface of the RenderScript API. In addition to advanced graphics, RenderScript supports high-performance computing using the compute APIs. These APIs are primarily found in the `rs_cl.rsh` header file.

USING **OPENGL**

Android provides full support for hardware-rendered graphics using the OpenGL ES 1.0/1.1 and OpenGL ES 2.0 standards. OpenGL APIs can be called through the Java framework and through the Native Development Kit (NDK). The Java framework provides an easy-to-use API but suffers from a small performance hit. For full accelerated graphics support, or to port existing graphics code, the NDK offers the best solution. However, this is outside the scope of this book.

NOTE: The Android emulator does not support OpenGL ES 2.0 graphics. You will need to test on a physical device to develop an app that uses the 2.0 standard.

OPENGL BASICS

A full explanation of OpenGL graphics would consume an entire book. However, a small example should give you a taste of the Java framework APIs that are available. Creating OpenGL graphics requires two classes: `GLSurfaceView` and `GLSurfaceView.Renderer`. The `GLSurfaceView` class is similar to `SurfaceView` and provides the glue between OpenGL-rendered graphics and Android's standard view framework. This class provides a separate rendering thread that generates graphics independently of the UI thread. In addition, `GLSurfaceView` provides some debugging tools that assist in tracking down errors in rendering code.

Typically, you will extend `GLSurfaceView` and override the `onTouchEvent` method to provide interactivity with your custom graphics. Here is an example that simply paints the screen black. This example will be compatible with the OpenGL ES 1.0 standard:

1. Create a class named `ExampleRenderer` that extends `GLSurfaceView.Renderer`:

   ```
   public class ExampleRenderer implements GLSurfaceView.Renderer {
   }
   ```

   Now implement the required callbacks.

2. Implement `onSurfaceCreated`. It's called when the `GLSurfaceView` is first created. Use it to do initial setup. For this simple example, it does nothing:

   ```
   public void onSurfaceCreated(GL10 gl, EGLConfig config) {
   }
   ```

3. Implement onDrawFrame. It's called every time the GLSurfaceView is updated. This is where the bulk of your code will go:

```
public void onDrawFrame(GL10 gl) {
    gl.glClear(GL10.GL_COLOR_BUFFER_BIT |
    → GL10.GL_DEPTH_BUFFER_BIT);
}
```

This is an OpenGL call that clears the specified buffers, which are referenced via their bit values. Here the color and depth buffers are cleared, making the screen black.

4. Implement onSurfaceChanged. It's called when the basic geometry of the GLSurfaceView changes. This is most often called when you rotate the device:

```
public void onSurfaceChanged(GL10 gl, int width, int height) {
    gl.glViewport(0, 0, width, height);
}
```

Here the view port is set to entirely fill the view dimensions.

5. Create a simple activity to display the OpenGL surface:

```
public class ExampleOpenGLActivity extends Activity {
    GLSurfaceView mGLView;
    @Override
    public void onCreate(Bundle savedInstanceState) {
        super.onCreate(savedInstanceState);
        mGLView = new GLSurfaceView(this);
        setContentView(mGLView);
    }
    @Override
    protected void onPause() {
        super.onPause();
        mGLView.onPause();
    }
```

```
    @Override
    protected void onResume() {
        super.onResume();
        mGLView.onResume();
    }
}
```

You should remember to call the appropriate life cycle methods on GLSurfaceView as your activity runs; OpenGL rendering can be very intensive, and this ensures that your app does not consume resources when it doesn't need them.

Run this example, and you'll see that it just paints the screen black on each frame. This isn't very interesting, so in the next section you'll add some graphics.

DRAWING GRAPHICS

You can easily re-create the example from the RenderScript section to rotate a triangle and set the background color as you slide your finger across the screen.

1. Update the ExampleRenderer, and add a new setColor method with member variables for color:

   ```
   private float mRed;
   private float mGreen;
   private float mBlue;
   public void setColor(float red, float green, float blue) {
       mRed = red;
       mGreen = green;
       mBlue = blue;
   }
   ```

2. Add member variables to draw a triangle, and initialize its vertices in the onSurfaceCreated method:

   ```
   private float mAngle;
   private long mLastFrameTime = 0;
   ```

```
float[] mVertices = {
    -1.0f, -1.0f, 0,
    1.0f, -1.0f, 0,
    0.0f,  1.0f, 0};
FloatBuffer mVertexBuffer;
public void onSurfaceCreated(GL10 gl, EGLConfig config) {
    // Set up the triangle vertices in FloatBuffers as needed
    ➥ by OpenGl
    ByteBuffer vertexByteBuffer = ByteBuffer.allocateDirect
    ➥ (mVertices.length * 4);
    vertexByteBuffer.order(ByteOrder.nativeOrder());
    mVertexBuffer = vertexByteBuffer.asFloatBuffer();
    mVertexBuffer.put(mVertices);
    mVertexBuffer.position(0);
}
```

3. Update the onSurfaceChanged method to set the projection matrix. OpenGL assumes a square display, so you need to change the aspect ratio of the graphics to match that of the screen:

```
public void onSurfaceChanged(GL10 gl, int width, int height) {
    gl.glViewport(0, 0, width, height);
    // Select the projection matrix
    gl.glMatrixMode(GL10.GL_PROJECTION);
    // Reset the matrix to default state
    gl.glLoadIdentity();
    // Calculate the aspect ratio of the window
    float ratio = (float) width/height;
    GLU.gluPerspective(gl, 45.0f, ratio, 0.1f, 100.0f);
    // Set the GL_MODELVIEW transformation mode
```

```
        gl.glMatrixMode(GL10.GL_MODELVIEW);
        gl.glLoadIdentity();
    }
```

4. Update the onDrawFrame method of ExampleRenderer to set the color of the view based on the color fields and to draw the triangle. This should look familiar if you have done any OpenGL graphics:

```
public void onDrawFrame(GL10 gl) {
    gl.glClearColor(mRed, mGreen, mBlue, 1.0f);
    gl.glClear(GL10.GL_COLOR_BUFFER_BIT | GL10.
GL_DEPTH_BUFFER_BIT);
    updateAngle();
    gl.glLoadIdentity();
    gl.glTranslatef(0.0f, 0.0f, -7.0f);
    gl.glRotatef(mAngle, 0.0f, 0.0f, 1.0f);
    gl.glEnableClientState(GL10.GL_VERTEX_ARRAY);
    gl.glColor4f(255f, 255f, 255f, 0.0f);
    gl.glVertexPointer(3, GL10.GL_FLOAT, 0, mVertexBuffer);
    gl.glDrawArrays(GL10.GL_TRIANGLES, 0, 3);
    gl.glDisableClientState(GL10.GL_VERTEX_ARRAY);
}
```

5. You need to implement the updateAngle() method:

```
private void updateAngle() {
    long now = System.currentTimeMillis();
    if (mLastFrameTime != 0) {
        mAngle += 10*(now - mLastFrameTime)/1000.0;
    }
    mLastFrameTime = now;
}
```

6. Create a new view named ExampleGLSurfaceView that extends GLSurfaceView:

```
public class ExampleGLSurfaceView extends GLSurfaceView {
    public ExampleGLSurfaceView(Context context) {
        super(context);
    }
}
```

7. Create an instance of the Renderer class, and set it as the renderer:

```
public class ExampleGLSurfaceView extends GLSurfaceView {
    public ExampleRenderer mRenderer;
    public ExampleGLSurfaceView(Context context) {
        super(context);
        mRenderer = new ExampleRenderer();
        setRenderer(mRenderer);
    }
}
```

8. Override the onTouchEvent method to implement the touch logic. This is almost identical to the version in the RenderScript example, but this time it will call the setColor method you just created:

```
@Override
public boolean onTouchEvent(MotionEvent event) {
    switch (event.getAction()) {
    case MotionEvent.ACTION_DOWN:
    case MotionEvent.ACTION_MOVE:
        final float x = event.getX()/getWidth();
        final float y = event.getY()/getHeight();
        queueEvent(new Runnable() {
            @Override
            public void run() {
```

```
                mRenderer.setColor(x, y, 0.5f);
            }
        });
        return true;
    }
    return super.onTouchEvent(event);
}
```

9. Use this new view in the ExampleOpenGLActivity:

```
public class ExampleOpenGLActivity extends Activity {
    GLSurfaceView mGLView;
    @Override
    public void onCreate(Bundle savedInstanceState) {
        super.onCreate(savedInstanceState);
        mGLView = new ExampleGLSurfaceView(this);
        setContentView(mGLView);
    }
    ...
```

This uses the queueEvent method of GLSurfaceView to schedule the background color change. GLSurfaceView performs all rendering on a separate thread from the standard Android UI, so you should be mindful of thread communication issues. The queueEvent method is a convenience that lets you post new tasks to run in the GLSurfaceView thread.

You should now have an example that works just like the RenderScript and SurfaceView examples. A single triangle slowly rotates on the screen. As you slide your finger across the screen, the background color changes in response. This is only scratching the surface of OpenGL development. In addition to using the Java APIs, Android supports running a fully OpenGL-compatible application through the NDK. This offers the maximum portability for high-performance graphics code.

WRAPPING UP

Android provides several advanced graphics options with increasing levels of performance. There are important tradeoffs to each API. The Canvas class offers the simplest API, but with limited performance. It's a good fit for basic graphics that don't require complex animations or user interaction. The newly introduced RenderScript API offers a good balance of performance with ease of programming, and it has the added advantage of easy portability across different device architectures. Finally, Android supports high-performance graphics using the OpenGL APIs. These are the most advanced graphics available on Android and should be used when you need to create high-performance applications like games.

- Use the `SurfaceView` class to achieve better performance by moving your drawing off the UI thread.
- The `TextureView` class provides the same API as `SurfaceView` but supports standard view transformations.
- RenderScript is an architecture-independent, high-performance computing API that uses a simple C-based syntax.
- Android's OpenGL implementation includes both a Java API and a Native Development API.

12

LOCALIZATION AND ACCESSIBILITY

Creating a successful Android application requires that you reach the largest audience possible. To that end, you should work from the beginning to make your app language agnostic and accessible to people with disabilities. Localization will help you launch your app in more countries, expanding your potential market to the whole world. Accessibility will also expand your target market, while helping those with special requirements utilize the next generation of computing. In this chapter, you will learn that using the `strings.xml` file allows you to create multiple copies of your app strings in different languages; that you can define plural strings that present different text based on the input number; that Android UI elements that have no text should include a content description for screen-reading software; and that accessibility events are sent by views, enabling the accessibility service to notify the user.

MAKING YOUR APP AVAILABLE IN MULTIPLE LANGUAGES

In Chapter 3, you learned about application resources and how Android uses folder structure to separate resources for different device configurations at runtime. This is very helpful in building apps that support multiple screen sizes. This same mechanism allows you to localize your app with alternate strings and resources for each locale.

OVERVIEW OF ANDROID LOCALIZATION

Throughout this book, you have been instructed to use string resources when displaying text in your UI. This may seem like a burden, but it greatly simplifies localization. By specifying all strings in the `strings.xml` file, you can create different versions of that file for each language you need to support. Android will then select the appropriate string resources at runtime, based on the user's selected language and region.

Android will mix and match strings from different `strings.xml` files. It will always select the most appropriate string based on the user's locale and your provided resources.

Android separates resources using the folders in the `res/` directory. For example, the `res/layout` directory is the default directory for layout files. But you can create a landscape-specific layout by placing a layout with the same name in the `res/layout-land/` folder. Similarly, when you create strings, you place them in the `res/values/strings.xml` file. These are the default strings that will be used throughout your application. When you want to create a Spanish-language version of your app, you first translate all the strings in the `strings.xml` file. Then you place the translated file in the `res/values-es/` folder. When your application references a string resource, the system will automatically use the Spanish-language version when the user's system default is Spanish. For French, you would create another `strings.xml` file and place it in the `res/values-fr/` folder.

NOTE: Android uses the ISO 639-1 language codes followed by an optional ISO 3166-1-alpha-2 region code for language and region qualifiers. Consult the Android documentation on providing resources (http://developer.android.com/guide/topics/resources/providing-resources.html) for the full list of qualifiers.

Try creating a simple example:

1. Open Eclipse and create a new Android project.

2. Open the res/values/strings.xml file. There should be a string named "hello":

```
<?xml version="1.0" encoding="utf-8"?>
<resources>
    <string name="hello">Hello World!</string>
    <string name="app_name">AccessibilityExample</string>
</resources>
```

3. Create a Spanish-language version of that string. Create a new folder named res/values-es/. Then create a new strings.xml file inside it, and add the following content:

```
<?xml version="1.0" encoding="utf-8"?>
<resources>
    <string name="hello">¡Hola Mundo!</string>
</resources>
```

   The app_name resource remains the same, so you don't need to create a translated version. Android will select resources from both files.

4. Run the app as you normally would, and you should see the standard Hello World app. Now change the emulator language to Spanish by choosing Settings > Language and Input > Language > Spanish. Rerun the app, and the displayed string is now in Spanish.

You are not limited to using language for localization; you can also create alternate resources for specific mobile country codes (MCC) and mobile network codes (MNC). Using these qualifiers allows you to create resources for specific geographic regions.

TIP: The MCC and MNC qualifiers take precedence over the language qualifiers. Make sure you understand resource loading precedence, and set up your resource folders appropriately.

Note that you do not need to alter your Java code for the correct string to be selected. You simply reference strings as normal, and Android will load the correct resource. In the previous simple example, the code to access the string is the same regardless of the language:

```
String translatedText = getResources().getString(R.string.hello);
```

In addition to translated strings, you can provide language-specific layouts for your application. Languages with longer words or a different text direction (such as right to left) may require you to rethink your layouts. In general, you should try to create layouts that are flexible enough to accommodate any language. When this is not possible, use alternative resources to change your UI to accommodate the alternative text.

In most cases, you should let the Android framework do the work of selecting the appropriate resources for you. But for those occasions when you need to access the locale yourself, you can do so as follows:

```
String locale = context.getResources().getConfiguration().locale;
```

TIP: Always create default resources for your application. If Android is unable to locate a suitable resource for the user's locale, an exception will be thrown indicating that the resource could not be found. Default resources are those that have no device-configuration qualifiers.

FORMATTING AND PLURALS

Beyond basic language selection, you should also leverage Android's ability to format strings for you. Android supports using string substitution (which is similar to string formatting in Java) to build strings.

```
<string name="example">A string: %1$s and a decimal: %2$d</string>
```

In this example, the first argument (numbered 1) is a string and the second argument (numbered 2) is a decimal. To format this string, you supply arguments to the getString method of Resources:

```
getResources().getString(R.string.hello, "Hello", 2);
```

In addition to basic string formatting, Android allows you to define alternative strings for different pluralizations. Android lets you define these using string resources. Here is an example:

```
<?xml version="1.0" encoding="utf-8"?>
<resources>
    <plurals name="planets">
        <item quantity="one">One planet.</item>
        <item quantity="other">%d planets.</item>
    </plurals>
</resources>
```

As you can see, when the quantity "one" is used, the string uses the singular "planet." When any other number is used, it becomes "planets." The full list of plural types is listed in **Table 12.1**.

TABLE 12.1 Plural Quantities

QUANTITY VALUE	DESCRIPTION
zero	Special handling of 0 in languages such as Arabic
one	Special handling of 1 in languages such as Russian and English
two	Special handling of 2 in languages such as Welsh
few	Special handling for small numbers in languages such as Polish
many	Special handling of large numbers in languages such as Maltese
other	Used when the language requires no special treatment of a number

To retrieve the proper string in code, you need to use the getQuantityString method:

```
Resources res = getResources();
String songsFound = res.getQuantityString(R.plurals.planets,
→ numPlanets, numPlanets);
```

The getQuantityString method takes three arguments: the string resource ID, a number to select the appropriate plural string, and the same number again to insert into the %d field of the string. If no substitution is necessary, the third parameter may be omitted.

NOTE: The plurals resources will only be selected in cases where the language requires it. In other cases, the default will be used. For example, in English, you would say "zero items," "one item," or "two items." The zero and two cases use the same plural. Android will ignore the zero quantity even if you create one.

TIPS FOR LOCALIZING

- Always include default resources in your app. If you fail to include them, your app will crash when running in an unsupported locale.
- Always define user-visible strings in the `strings.xml` file. Use the default `strings.xml` when you start developing your application. You can add translated versions later.
- Use quantity strings to handle any plural strings in your app.
- Design your layouts to be as flexible as possible to accommodate languages that may have different space requirements.
- Test your application in the alternative languages you support, and check for any formatting errors. Consider creating alternative resources for those cases.

MAKING YOUR APP **ACCESSIBLE**

Android is part of the next generation of personal computing—a generation that is defined by natural user interfaces such as touchscreens. While this has been a boon to most, many users have disabilities that prevent them from using touchscreens. Android features accessibility support that developers should use to ensure that all users can enjoy their work. This section covers the basics of ensuring that your application is accessible.

NAVIGATION AND FOCUS

The first step to making your Android app accessible is allowing use without a touchscreen. This generally takes the form of a directional pad (d-pad) for selecting UI elements before activating them. Luckily, Android was designed from the beginning to support phones with directional input. All views in Android support a focused state, allowing navigation without a touchscreen. When a view is focused, it is highlighted in the UI and a primary button press will trigger an `onClick` event.

Android's built-in views already provide focus behavior, and any custom views you create that inherit from `View` will retain that ability. However, if you create a custom UI for your view (custom button drawables, for example), you should provide focused states along with pressed states. In addition, you should test navigating your app UI using only the d-pad. Pay special attention to the order in which views are focused. Does it make sense that this view is in focus after the previous one? If not, you can change the focus ordering in your layout files by using the `android:nextFocus*` attributes. These attributes let you define which view will be the next to receive focus. This is useful for more than just accessibility: Using focus lets you define which fields are selected when the user tabs through your UI using a keyboard.

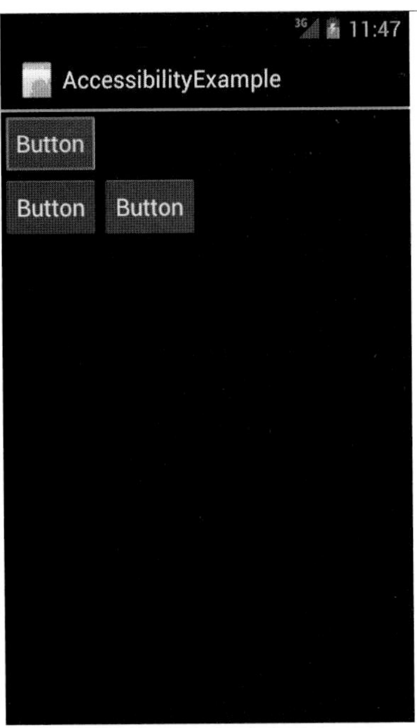

FIGURE 12.1 To navigate between these buttons using the directional pad, use the `android:nextFocus*` attributes to configure which button will gain focus.

Here is an example layout that contains three buttons (**Figure 12.1**):

```
<?xml version="1.0" encoding="utf-8"?>
<LinearLayout xmlns:android="http://schemas.android.com/
→ apk/res/android"
    android:layout_width="match_parent"
    android:layout_height="match_parent"
    android:orientation="vertical" >
    <Button
        android:id="@+id/button1"
        android:layout_width="wrap_content"
        android:layout_height="wrap_content"
        android:text="@string/button" />
    <LinearLayout
        android:layout_width="match_parent"
```

```
        android:layout_height="wrap_content" >
        <Button
            android:id="@+id/button2"
            android:layout_width="wrap_content"
            android:layout_height="wrap_content"
            android:text="@string/button" />
        <Button
            android:id="@+id/button3"
            android:layout_width="wrap_content"
            android:layout_height="wrap_content"
            android:text="@string/button" />
    </LinearLayout>
</LinearLayout>
```

Run the example on the emulator, and use the navigation buttons to cycle through the buttons. Notice that if you press just the up and down buttons, you cannot reach the button on the right. To fix this, add the nextFocus attributes:

```
<?xml version="1.0" encoding="utf-8"?>
<LinearLayout xmlns:android="http://schemas.android.com/
→ apk/res/android"
    android:layout_width="match_parent"
    android:layout_height="match_parent"
    android:orientation="vertical" >
    <Button
        android:id="@+id/button1"
        android:layout_width="wrap_content"
        android:layout_height="wrap_content"
        android:text="@string/button" />
    <LinearLayout
```

```
        android:layout_width="match_parent"
        android:layout_height="wrap_content" >
        <Button
            android:id="@+id/button2"
            android:layout_width="wrap_content"
            android:layout_height="wrap_content"
            android:text="@string/button"
            android:nextFocusDown="@+id/button3" />
        <Button
            android:id="@+id/button3"
            android:layout_width="wrap_content"
            android:layout_height="wrap_content"
            android:text="@string/button"
            android:nextFocusUp="@id/button2" />
    </LinearLayout>
</LinearLayout>
```

Now when you use the down and up keys to navigate, you will cycle through all the buttons.

TIP: Test your UI using both up/down directions and left/right directions to ensure that it properly responds to all directional input.

CONTENT DESCRIPTION

Beyond making your UI navigable by d-pad, you should strive to make it usable by users with impaired vision. Vision-impaired users will not be able to navigate your UI solely via a touchscreen interface. To work around this, users with vision disabilities rely on screen readers to speak the UI elements as they slide their fingers over the display. The screen reader reads the text of the view that the user is touching. However, many UI elements convey their meaning visually rather than via text. For those elements, you should set the `android:contentDescription` attribute to provide a description of the view. Here is an example that sets the `android:contentDescription` attribute on an `ImageView`:

```
<ImageView
    android:id="@+id/image"
    android:src="@drawable/example_drawable"
    android:contentDescription="@string/description" />
```

When accessibility features are enabled, users who touch the image will hear the contents of the `android:contentDescription` attribute read aloud. By sliding a finger across the screen, visually impaired users can navigate and use your application with just spoken text.

ACCESSIBILITY EVENTS

Accessibility features are provided by Android's accessibility service. For the service to work, all views need to implement the `AccessibilityEventSource` interface and emit `AccessibilityEvents` when the state of the view changes. These events are used by the `AccessibilityService` to provide users with awareness of events in the UI. Changes in text, changes in focus state, and changes in click state are all examples of events. The `View` class and its descendants already send `AccessibilityEvents` at the appropriate times. However, when you implement a custom view, you may want to generate `AccessibilityEvents` yourself, to handle any new functionality the base class may be missing.

Accessibility events include properties that describe the event and its source. If you extend a built-in view class, the base view will supply these properties for you. Use the `sendAccessibilityEvent` method to send the event with the default properties:

```
sendAccessibilityEvent(AccessibilityEvent.TYPE_VIEW_CLICKED);
```

And if you need to change or add event properties, implement the `dispatchPopulateAccessibilityEvent` method to adjust the event properties:

```
@Override
public boolean dispatchPopulateAccessibilityEvent
➥ (AccessibilityEvent event) {
    boolean populated = super.dispatchPopulateAccessibilityEvent
    ➥ (event);
    if (!populated) {
        event.setChecked(mChecked);
    }
    return populated;
}
```

The Android documentation contains the full list of accessibility events that you should be emitting. Take care to test your app using accessibility features to verify that you are properly serving users with disabilities.

TIPS FOR MAKING YOUR APP ACCESSIBLE

- If possible, use the standard views provided by Android. They already follow accessibility guidelines.
- Always use the `android:contentDescription` attribute on visual elements that don't include text, such as `ImageViews`.
- Always follow the platform guidelines on proper usage of the Back button. This is especially important for users with disabilities, who may be using your app without using the touchscreen.
- Test your application on your phone or emulator by choosing Settings > Accessibility and enabling accessibility features.
- Download a screen reader from the Android Market to test your app using voice-only navigation; the TalkBack app by the Eyes-Free Project is a good choice. Note that this may be unnecessary, as some devices have TalkBack installed by default.

WRAPPING UP

Localizing your app is required if you want to expand your market reach into other countries. And ensuring that your app is accessible not only expands your potential market, it helps people with disabilities make better use of technology. By following Android best practices, you can achieve both with minimal effort. In this chapter, you learned that

- You should use Android's resource qualifiers to provide translated strings for your app.
- You should always provide default resources; otherwise, your app may crash.
- You should add focus and content description attributes to your views to make them navigable by users with impaired vision.
- When creating a custom view, you should make sure you emit the proper accessibility events so that the accessibility service can properly handle UI events.

As a final wrap up, I want to encourage you to take any knowledge you've gained here and use it to create something awesome. Throughout this text, I've tried to show you how to build fluid, beautiful software. It's not always easy, but your users will thank you for the effort. If you do find this book helpful, and you go on to create an Android application, please let me know via Twitter (@jasonostrander). I love trying new apps and would love to see what you've come up with. Good luck!

INDEX

H

I

J

K

L